# ROUTE SUMMARY TABLES

| Stage number | Start/finish | Distance | Total ascent | Total descent | Duration | Page |
|---|---|---|---|---|---|---|
| 1 | Florence to Pontassieve | 18.4km | 271m | 215m | 5hr | 41 |
| 2 | Pontassieve to Consuma | 16.8km | 999m | 74m | 5½hr | 49 |
| 3 | Consuma to Stia | 14.6km | 640m | 829m | 6hr | 55 |
| 4 | Stia to Badia Prataglia | 23.8km | 1116m | 718m | 7¾hr | 60 |
| 5 | Badia Prataglia to Santuario della Verna | 15.9km | 1084m | 791m | 6hr | 66 |
| 6 | Santuario della Verna to Pieve Santo Stefano | 14.6km | 236m | 930m | 4¾hr | 85 |
| 7 | Pieve Santo Stefano to Montagna | 22.6km | 838m | 591m | 7¼hr | 90 |
| 8 | Montagna to Sansepolcro | 11.2km | 149m | 502m | 3½hr | 97 |
| 9 | Sansepolcro to Citerna | 12.2km | 229m | 84m | 3½hr | 102 |
| 10 | Citerna to Città di Castello | 19.1km | 621m | 799m | 6¼hr | 107 |
| 11 | Città de Castello to Pietralunga | 28.7km | 834m | 566m | 8½hr | 116 |
| 12 | Pietralunga to Gubbio | 26.2km | 623m | 694m | 7¾hr | 122 |
| 13 | Gubbio to Valdichiascio | 15.9km | 354m | 390m | 4¾hr | 130 |
| 14 | Valdichiascio to Valfabbrica | 20.8km | 570m | 732m | 6½hr | 135 |
| 15 | Valfabbrica to Assisi | 13.2km | 568m | 497m | 4½hr | 142 |
| 16 | Assisi to Spello | 12.9km | 234m | 322m | 3¾hr | 156 |
| 17 | Spello to Trevi | 19.0km | 329m | 190m | 5¼hr | 162 |
| 18 | Trevi to Spoleto | 27.1km | 952m | 969m | 8¾hr | 168 |
| 19 | Spoleto to Macenano | 19.7km | | | | 176 |
| 20 | Macenano to Piediluco | | | | | 182 |
| 21 | Piediluco to Poggio Bustone | | | | | 189 |
| 22 | Poggio Bustone to Rieti | | | | | 196 |

## THE WAY OF ST FRANCIS – VIA DI FRANCESCO

| Stage number | Start/finish | Distance | Total ascent | Total descent | Duration | Page |
|---|---|---|---|---|---|---|
| 23 | Rieti to Poggio San Lorenzo | 20.5km | 359m | 266m | 6hr | 210 |
| 24 | Poggio San Lorenzo to Ponticelli Sabino | 19.9km | 568m | 732m | 6¼hr | 216 |
| 25 | Ponticelli Sabino to Monterotondo | 29.4km | 536m | 716m | 8½hr | 222 |
| 26 | Monterotondo to Monte Sacro | 18.9km | 286m | 401m | 5½hr | 229 |
| 27 | Monte Sacro to Vatican City, Rome | 15.0km | 59m | 66m | 4hr | 234 |
| **Total** | | 517.6km | | | | |

| Variant number | Start/finish | Distance | Total ascent | Total descent | Duration | Page |
|---|---|---|---|---|---|---|
| Variant 1.1 | Florence to Santuario della Verna – southern route | 89.2km | 3243m | 2234m | 28hr | 74 |
| Variant 1.2 | Cortona and Arezzo to Santuario della Verna | 106.4km | 3608m | 2991m | 33hr | 79 |
| Variant 2.1 | Valfabbrica to Assisi via Perugia | 54.7km | 1056m | 985m | 17½hr | 150 |
| Variant 3.1 | Arrone to Terni, Greccio, and Rieti | 61.1km | 1754m | 1600m | 19hr | 204 |
| Variant 4.1 | Poggio San Lorenzo to Monterotondo via Farfa Abbey | 62.2km | 1436m | 1785m | 18½hr | 244 |

# THE WAY OF ST FRANCIS: VIA DI FRANCESCO

## FROM FLORENCE TO ASSISI AND ROME

by Sandy Brown

JUNIPER HOUSE, MURLEY MOSS,
OXENHOLME ROAD, KENDAL, CUMBRIA LA9 7RL
www.cicerone.co.uk

© Sandy Brown 2025
Second edition 2025
ISBN: 978 1 78631 167 2
eISBN: 978 1 78765 184 5
First edition 2015

Printed in Czechia on responsibly sourced paper on behalf of Latitude Press Ltd.
A catalogue record for this book is available from the British Library.
All photographs are by the author unless otherwise stated.

Route mapping by Lovell Johns www.lovelljohns.com

Contains OpenStreetMap.org data © OpenStreetMap contributors, CC-BY-SA.
NASA relief data courtesy of ESRI

### Updates to this guide

While every effort is made by our authors to ensure the accuracy of guidebooks as they go to print, changes can occur during the lifetime of an edition. Any updates that we know of for this guide will be on the Cicerone website (www.cicerone.co.uk/1167/updates), so please check before planning your trip. We also advise that you check information about such things as transport, accommodation and shops locally. Even rights of way can be altered over time.

The route maps in this guide are derived from publicly available data, databases and crowd-sourced data. As such they have not been through the detailed checking procedures that would generally be applied to a published map from an official mapping agency, although naturally we have reviewed them closely in the light of local knowledge as part of the preparation of this guide.

We are always grateful for information about any discrepancies between a guidebook and the facts on the ground, sent by email to updates@cicerone.co.uk.

**Register your book:** To sign up to receive free updates, special offers and GPX files where available, create a Cicerone account and register your purchase via the 'My Account' tab at www.cicerone.co.uk.

*Front cover:* Pilgrims descend a final hill into the ancient town of Spello (Stage 16)

MAP KEY

## Dedication

*Since 2014 when we first walked together on this trail it was clear to me there could be no better walking partner than my wife. To Theresa, my partner in everything.*

*Morning sun illuminates the Duomo of Florence above the city streets. (Stage 1)*

# CONTENTS

Route summary tables . . . . . . . . . . . . . . . . . . . . . . . . . . . . . . . . . . . . . . . . . . 1
Map key . . . . . . . . . . . . . . . . . . . . . . . . . . . . . . . . . . . . . . . . . . . . . . . . . . . . . 5
Overview profile . . . . . . . . . . . . . . . . . . . . . . . . . . . . . . . . . . . . . . . . . . . . . 10

**INTRODUCTION** . . . . . . . . . . . . . . . . . . . . . . . . . . . . . . . . . . . . . . . . . . . 13
The Ways of St Francis . . . . . . . . . . . . . . . . . . . . . . . . . . . . . . . . . . . . . . . . 15

**PLANNING YOUR WALK** . . . . . . . . . . . . . . . . . . . . . . . . . . . . . . . . . . . . 18
Where to begin . . . . . . . . . . . . . . . . . . . . . . . . . . . . . . . . . . . . . . . . . . . . . . 18
When to walk . . . . . . . . . . . . . . . . . . . . . . . . . . . . . . . . . . . . . . . . . . . . . . . 20
Choosing a schedule . . . . . . . . . . . . . . . . . . . . . . . . . . . . . . . . . . . . . . . . . 21
Where to stay . . . . . . . . . . . . . . . . . . . . . . . . . . . . . . . . . . . . . . . . . . . . . . . 21
What and where to eat . . . . . . . . . . . . . . . . . . . . . . . . . . . . . . . . . . . . . . . 23
How much money should I budget? . . . . . . . . . . . . . . . . . . . . . . . . . . . . 24
How do I get to the route? . . . . . . . . . . . . . . . . . . . . . . . . . . . . . . . . . . . . 24
How do I return from Assisi or Rome? . . . . . . . . . . . . . . . . . . . . . . . . . . . 25
How do I secure my credential and testimonium? . . . . . . . . . . . . . . . . . 26

**TIPS FOR MAKING THE MOST OF YOUR WALK** . . . . . . . . . . . . . . . . . 27
Topography of the Way of St Francis in Central Italy . . . . . . . . . . . . . . . . 27
Weather patterns . . . . . . . . . . . . . . . . . . . . . . . . . . . . . . . . . . . . . . . . . . . . 27
Post, phones, and internet . . . . . . . . . . . . . . . . . . . . . . . . . . . . . . . . . . . . . 28
Other tips . . . . . . . . . . . . . . . . . . . . . . . . . . . . . . . . . . . . . . . . . . . . . . . . . . 29
Training for your walk . . . . . . . . . . . . . . . . . . . . . . . . . . . . . . . . . . . . . . . . 30
What and how to pack . . . . . . . . . . . . . . . . . . . . . . . . . . . . . . . . . . . . . . . . 31
Baggage transport and storage . . . . . . . . . . . . . . . . . . . . . . . . . . . . . . . . . 32
Language aids . . . . . . . . . . . . . . . . . . . . . . . . . . . . . . . . . . . . . . . . . . . . . . 32
Health and well-being . . . . . . . . . . . . . . . . . . . . . . . . . . . . . . . . . . . . . . . . 32

**HOW TO USE THIS GUIDE** . . . . . . . . . . . . . . . . . . . . . . . . . . . . . . . . . . 34
Stage descriptions . . . . . . . . . . . . . . . . . . . . . . . . . . . . . . . . . . . . . . . . . . . 34
GPX tracks and accommodation downloads . . . . . . . . . . . . . . . . . . . . . . 38

## SECTION 1: FLORENCE TO SANTUARIO DELLA VERNA
| | | |
|---|---|---|
| Stage 1 | Florence to Pontassieve | 41 |
| Stage 2 | Pontassieve to Consuma | 49 |
| Stage 3 | Consuma to Stia | 55 |
| Stage 4 | Stia to Badia Prataglia | 60 |
| Stage 5 | Badia Prataglia to Santuario della Verna | 66 |

## SECTION 1A: VARIANT ROUTES TO SANTUARIO DELLA VERNA
| | | |
|---|---|---|
| Variant 1.1 | Florence to Santuario della Verna – southern route | 74 |
| Variant 1.2 | Cortona and Arezzo to Santuario della Verna | 79 |

## SECTION 2: SANTUARIO DELLA VERNA TO ASSISI
| | | |
|---|---|---|
| Stage 6 | Santuario della Verna to Pieve Santo Stefano | 85 |
| Stage 7 | Pieve Santo Stefano to Montagna | 90 |
| Stage 8 | Montagna to Sansepolcro | 97 |
| Stage 9 | Sansepolcro to Citerna | 102 |
| Stage 10 | Citerna to Città di Castello | 107 |
| Stage 11 | Città di Castello to Pietralunga | 116 |
| Stage 12 | Pietralunga to Gubbio | 122 |
| Stage 13 | Gubbio to Valdichiascio | 130 |
| Stage 14 | Valdichiascio to Valfabbrica | 135 |
| Stage 15 | Valfabbrica to Assisi | 142 |

## SECTION 2A: VARIANT ROUTE TO ASSISI
| | | |
|---|---|---|
| Variant 2.1 | Valfabbrica to Assisi via Perugia | 150 |

## SECTION 3: ASSISI TO RIETI
| | | |
|---|---|---|
| Stage 16 | Assisi to Spello | 156 |
| Stage 17 | Spello to Trevi | 162 |
| Stage 18 | Trevi to Spoleto | 168 |
| Stage 19 | Spoleto to Macenano | 176 |
| Stage 20 | Macenano to Piediluco | 182 |
| Stage 21 | Piediluco to Poggio Bustone | 189 |
| Stage 22 | Poggio Bustone to Rieti | 196 |

## SECTION 3A: VARIANT ROUTES TO RIETI
| | | |
|---|---|---|
| Variant 3.1 | Arrone to Terni, Greccio, and Rieti | 204 |

## SECTION 4: RIETI TO ROME

| Stage 23 | Rieti to Poggio San Lorenzo | 210 |
| Stage 24 | Poggio San Lorenzo to Ponticelli Sabino | 216 |
| Stage 25 | Ponticelli Sabino to Monterotondo | 222 |
| Stage 26 | Monterotondo to Monte Sacro | 229 |
| Stage 27 | Monte Sacro to Vatican City, Rome | 234 |

## SECTION 4A: VARIANT ROUTE TO MONTEROTONDO

| Variant 4.1 | Poggio San Lorenzo to Monterotondo via Farfa Abbey | 244 |

| **Appendix A** | Stage planning table | 246 |
| **Appendix B** | Useful contacts | 249 |
| **Appendix C** | Language tips | 252 |
| **Appendix D** | Index of St Francis stories | 255 |
| **Appendix E** | Further reading | 256 |

*The 13th-c. Torre della Fiora was a peripheral fortification of the city of Rome (Stage 25)*

# THE WAY OF ST FRANCIS — VIA DI FRANCESCO

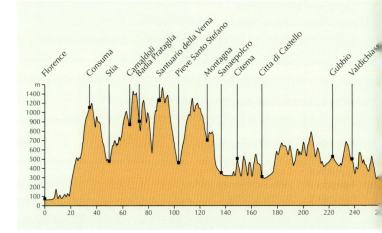

## Acknowledgments

This volume was conceived in 2013 after walking the Via di Francesco with friends Jacqueline, Sebastian, and Andreas. We had walked the Camino de Santiago the year before and it was Jacqueline's idea to move our saintly patronage for a time from James to Francis. The subsequent book proposal was hatched with the encouragement of my sister, Lori McCarney, and her husband, Rick Keene. Jonathan Williams of Cicerone saw possibilities in it and has been a guide and mentor ever since.

Jacqueline returned to Italy in 2014 to scout the walk with me, then I took language classes in Perugia and rewalked the route with Theresa Elliott, after which the first edition went to press. Chiara dall'Aglio and Gigi Bettin of Sviluppumbria helped promote the book at the World Travel Market in London in 2015, and three printings later the second edition is here and in your hands. Chiara and Gigi are dear friends, and Gigi remains an inspiration and source of information (the accommodation listings are largely based on his work), as does Don Paolo Giulietti also one of the team of the Perugia collaborators, and, now Archbishop of Lucca. Gigi and Don Paulo are coauthors of the excellent Italian guidebook that covers the route.

*OVERVIEW PROFILE*

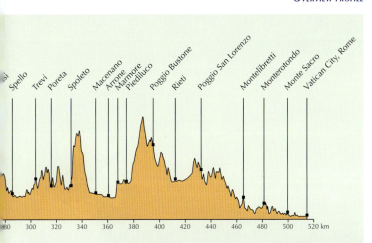

Over the years I've come to appreciate the many volunteers who work to support the route, and at the top of that list are Andrea Morbidelli and Simone Minelli, who stand out for their love of Francis and devotion to the path. Raffaele Manelli of Tuscany saw to it that the Region of Tuscany would officially add walking itineraries to Santuario della Verna. I have found it a true pleasure to lead groups on this route with outstanding outdoor guides Giovanni Ramaccioni of Sansepolcro and Mauro Cappelletti of Poggio San Lorenzo, both of whom have taught me so much and whom I count as dear friends. Giovanni guided me through the new Tuscan routes from Cortona and through Bibbiena and Poppi. Every walker I've shared the path with has taught me, so my thanks to the many I've walked with, talked and laughed with, and learned from over my ten years of walking and studying this path.

Kudos to Joe Williams and Maddy Williams, who gave the green light to this second edition, and to the talented team at Cicerone Press, led by editor Nicole Spray, copy editor Pat Dunn, and designer Avery Mitchell who worked to make these scratchings into a guidebook.

*A statue of St Francis sits at the edge of a terrace at Montecasale (Stage 8)*

# INTRODUCTION

*The author overlooks the Upper Tiber Valley from a vantage point on the trail near Cerbaiolo (Stage 7)*

Italy has had its share – and more – of people with genius. There have been great writers – Dante and Machiavelli; great artists – Michelangelo and Raphael; great scientists – da Vinci and Galileo; great architects – Brunelleschi and Bernini; great political leaders – Augustus and Marcus Aurelius; and great musicians – Puccini and Verdi. Together they left a legacy of words, thoughts, artworks, buildings, inventions, empires, and musical masterpieces.

Those who have come to know Francis of Assisi recognize this same kind of genius in him. An Italian genius before there was an Italy, his brilliance is unlike that of the others, for it is one of soul rather than intellect. Even today, Francis' work embodying faith is definitive. He found something in the life of humility, prayer, and service that jumps off the page of dusty history books and brings a smile to the faces of Italians in the villages of Umbria, where he is revered as a neighbor and friend.

A year after he began his ministry, his followers numbered eleven. Within ten years there were 5000. Today – even 800 years after his death – there are as many as 650,000 friars, cloistered nuns, and secular members, making Franciscans the largest Catholic order. Popes honored Francis during his life and at his death,

## THE WAY OF ST FRANCIS — VIA DI FRANCESCO

and when Cardinal Jorge Bergoglio was elected pope in 2013, he chose the name of Pope Francis to send a strong and unmistakable message to the world that his papacy would be about the virtues of deep humility, prayer, service, and respect for nature – virtues that lift the name of Francis among the greatest Italians of all time.

To walk Italy's Way of St Francis – its Via di Francesco – is to come to know this man. This mountainous, green, and natural itinerary offers the solitude that Francis loved, the nature he adored, and the simplicity he embodied.

The modern Way of St Francis connects places and paths important in the life of this beloved saint and makes them available to pilgrim walkers who seek to retrace his steps and capture his love of this land. Indeed, the ministry of Francis of Assisi began with a walk, when in 1209 he and his friends walked from Assisi to Rome to meet Pope Innocent III. His travels north of Assisi and in Tuscany inspire stories that are told to this day, while, closer to Rome, he loved to visit the Holy Valley of Rieti for rest and prayer. The Way of St Francis links these travels and destinations into a month-long walk that even after many centuries echoes with his presence.

Today, as you walk from Florence to Rome via Assisi, it is easy to imagine the Italy of Francis' time. Still present are the thick, gray-brown walls of medieval hill towns, the quiet mountain pathways, the sweeping vistas of fertile farmland where wheat and herbs are grown, and the ancient olive groves where locals know to find the tender stalks of the wild asparagus they gather by hand and toss with the pasta of their evening meal. These Central Apennines contain some of Italy's most beautiful mountains and valleys, what Italians call *il cuor verde d'Italia* – the green heart of Italy.

If the mountains of Umbria, Tuscany, and Lazio could speak of all that has happened in their shadow, they would tell a rich and colorful story of armies and conquerors, of mysterious Etruscans and crafty Romans, of Christian princes and worldly bishops, of invading hordes and bumbling dictators – all who made marks on the land that today are still visible to the observant pilgrim walker. Every day of this walk brings evidence of another historic episode to see and touch: an Etruscan archway, a Roman road, a papal castle, a monument to soldiers lost in a war, a gleaming new European Union highway. But perhaps the most famous mark of all was made by one who left the land undisturbed and instead fashioned his feelings about it into a song about our brotherhood and sisterhood with the sky, the sun, the moon, the land, its plants, and animals as fellow creatures. For those with ears to hear, that song is sung again to the rhythm of your footsteps as you walk the green paths of this route.

In this book, the story of St Francis is laid out geographically, with portions of his tale sprinkled among the towns and villages where the events

# THE WAYS OF ST FRANCIS

took place. Parts of his story that happened in other places are added in between, fleshing out the life of this humble man and adding a daily reminder of the saint to the journey. Many of the stories and legends come from Francis' biographers, many are depicted in frescoes in Assisi's Basilica di San Francesco. They are offered here without comment or modern appraisal, and you are invited to read the lines and between the lines to discover how the stories might speak to you. (An index of these stories is provided in Appendix D, while Appendix E suggests further reading.)

## THE WAYS OF ST FRANCIS

Since the death of Francis in the early 13th c., pilgrims from all over Italy and Europe have traveled to Umbria to venerate him and his friend and collaborator, Clare. This steady stream of pilgrims has only grown over the years, now numbering over four

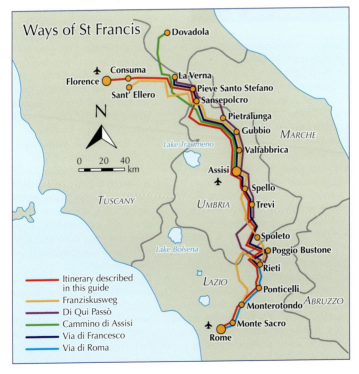

## The Way of St Francis — Via di Francesco

*A robe of St Francis is one of the relics on display at Santuario della Verna (Stage 5)*

million each year arriving in the pinkish-white streets of Assisi.

With the growing popularity of long-distance walking in the late 20th c., interest arose in a walking itinerary in Central Italy that would link together the sites associated with St Francis. Unlike other pilgrimages such as the Camino de Santiago and Via Francigena, there is no historic text that documents a specific route, so several itineraries have sprung up, linking together beloved St Francis sites. Among the main routes are:

- The **Via Francigena di San Francesco (Via di Francesco)** is a joint project of the region of Umbria, the Franciscan family of orders in Assisi, and the Umbrian Conference of Catholic Bishops. (The name 'Via Francigena' is a mistake of history and is no longer used, although it persists on signage planted two decades ago.) A northern route (originally beginning at Santuario della Verna) and a southern route (starting in Rome) converge in Assisi. Large blue-and-yellow metal signs and blue-and-yellow painted stripes mark the way. While Santuario della Verna had traditionally been seen as the northern starting point of the Via di Francesco, in 2018 the region of Tuscany joined the Via di Francesco network and gave official recognition to four routes leading to Santuario della Verna: from Florence through Stia and Badia Prataglia; from Cortona, Arezzo, and Anghiari; from Florence through Poppi and Bibbiena; and from Rimini. These are marked with red-and-white blazes, and small red-and-white signs with the Tau symbol.
- The **Cammino di Assisi** begins at the tiny town of Dovadola in Emilia-Romagna. It visits sites of St Anthony of Padua, an important Franciscan leader, before reaching Santuario della Verna where it connects with a Franciscan itinerary that ends in Assisi. Green arrows and a dancing Tau figure mark the route.
- **Di Qui Passò San Francesco** is the brainchild of pilgrim pioneer Angela Seracchioli and leads from Santuario della Verna through Greccio to Poggio Bustone. Look for yellow Tau markers and yellow arrows marking this route.

## THE WAYS OF ST FRANCIS

- The **Cammino di Francesco** is a project of the Rieti tourism office, which maintains a ring of trails among the holy sites of the Sacred Valley of Rieti in a circular route between the sanctuaries at Poggio Bustone, La Foresta, Fonte Colombo, and Greccio. Carved wooden signs and X-framed fences mark the route.
- The **Via di Roma/Via di Francesco** is the portion of the Via di Francesco overseen by the region of Lazio and leads from Poggio Bustone to Rome. Its blue-and-yellow signs are similar to those of the Via di Francesco. In Rome, the route is also marked with images of St Francis and the two keys of St Peter stencilled in yellow paint on sidewalks, and with round stickers in blue and yellow.
- The **Sentiero Francescano della Pace** traces the route walked by Francis from Assisi to Gubbio after his parents disowned him. Large kiosks mark the route.
- **Franziskusweg** routes beginning near Florence and ending just before Rome are described in guidebooks by authors Kees Roodenburg of the Netherlands and Simone Ochsenkühn of Germany. Before La Verna, they follow pre-existing Club Alpino Italia (CAI) trails, which are marked in painted red-and-white stripes, and after La Verna they select from among the Franciscan options to find the most favorable itineraries.

Since the goal of this book is to provide the best and most widely accepted itinerary linking sites associated with St Francis, the Via di Francesco seems the obvious choice. It is backed by governmental agencies in Tuscany, Umbria, and Lazio, and includes the best St Francis locations and optimal walking trails, making it stand out as the itinerary most likely to thrive in coming years. Statistics show that four to five thousand pilgrims walk all or part of the Via di Francesco each year.

*A pilgrim walks the narrow path into the Valnerina before Ceselli (Stage 19)*

# PLANNING YOUR WALK

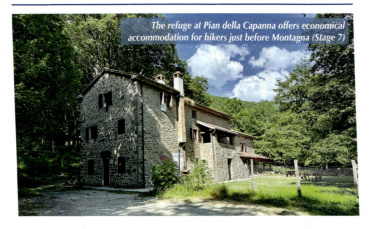
*The refuge at Pian della Capanna offers economical accommodation for hikers just before Montagna (Stage 7)*

## WHERE TO BEGIN

The route and schedule in this book are designed with the notion that a person might want a similar experience to walking the Camino de Santiago/Camino Francés, which lasts about one month. Since the Via di Francesco sites can all be strung together in one journey from north to south, the book is laid out in this fashion. A few of the major options for approaching the route are discussed below. Consult Appendix A (stage planning table) for a list of distances that may help in your planning.

### Southbound options
- **Beginning in Florence – this book's route:** The entire itinerary is accessible in this option, with a few days of mountain hiking before experiencing the beautiful Santuario della Verna. Florence enjoys excellent transit connections with the rest of Europe by plane or train, so travel from here is simple.
- **Beginning at Santuario della Verna:** This option begins at one of the scenic highlights of the entire route, but getting here involves a train to Arezzo, transfer to another train to Bibbiena, then a bus trip to Chiusi della Verna followed by a 1km uphill walk or a wait for the infrequent bus directly to Santuario della Verna. From here, a person can walk the remaining itinerary to Assisi or on to Rome.
- **Beginning at Assisi:** A start here offers an instant immersion into the life of St Francis. From here, it is most common to continue on

## WHERE TO BEGIN

Example signage that you'll see along the route

to Rome, incorporating the important Spoleto and Rieti valleys. This option misses all of the northern sites, although it is also possible, but uncommon, to walk from Assisi northward to La Verna.

### Northbound options
- **Beginning at Rieti:** From here, you can walk north to Assisi and stop at many of the most important Franciscan locations. In fact, the Via di Francesco assumes it is most common to walk to Assisi from the north or south. Again, it would be uncommon, but not impossible, to walk northward all the way to La Verna or Florence from here, or to walk only from Rieti to Rome.
- **Beginning at Rome:** This is the choice of about four percent of walkers. It allows people to enjoy the excellent travel connections from the Italian capital and then end in the birthplace and resting place of St Francis at Assisi. Again, it is uncommon to walk northward beyond Assisi, but not impossible.

## WHEN TO WALK

April to June and mid August through October are the best times to walk the Way of St Francis. During these months the temperatures range from mild to hot and the rainfall is at its lowest average. The weeks between 1 July and 15 August are historically the hottest of the year and are best avoided unless you're ready for very warm temperatures.

For the last 2000 years, Italians have celebrated *ferragosto* – a two-week holiday at the end of August when Italians close their shops and retreat to the mountains and beaches. Except in tourist areas, small businesses and restaurants may be closed for half of August or longer.

Due to the winter climate of the highlands, the likelihood of heavy rain and snow, and shorter hours of daylight, a pilgrimage between November and March on certain portions of the Way of St Francis is unwise. The possibility of trail washouts, overflowing streams, and signage lost due to snow – not to mention the danger of hypothermia and getting lost – outweigh any advantages of walking in these months. Likewise, walking in the shoulder months of November and April can mean that some accommodations are not yet open for the season and that tiny streams mentioned here may be swollen with the rains and snowmelt.

Pilgrims may want to coordinate their journey around special holidays in the Italian communities on the pilgrimage. On 4 October, the Feast Day of St Francis, Assisi is filled with pilgrims, excitement is high, and accommodations can be hard to find. Gubbio's Corsa dei Ceri (Candle Race) is held on 15 May each year, and Spello's Infiorata (a flower festival) lands on the ninth Sunday after Easter.

## WHERE TO STAY

*Local residents buy groceries at a shop in Spoleto's Piazza del Mercato (Stage 18)*

Near Assisi are Perugia's Umbria Jazz in July and EuroChocolate in October, and Spoleto's Due Mondi (Two Worlds) in June/July attracts classical musicians from around the world. Although the festivals are a real treat, pilgrims should be aware that accommodations might be scarce without adequate advance reservations and should plan accordingly.

### CHOOSING A SCHEDULE

While the complete walk of 27 stages could be accomplished in 27 walking days, that's not nearly enough time to enjoy and appreciate this important pilgrimage and its many wonders. Unless you have already toured Rome and Florence, you would want to spend at least one or two extra days in each. You can't enjoy Assisi in what's left of the day it took to walk there, so add another day for St Francis' hometown. It's good to allow for a day of rest every week anyway, which means that a realistic, complete itinerary would be in the realm of 31–32 days, not including travel to and from Italy. There are two long stages with significant ascents and descents (Stia to Badia Prataglia, and Trevi to Spoleto), which you may want to break up into one and a half days instead, adding another day or two to your trip.

If a journey of 30–35 days is unmanageable, the journey could be broken into several parts to be completed as time permits:

Florence to Assisi – 15 or more days
La Verna to Assisi – 17 or more days
Assisi to Rieti – 8 or more days
Assisi to Rome – 12 or more days

### WHERE TO STAY

Stages in this book have been arranged to coincide with available lodging. Where possible, at least three accommodation options are listed per daily stage. The daily listings include low-cost hotels, *agriturismi* (farm accommodations: see below for details), and *foresterie* (guest houses), and at least one hostel, if available.

Unlike on the Camino de Santiago, it is expected that pilgrims will reserve ahead. Make your reservations at least 2–3 days in advance so you know you'll have a suitable place to stay. Hostels often do not use email, so telephone is sometimes the only option. Try not to make reservations more than 4–5 days in advance, so that you maintain some flexibility in your plans.

See Appendix B (Useful contacts) for a list of tourist information offices along the route; if you find yourself struggling to make a booking, they may be able to help.

### Ostelli

A growing number of local parishes, monasteries, and convents along the route have opened small *ostelli* (hostels) or spare rooms for use by pilgrims. A sleeping bag is only required when specified since virtually every hostel makes pillows and blankets available for free or for a small cost. Do plan on bringing a sleeping bag liner though, since sheets are seldom included.

### Rifugi

These are mountain huts found in national parks (such as the Casentino) and they are maintained by the local chapters of the Club Alpino Italia (CAI). Extremely basic, there may simply be a bare cot, table, and fireplace, and no restaurant nearby. With only one *rifugio* along the way – just after Camaldoli – it's likely not worth it to plan to stay there since an overnight would require a sleeping bag, food, cooking utensils, and a gas stove.

Some lodgings along the way use the name *rifugio* to denote their rustic location or their heritage (eg Rifugio Casa Santicchio, Rifugio Asqua), but they offer linens, plumbing, and meals. The particulars of their offerings are spelled out in their individual listings in the route description.

### Agriturismi

An *agriturismo* is a country house set on a farm, with eating accommodations

*'Bread of the Pilgrim' from Camaldoli makes a hearty snack for pilgrims climbing to Badia Prataglia.*

that range from small dining rooms with prepared meals to apartments with kitchens. An overnight at an *agriturismo* with breakfast and dinner can be in the €70–90 range, and if it is remotely located there may be no other dining options. It's always best to check in advance about the eating options so you can make the meal choice that best meets your budget. In a few cases, this means opting out of the *agriturismo* dinner in favor of a walk or hitched ride to a nearby restaurant.

### Hotels
Hotels in Italy almost always include a continental-style breakfast. Those featured in this guide usually range from €40–60 per person per night. Reduce the cost by sharing a double room with a companion. Expect to be asked for your passport when you check in, but not to pay until you check out; if you plan to leave early in the morning, ask to pay the night before. And don't forget to pick up your passport before you leave.

### Foresterie
A *foresteria* is a hotel run by a convent or monastery (such as Camaldoli and La Verna) that offers hotel-like rooms with breakfast and a large group, one-menu dinner included in the price.

### Camping
While it is possible to camp, you would need a tent or other gear for outdoor sleeping, which would mean unnecessary extra weight. In Italy, camping is legal only in designated campgrounds.

## WHAT AND WHERE TO EAT

It may be tough for non-Europeans to get used to the idea that a meager espresso with perhaps a croissant (*cornetto* in Italian) is meant to suffice as breakfast in Italy. Lunch is served in early afternoon and is followed by the *riposo* (see 'Business hours and the riposo' below). Early evening is time for a snack – a glass of beer or wine with tiny bites of food. Although restaurants generally open around 7:30pm, Italians usually enjoy dinner from around 8:00pm until 10:30pm. Restaurants are often open until midnight, although the kitchen may close sooner. Efficiency-loving Northern Europeans and Americans may need to learn the 'slow food' pattern of Italian restaurant meals, where the kitchen expects you to take your time enjoying food, wine and conversation and it is considered rude for the server to rush you off by bringing the bill without being asked.

Pizza and pasta are, of course, omnipresent in Italy. However, almost every town has its special take on pasta, and you will endear yourself to your server by ordering the local specialty. In Tuscany and Umbria, beef and pork are highly prized and the many varieties of cured meats are famous the world over.

Even in a plain-looking restaurant, a full Italian meal of *antipasto*, *primo, secondo,* and *dolci* (starter, first and second course, and dessert) can be expensive, so, if you're on a budget (or simply can't eat that much food), feel free to pick and choose from any of the courses. If you do, the server will want to know in what order you'd like your food.

## HOW MUCH MONEY SHOULD I BUDGET?

If you're on a tight budget, planning ahead to take advantage of private and parochial hostels is a wise move. If you prefer to stay in hotels, you can save some money by having a companion or two to share the cost. You can cut down on food expense by shopping for your lunch at a grocery store the night before. Only occasionally will you find a room or hostel with a kitchen, so you'll want to learn to study restaurant menus carefully for the most economical choices.

A moderate daily budget per person in double hotel rooms will look something like this:
- Breakfast incl. with room, otherwise €5.00 for coffee and *cornetto*
- Lunch €8.00
- Dinner €20.00
- Overnight €40.00
- Incidentals €5.00
- Total €78.00

When it comes to cash, rather than bringing a large stash of euros it's easiest to have an ATM card with you to get cash from your bank account as needed. Check with your bank to see what the fees are, whether there's a maximum daily withdrawal, and to make sure you're getting a favorable exchange rate. It's also a good idea to bring a second ATM card so you have a backup. A credit card is usually best for hotel reservations, since it is common for hotels to place a hold for an amount larger than the actual bill. When using a credit/debit card, if given the option of paying in euros or your own currency, choose euros so that you can avoid pricey conversion fees.

## HOW DO I GET TO THE ROUTE?

### Florence

Florence has a mid-sized international airport (FLR – Florence/Peretola, formally Aeroporto Amerigo Vespucci) that can be reached from major airline hubs in Europe. Upon arrival, pilgrims can easily take the T2 tram from the airport to the end of the line at the city center for €1.50; the tram is directly north of the airport terminal. Santa Maria Novella is the main train station in Florence and is served by trains from all over Europe. Florence's main attractions are all a quick walk from here, as is the Basilica of Santa Croce, start of the pilgrimage.

You can also get to Florence from Rome, whose Fiumicino airport (FCO) has excellent connections to cities around the world. The 30min express train from the airport to Rome's

Termini station costs €14, and from there the 1hr 36min ride to Florence on the high-speed Frecciarossa costs about €36.

### Santuario della Verna
Without a car, a trip to La Verna requires a train and/or bus, most often through Arezzo and Bibbiena. From Florence, Assisi, or Rome, take the train to Arezzo. From there, transfer to the Bibbiena train. At Bibbiena, you then transfer at the train station to the Autolinee Toscane bus line H12 (www.at-bus.it) for the 49min ride to Chiusi della Verna. From there, it is a 1km hike uphill on a path to Santuario della Verna (walking the road is 3km longer). In summer, the sanctuary is served on this same bus route.

### Assisi
Most travelers to Assisi choose to fly to Florence or Rome and then take the train to Assisi's nearest station, Santa Maria Degli Angeli. From the station, there is a €1.50 bus trip every 30min for the last 2.5km uphill to Assisi. If you want to exercise your legs, it's a 45min ascent on the 'Pax et Bonum' pedestrian walkway from the train station.

Assisi also shares the Aeroporto San Francesco d'Assisi (PEG) with Perugia at Sant'Egidio, about 10km out of town (www.airport.umbria.it). The airport has direct links to several European cities, including London (Stansted), Catania, Tirana, Brussels (Charleroi), and Malta. Information on the infrequent local bus (number E007, Assisi–Petrignano–Perugia) can be found at www.fsbusitalia.it, but lack of frequent runs makes it more convenient to pay the approximately €25 cab fare for the 15min trip to Assisi.

## HOW DO I RETURN FROM ASSISI OR ROME?

A downhill walk, bus, or taxi ride from Assisi to its train station at Santa Maria degli Angeli brings you to the Italian railroad system, which has links to all of Italy and Europe. From Assisi's station, it is easy to take trains directly to Florence's airport (via Santa Maria Novella station and the airport T2 tram) or to Rome (via Termini station and the Leonardo Express to Rome's Fiumicino airport).

*St Peter's Basilica, Vatican City, Rome (Stage 27)*

A trip to Rome airport from the Vatican can use the city's subway system to get to Rome Termini station, or a person can walk from the Vatican to the Trastevere train station (Piazza Flavio Biondo 1) and take a 27min train directly to the airport. Rome taxis are required by law to charge a maximum rate of €48–50 from Rome's city center to Fiumicino airport, which may make taxis the best option for early departures, particularly if you can share a ride.

### HOW DO I SECURE MY CREDENTIAL AND TESTIMONIUM?

As well as booking your travel arrangements to Italy, it is important to secure your credential (or *credenziale*) – a pilgrim 'identity card' – within two months of your departure. Pilgrims need a credential to certify their status and to receive a completion certificate (*testimonium* in Latin) at the end of the walk.

While there are several credentials for the various Francesco walks, this guide recommends the credential of the Via di Francesco because of its many institutional sponsors. The credential is free, but a donation is requested to cover the cost of postage. Go to the website www.piccolaccoglienzagubbio.it/credenziale and fill out the form online, or write directly to the volunteers at piccolaccoglienzagubbio@gmail.com. This wonderful service is run by volunteers in Gubbio, Italy, who send credentials out each week. Take care to show your address exactly as it should appear, to ensure that it is correctly mailed by your national postal service. Allow 6–8 weeks for delivery.

It is also possible to secure a credential in person at the Pilgrim Office adjacent to the Lower Basilica di San Francesco in Assisi. Credentials are available in Florence at St James Episcopal Church (Via Rucellai 9, tel 055 294417).

Once you have your credential, keep it safe and dry while you are walking, and have it stamped each day at the front desk of the lodging where you spend the night, or by the priest or staff member at a local church. Some bars, restaurants, and tourist offices also have credential stamps. Plan carefully so there are adequate blank spots on the credential to last your entire walk.

A *testimonium* is offered at the Basilica di San Francesco in Assisi for those who walk at least 100km to Assisi, and a separate one is offered at the Vatican for those who walk at least 100km to Rome. To receive your *testimonium* in Assisi, go to the entrance of the Lower Basilica and look for a door opposite marked 'Statio Peregrinorum.' Present your credential to receive your *testimonium*. To receive a *testimonium* in Rome, follow the steps listed at the end of Stage 27 in this guidebook.

# TIPS FOR MAKING THE MOST OF YOUR WALK

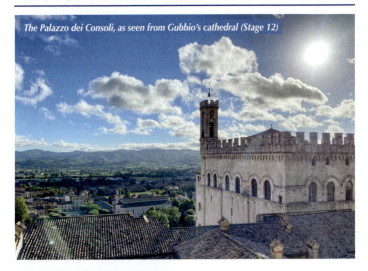

*The Palazzo dei Consoli, as seen from Gubbio's cathedral (Stage 12)*

## TOPOGRAPHY OF THE WAY OF ST FRANCIS IN CENTRAL ITALY

So that you won't be surprised by the difficulty of this route, it's important to understand that the Apennine range is the thick spine of the Italian peninsula, and the forested foothills of the Central Apennines form the heart of the Way of St Francis. The average daily ascent is 540m on this route, with a similar 540m descent. Four stages have an ascent of over 900m. Because of this rugged topography, the Way of St Francis is best considered as a much more challenging course than other pilgrimage walks. Veteran Camino de Santiago pilgrims often compare several of the days of this route to a walk over the Route Napoléon that crosses the Pyrenees. The challenge has its benefits, of course, and those who conquer the Francesco may end up stronger and fitter than when they began.

## WEATHER PATTERNS

Mount Terminillo and other snowy peaks in the Central Apennines create weather patterns that ensure regular rainfall. For pilgrims, this means that sporadic and sometimes heavy rain is assured in any season of the year.

Some who haven't visited Central Italy are surprised to discover this region has four distinct seasons, with frequent freezing temperatures in the winter as well as very hot temperatures in the summer. Snow is common at the higher elevations included on this itinerary, with chilly temperatures and more rain in the lowlands. Summers bring the high temperatures expected of Italy, but rainfall averages year-round show why the region remains green.

For pilgrims, the geography and climate offer rewards as well as challenges – breathtaking views from lofty mountain ridges and long walks in ancient forests or among green fields in quiet valleys.

### POST, PHONES, AND INTERNET

Italy's state-owned **public postal service**, Poste Italiane, has offices in towns and cities throughout the country, where you can post letters and postcards; there is usually an ATM outside.

To make accommodation reservations in real time it's very handy to have a **telephone** – and even more handy to have a smartphone with Internet capability for email. If you have a smartphone, contact your carrier prior to departure to ask for an international voice and data plan. If this is too expensive – and if your smartphone is unlocked from your local carrier – you can purchase a prepaid Italian SIM card on arrival in Italy at the office of one of the major carriers (TIM, Vodaphone, Windtre, for example). Whether it's a physical SIM card or an e-SIM, the clerk will install a new card for you and offer you prepaid voice and data plans. Make certain to retain your old SIM card so you can use it back home when you return.

For international calling, remember Italy's country code is +39. It takes a little time to get used to the variety of Italian phone numbers, which range in length from eight to eleven digits. Landline phone numbers all start with a 0, whereas mobile numbers generally start with a 3.

You can save on the cost of cell-based data by using the **Wi-Fi** capability of your phone when Wi-Fi is available, as it frequently is in public establishments in cities and towns throughout Italy. Your smartphone can also allow you to easily use the GPX tracks available for this walk (see 'GPX tracks and accommodation downloads' below).

As with most of the world, **Italian electricity** operates at 220v. With the dawn of international electronic appliances, most phones, cameras, and computers have a 110/220v transformer built into the 'power brick.' This means that usually only a plug adapter is necessary, whether you are coming to Italy from places that use 110v or non-European plugs, or from countries that use 220v power. In both cases, be aware that older Italian power outlets have a slightly smaller, narrower inlet than the standard European plug, so you may have to improvise with a trip to the hardware store.

## OTHER TIPS

Italians are justifiably proud of their way of life. Indeed, the lifespan of Italians, which is among the world's top ten longest, suggests that they may not be wrong in how they approach life.

### Business hours and the riposo

Northern Europeans and Americans are often surprised to find Italian stores and businesses closed at midday. This is the *riposo*, the mid-afternoon rest observed in much of Italy. If you live in Italy during the summer, you'll see the value of this custom – the mid-afternoon Italian sun can be unbearably hot. Businesses typically close around 1:30pm and reopen around 4:30–5:30pm, once the day has cooled off.

There is a sort of weekly *riposo*, too: stores often close on Saturday at noon and then won't reopen until Monday afternoon or even Tuesday morning. In small towns and villages, this can make it a challenge to find groceries on Sunday mornings, so be sure to plan ahead.

### Laundry

In large cities there are almost always coin-operated laundromats. Ask the hotel or hostel clerk for the nearest location. Laundry is most reliably washed in the sink, so plan to have soap, clothespins, and a clothesline with you.

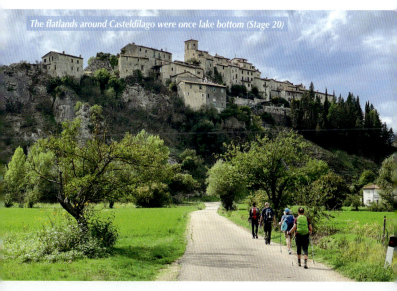
*The flatlands around Casteldilago were once lake bottom (Stage 20)*

## THE WAY OF ST FRANCIS — VIA DI FRANCESCO

### Water fountains
Only occasionally are there water fountains in the middle of a stage and, when there are, they are seldom marked for drinkability. Our maps show locations of water fountains that are confirmed as potable, but it is wise to carry a 2-liter water capacity in fall and spring, and a 3-liter capacity in the summer.

### Street and highway names
*Strada statale* (*SS*) is a national road, while *strada provinciale* (*SP*) is a provincial highway, *strada comunale* (*SC*) is a local highway, and *strada regionale* (*SR*) is a regional highway that crosses provincial borders. All usually have a number and often are designated by the places they connect, like SP Stia–Londa.

Italians have many names for streets, for example *via*, *viale*, and *strada*, and for pathways, including *sentiero*, *passeggiata*, and *cammino*.

### TRAINING FOR YOUR WALK
It's helpful to train in advance of the walk, and this should be part of your careful preparation. The steep hills will challenge anyone who hasn't trained adequately in advance, although almost anyone will find themselves stronger and fitter after walking for several days.

People who are significantly overweight and have a hard time climbing a stairway or hill will have a difficult time on this itinerary. Likewise, because of the frequent and sometimes-steep hills, people with knee or hip problems will find this a difficult walk.

Most important in the training regime is being sure your feet and your boots and socks are adequate for the journey. You should plan to test your shoe/sock combination with a few long walks before you leave, preferably on varied terrain, so blisters along the way won't sideline you.

*Perugia's Corso Vannucci runs through the center of the city, capital of Umbria (Section 2A)*

## WHAT AND HOW TO PACK

The first rule of packing for a long hike is to have exactly the right amount of gear and no more. A light pack is a gift that keeps on giving. The second rule is never to bring anything made of cotton – it's cold when wet and takes too long to dry. Keeping those rules in mind, here is a recommended gear list that works for summer. Heavier layers are required, of course, in spring and fall.

- **Backpack** – 35-liter size is fine for the average build
- **Backpack rain cover** – some backpacks come pre-equipped
- **Emergency foil blanket** – basic survival gear and a must for all outdoor hikes in case of an injury or unintended overnight
- **Hiking shorts** – one or two pairs
- **Long pants** – lightweight and quick-drying for rain and suitable for churches and restaurants – one pair
- **Technical T-shirts** – two short-sleeve, one long-sleeve (jogging shirts work nicely)
- **Shirt/blouse or no-iron dress** – one for dinner and/or church
- **Underwear** – shorts/panties and bras (stretch poly material for quick dry) – two or three pairs
- **Socks** – wool trekking socks, lightweight for summer, heavier for cool weather – three pairs
- **Hiking shoes or boots** – extremely rugged soles with excellent traction are best in this mountainous terrain; consider waterproof material in the spring and fall
- **'Camp shoes'** – a second pair of shoes comfortable enough for evenings and walking on asphalt; trainers or hiking sandals work fine
- **Rain jacket** – of breathable material such as Gore-Tex®
- **Warm layer fleece or light down jacket** – to be worn as a middle layer
- **Sun/rain hat** – wide brim to protect face, ears and back of the neck from sun exposure
- **Toiletries and toiletry bag** – toothbrush, deodorant, etc
- **Multi-purpose soap** – one small bar of soap works in the shower and also for washing laundry
- **Camera, camera pouch and charger** – if you take special care with your photos, and/or:
- **Phone (with camera) and charger**
- **Water storage system** – a bladder or bottles with 2-liter (spring/fall) or 3-liter (summer) capacity; lack of drinking fountains along the way means it's important to carry adequate water
- **Clothespins and clothesline**
- **Passport, airline ticket, waterproof bag for documents**
- **Sunblock lotion**
- **Pen and paper and/or journal**
- **Blister kit** – blisters need prompt attention, so plan to carry the ingredients necessary to treat your blisters before they damage your pilgrimage; this may include sterile wipes, bandages, a small scissor or razor blade, and Compeed® to cover hotspots

## THE WAY OF ST FRANCIS — VIA DI FRANCESCO

- **Partial toilet paper roll and two plastic bags** – the paper is for use when needed; one bag is for keeping the roll dry, and the second is for carrying the used paper to proper disposal
- **Debit/credit card(s)**
- **Copies of important documents** – scans or hard copies of your passport, travel arrangements, and credit/debit cards are priceless in case of theft or loss of the originals
- **Walking poles** – many pilgrims swear by these to help with balance and to take weight off the knees and hips
- **Swimsuit** – it's lightweight, and you'll miss it if your lodging includes a pool
- **Mosquito repellant** – very helpful in a few swampy areas

Layers are the key to staying warm on cold days. A cold weather set-up is:

- technical long-sleeve T-shirt closest to the body
- fleece or down jacket layer for warmth
- rain jacket on top.

Add or subtract layers depending on the temperature.

### BAGGAGE TRANSPORT AND STORAGE

Given the smaller population of pilgrims along this route, the options for baggage handling are fewer and more expensive. Since you can expect to pay €50 for transporting up to five bags over one stage, it makes baggage transport much more economical for groups than for individuals.

Between Florence and Assisi (including the Cortona–Arezzo–Anghiari variant), baggage transport is available through www.beppino.net. From Assisi to Rome, bags can be transported through www.bagsfree.com. Storage of luggage is available near the airports at Florence and Rome, and in Assisi through www.usebounce.com and other providers.

### LANGUAGE AIDS

In tourist centers it's easy to find someone who speaks English, but in the small towns which are at the heart of this walk, Italians may know little or no English. For this reason, it's a great idea to know a few helpful Italian phrases and to learn the rudiments of Italian pronunciation, which, compared to English pronunciation, is surprisingly easy and consistent. Translation apps like Google Translate are an indispensable and free resource on your smartphone, and in Appendix C you'll find a brief guide that will help you get started.

### HEALTH AND WELL-BEING

Italy has a state-of-the-art national telephone system to contact ambulance and police, with English-speaking operators available 24/7 to answer emergency calls.

## HEALTH AND WELL-BEING

If you become sick or injured and don't feel it's an emergency, a good starting place for information is the local pharmacy, which is marked in Italy with the sign of a green cross above the storefront. If he or she can't help you, the pharmacist will recommend a nearby clinic (*guardia medica*) or hospital. Your overnight host is a valuable source of information about local transportation, clinics, hospitals and doctors.

### EMERGENCY HEALTH AND SAFETY PHONE NUMBERS

112 – One-call emergency service phone line
113 – Direct line to local police
115 – Fire department
117 – Finance police (if you've been cheated)
118 – Medical emergencies: this is the best number to call if you have a health-related emergency and need an ambulance or emergency room
1515 – Forest fires

*A field of poppies after Macenano makes a colorful setting for minor repairs to gear (Stage 20)*

# HOW TO USE THIS GUIDE

*Pilgrims cross a stone bridge at the valley floor below Poggio Moiano (Stage 24)*

## STAGE DESCRIPTIONS

As part of Cicerone's pilgrimage series, this guide provides a lot of helpful information for your walk. Each stage is laid out in the following format:

### Route summary information

An **information box** at the start of each stage provides the specific start and end points of the stage as well as the following key statistics:

- **Duration:** No two walkers share an identical pace, so this book uses an algorithm that calculates duration based on 4km/hr pace with an additional 5min added for every 100m of ascent, rounding the result to the nearest ¼hr. Rest stops are not included in the duration total.
- **Distance:** Unless otherwise specified, the number given is always based on the official route with all extraneous waypoints carefully edited out and the tracks smoothed to one waypoint for each 30 metres in distance. Expect the unedited tracks from your recreational GPS, smartphone app, or step counter to add about 10–15% to the total.
- **Total ascent and descent:** These figures record the up and down bumps that occur as you gain and lose elevation through the day.

Elevation figures for GPS tracks in this book are provided by www.ridewithgps.com.
- **Difficulty:** Using a formula that balances total distance, steepness, and ascent/descent statistics, all stages are awarded one of four designations: 'Easy,' 'Moderate,' 'Moderately hard,' and 'Hard.'
- **Percentage paved:** This percentage shows how much of the walk is carried out on hard (paved) surfaces like concrete, tarmac, asphalt, and cobblestones rather than unpaved, softer surfaces like gravel, dirt roads, and dirt paths.
- **Lodgings:** Distances to most lodgings between the start and end points are included, to help you plan your stages.

Following the information box, an **overview** paragraph summarizes the stage and shares any special tips, recommendations, or warnings that walkers should know before beginning the walk.

## Walking directions, distances, and municipality information

Since the Way of St Francis/Via di Francesco is fairly well marked, only moderately detailed walking directions are given for each stage. Within the directions, **bold** is used to highlight landmarks that are labeled on the route maps, and intermediate distances between key landmarks are provided. Because underlying distance calculations are based on 100ths of a kilometer while intermediate distances are shown at 10ths of a kilometer, some minor decimal rounding discrepancies naturally result when intermediate distances are added together.

Municipalities with pilgrim lodgings are featured in boxes throughout the route directions. The box headings provide key information,

*An early morning mist covers a pasture in the Valdichiascio (Stage 13)*

# *The Way of St Francis — Via di Francesco*

## Figure 1: Example of stage description and municipal information

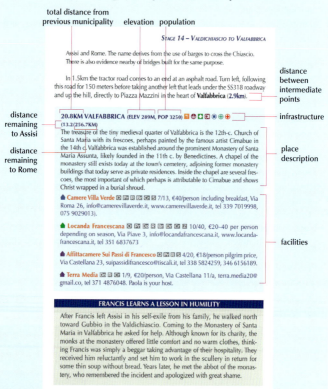

## Infrastructure symbols

# STAGE DESCRIPTIONS

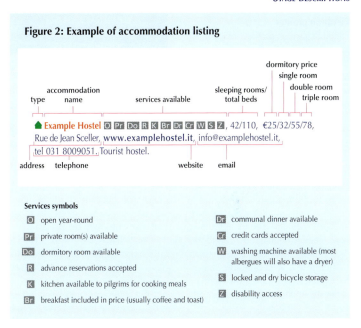

Figure 2: Example of accommodation listing

including a set of infrastructure symbols indicating available services. Distance from the previous municipality is shown, as well as distance remaining: for the stages before Assisi, the distance remaining to both Assisi and Rome is shown; after Assisi, only the distance to Rome is shown. Figure 1 provides a key to the municipal information boxes and their symbols.

## Accommodation listings

The Via di Francesco and its volunteer organizations have done an excellent job of creating a network of pilgrim-specific lodgings located in churches, monasteries, convents, municipal facilities, and church retreat houses, with a preference for low-cost options – these types of lodgings are invisible in typical tourist resources like Booking.com. With help from the Via di Francesco organization, important information is provided about each lodging, to help you make your choice. This includes names, contact information, cost, and symbols indicating available services. See Figure 2.

## Elevation profiles
Helpful elevation profiles are included for each stage, so that you can see a representation of distances and topography. When stages have two route options, one of the profiles will often be superimposed on the other to make comparison easier.

## Maps
All Cicerone guidebook maps are 'north up' and show the entire stage route at 1:100,000 resolution. Six cities – Florence, Gubbio, Assisi, Spoleto, Rieti, and Rome – are shown at about 1:25,000. The main route of each stage is depicted by a solid red line, and options within a stage are in dashed red; a solid blue line is used for variant stages. Check the map key at the start of the book for more details about map symbols.

### GPX TRACKS AND ACCOMMODATION DOWNLOADS

The Pilgrim Paths Navigo App includes GPS tracks corresponding to the route of this book. Full and current accommodation listings are also included in the app, which is available on both the Apple App Store and Google Play Store (for more information see www.pilgrimpaths.com/navigo).. Reservations at many lodgings can be made directly from the app, either with hot links to phone numbers or with live hyperlinks to reservation sites when they are available.

You will also find Way of St Francis GPX tracks at the Cicerone website (www.cicerone.co.uk/1167/gpx), offered free to book purchasers. A printout of the accommodation listings is downloadable from this book's web page at www.cicerone.co.uk/1167. For the latest book updates, always remember to visit the book's Cicerone web page as well as the author's site at www.sandybrownbooks.com.

# SECTION 1: FLORENCE TO SANTUARIO DELLA VERNA

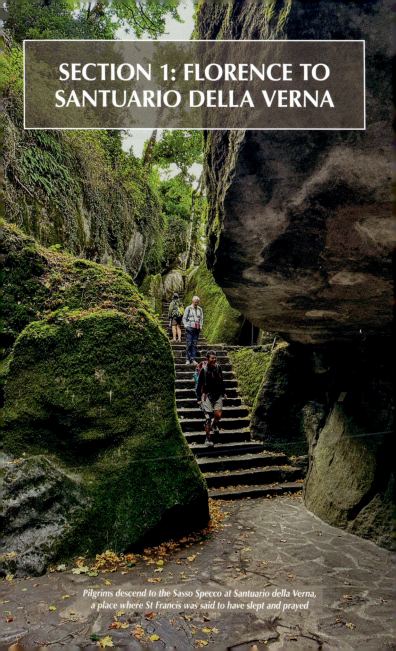

*Pilgrims descend to the Sasso Specco at Santuario della Verna, a place where St Francis was said to have slept and prayed*

## THE WAY OF ST FRANCIS – VIA DI FRANCESCO

This mountainous portion of the route is best suited to hardy hikers who are undeterred by remote and solitary mountain pathways. Walkers enjoy a progressively more secluded and rugged journey, first on well-groomed forest roads and then on the steep and narrow mountain paths of the Casentino National Forest. The climactic hike crosses three tall hills after Badia Prataglia before coming to the lofty and serene mountaintop retreat of Santuario della Verna. Along the way is the secluded twin Monastery/Hermitage of Camaldoli, where the quiet forest has overheard the prayers of Benedictine monks and hermits for over 1000 years.

See Variant 1.1 for details on the southern Florence to Santuario della Verna route.

# STAGE 1
*Florence to Pontassieve*

| | |
|---|---|
| **Start** | Basilica Santa Croce, Florence |
| **Finish** | Piazza Vittorio Emanuele II, Pontassieve |
| **Duration** | 5hr |
| **Distance** | 18.4km |
| **Total ascent** | 271m |
| **Total descent** | 215m |
| **Difficulty** | Easy |
| **Percentage paved** | 50% |
| **Lodgings** | Pontassieve 18.4km |

Memories of Renaissance masterpieces fade quickly as this stage travels along quiet bends of the scenic Arno River and briefly among olive groves before coming to modern Pontassieve. Prepare for lack of shade and water fountains on the 6.5km river walk. Afterward, the towns of San Jacopo al Girone, Compiobbi, and Sieci offer services.

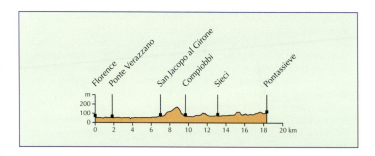

**FLORENCE (ELEV 50M, POP 367,150)** 🍴 🛏 🛒 🏧 🚌 🚉 ➕ ✚ 🏥 ℹ️ **(274.1/517.6KM)**
Birthplace of the Renaissance and seat of Italian culture, Florence is visited each year by over five million people, who crowd into the city to see Michelangelo's *David*, to marvel at Brunelleschi's dome, and to admire the world's premier collection of Renaissance art at the Uffizzi Gallery. Florence is also home to the venerable Basilica Santa Croce, the largest Franciscan church in the world, a fitting place to begin a journey to discover St Francis of Assisi.

*The Way of St Francis — Via di Francesco*

The Romans established Florence, Pisa, Lucca, and Siena in the 1st c. BC as colonies in the newly Roman territory of Etruria. In the late Middle Ages, Florence's rise as an economic center helped it eclipse its Tuscan rivals to become one of the largest and most prosperous cities of Europe. With prosperity came a rich cultural life, and Florence became home to poets, artists, and philosophers like Ghiberti, Brunelleschi, Giotto, Michelangelo, Leonardo da Vinci, Raphael, Botticelli, Dante, Machiavelli, Galileo, and many others. Because of its literary primacy in Italy, the Tuscan dialect would become the basis of the modern Italian language. After the unification of Italy, Florence served six years (1865–1871) as the nation's capital.

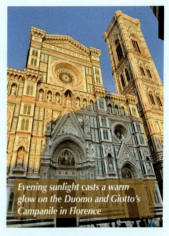
*Evening sunlight casts a warm glow on the Duomo and Giotto's Campanile in Florence*

The most visible symbol of the city is its domed cathedral, the **Florence Duomo**, whose 15th-c. dome by Filippo Brunelleschi is widely considered a masterwork of architecture. While the Duomo may receive the most attention, the interior of its adjacent 11th–12th-c. **Baptistery of San Giovanni** is covered in rich mosaics, and its doors, including Ghiberti's *Gates of Paradise*, are treasured as masterpieces of Renaissance art. The ensemble is completed by **Giotto's Campanile**, the adjacent 15th-c., 85m-tall bell tower, making the Duomo complex one of Christendom's most beautiful and beloved architectural treasures. (Purchase tickets at the office across from the Duomo's south entrance or online at https://duomo.firenze.it/en.)

Florence's many works of art are scattered among its ample museums. The famed **Uffizi Gallery** is home to treasures of the Middle Ages and Renaissance, including *Birth of Venus* by Botticelli and *Doni Tondo* (*Holy Family*) by Michelangelo. Across the **Ponte Vecchio**, with its glittering jewelry shops, is the **Pitti Palace**, home to art by Raphael and Titian, as well as the Gallery of Modern Art. The adjacent **Boboli Gardens** are a fine example of the beauty of Italian gardens. (Go to www.uffizi.it for individual or combined tickets.)

The single most prized artwork is certainly **Michelangelo's** *David*, the original housed at the Accademia Gallery (www.galleriaaccademiafirenze.it) and a copy set in front of the town hall – **Palazzo Vecchio** in **Piazza della Signoria**. The storied statue is the biggest single draw in Florence, and in many ways is the symbol of the Renaissance of classical ideas in art.

## STAGE 1 – FLORENCE TO PONTASSIEVE

As with all of Italy's medieval cities, Florence is a town rich in beautiful churches. After the Duomo, **Basilica Santa Croce** stands out for its Franciscan connection; see 'Basilica Santa Croce and the start of the Way of St Francis in Florence' for a more complete description. The Dominican **Basilica Santa Maria Novella** holds artworks by Brunelleschi and Giotto, while the Basilica of San Lorenzo, called the **Medici Chapel** for its primary benefactors, astounds with its glorious interior, hidden by a humble, unfinished exterior.

The pace of touristy Florence slows a bit after sundown, when its piazzas become the center of life. Along with **Piazza della Signoria**, the **Piazza della Repubblica** is abuzz with activity after dark. Hidden across the Arno is the quieter and less touristic **Piazza Santa Spirito**, whose restaurants offer their wares mostly to the local population. For dinner, look for a quiet restaurant serving local favorites like *zuppa di cipolle* (onion soup). The bold can try *trippa al Fiorentina* (tripe) for a main course, or perhaps a *bistecca Fiorentina* – the famous local version of the classic T–bone steak. Best of all may be to find a café before the crowds are awake and enjoy a breakfast of *cappuccino*, *cornetto* (croissant), and *spremuta d'arancia* (freshly squeezed orange juice) to begin your day.

🏠 **Casa per Ferie – Oblate Sisters of the Assumption** O Pr Do R Br Cr S 26/46, €-/55/100/135, Borgo Pinti 15, info@oblate.it, www.oblate.it, tel 055 2346291.

🏠 **7 Santi Hostel** O Pr Do R K Br Cr S Z 83/141 €51/55/100/135, Viale dei Mille 11, www.hostel7santi.com, info@hostel7santi.com, tel 055 218510.

### BASILICA SANTA CROCE

#### The start of the Way of St Francis in Florence
According to tradition, Francis of Assisi came to Florence in 1211, and was given a small chapel dedicated to the Holy Cross on an island in the Arno. When Francis' followers returned to build a church, they took the chapel's name for their parish, building its first structure near the river in a flood-prone neighborhood of poor homes. Their church, now Basilica Santa Croce, is the largest Franciscan church in the world.

Sometimes called the 'Pantheon of Italy' because of the many notables entombed inside, the church is also a celebration of the life and accomplishments of the humble saint of Assisi. The medieval frescoes inside the basilica tell his story in rich detail, and it's only fitting that a pilgrim on this route begin the walk with these priceless images in mind. Pietro Nelli's late-14th-c. *The First Franciscans Come to Florence* depicts their story in the city. Giotto's cycle of frescoes in the chancel illustrates seven scenes

## THE WAY OF ST FRANCIS — VIA DI FRANCESCO

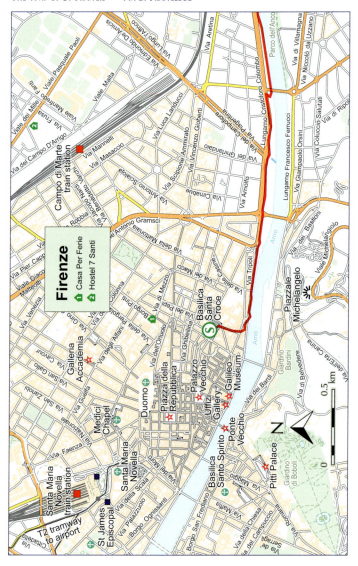

## STAGE 1 – FLORENCE TO PONTASSIEVE

from the life of St Francis, as well as his friends kneeling before the Pope in Rome, while Gaddi's 1340 *Crucifixion* in the sacristy shows Francis in an intentional anachronism at the crucifixion of Jesus. Look for Gaddi's depiction of St Francis and the stigmata in the 1350 *Tree of Life and Last Supper* (refectory). Go to the pulpit to see bas-relief carvings by Maiano with scenes from the life of St Francis from the late 15th c.

Francis' legacy through the centuries is also represented in the Third Order Franciscans buried or memorialized here. Among them are Dante Alighieri and Michelangelo. A gilded reliquary holds the relics of Umiliana de' Cerchi, the first woman to become a member of the Third Order. These tombs and the great works of art inside Basilica Santa Croce are signs of the deep admiration and respect earned by Francis and his followers during his lifetime and in later centuries. (For more information, go to www.santacroceopera.it/en.)

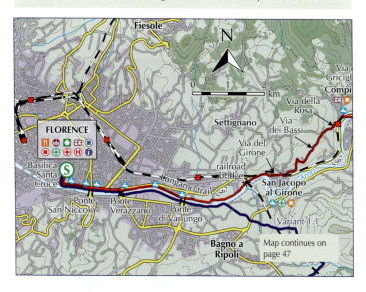

At the steps of Basilica Santa Croce, facing the church, turn right and walk 1½ blocks to the raised sidewalk alongside the **Arno River**. Cross the street and follow this sidewalk past the busy riverside hotels, with the old tower of Florence's original walls visible across the river. Car traffic crosses the Arno on successive bridges; before the second auto bridge, the **Ponte Verazzano** (**1.8km**), find a

## THE WAY OF ST FRANCIS — VIA DI FRANCESCO

footpath down to the dirt trail by the river, the **Lungarno**, which will take you alongside the river all the way out of urban Florence.

After crossing under the **railroad bridge**, come to a children's play area at a turn of the river, where you turn left off the path and follow Via del Girone alongside the SS67 Via Arentina Nuova for two long blocks to the stoplight and piazza at the center of **San Jacopo al Girone** (5.2km, café, pharmacy). Cross left, under the tracks, and then veer right onto the white brick sidewalk of Via San Jacopo. At the end of the sidewalk, turn left and follow **Via dei Bassi** as it winds its narrow way uphill along stone walls and through olive groves in the stage's longest climb. At the second right, turn onto **Via della Rosa**, which traverses the hillside then descends with views of Compiobbi below. Follow the road downhill, coming alongside the railroad tracks, until it finally ends at Strada Provinciale 110. Now turn right, cross under the railroad tracks, and then cross the SS67 Via Arentina highway into central **Compiobbi** (2.7km, bank, restaurant, café).

Continue to the riverside and take the trail just past the newspaper kiosk along the slow and lazy Arno River. In a few minutes turn left at a yellow utility tower and walk up the steps to the protected walkway beside the highway. Fork

*A group of pilgrims make their way along the Lungarno walking path on their way toward Pontassieve*

## STAGE 1 – FLORENCE TO PONTASSIEVE

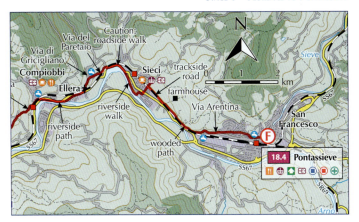

right to the residential suburb of **Ellera** (no services) and continue as you briefly rejoin the highway at a traffic circle. Just after the traffic circle, look for a modern, nondescript, yellow church on the left side of the road. Immediately after this, turn left onto tiny Via Le Folle. Cross under the railroad tracks and cross the pedestrian bridge that spans the creek to the right.

Follow the walkway, then turn left at its end and follow **Via di Gricigliano** uphill beside a yellow apartment building. At the first fork, turn right onto **Via del Paretaio**. The road veers to the right and soon crosses back under the railroad bridge. Turn left at the highway and carefully follow it on the left shoulder to the town of **Sieci** (**3.5km**, groceries, café, train, bank).

Walk on the highway's sidewalk and cross the Arno tributary on the highway bridge. Just after the bridge, turn right onto the pedestrian walkway along the river. Follow this trail, enjoying the last quiet moments along the beautiful Arno. After the park, turn left at Via Toscanini, away from the river, and continue across the Via Arentina highway at a roundabout. Cross under the railroad tracks on the right side of the road and in 100 meters make a hard right, doubling back to a dirt road that follows alongside the tracks.

Follow this road alongside the tracks, diverting briefly uphill for a few hundred meters toward a **farmhouse**. Before a hairpin turn under the track, go straight onto a wooded path that briefly enters woods. Soon come to a gravel road, which you follow right and downhill. The gravel road becomes concrete as it enters the outskirts of **Pontassieve**. Stay on this road as it passes a small piazza and then veers right and downhill, ending at the Via Gualdo Reni. Turn left here and follow the road through the Porta Fiorentina city gate, finding Piazza Vittorio Emanuele II on the right (**5.2km**).

*The Way of St Francis — Via di Francesco*

**18.4KM PONTASSIEVE (ELEV 108M, POP 20,622)** 🍴 🏨 🛖 🚌 🚏 🚉 ✚ (255.7/499.2KM)
In the Middle Ages, Pontassieve was called Castel Sant'Angelo for the Florentine castle built here. The town later became known for its strategic bridge across the Sieve River, which opened to Florence the territories of Mugello and Casentino. By the 18th c., Pontassieve's location made it a regional economic hub, and in the 19th and 20th c. the railroad made it an industrial center. Its economic importance led the Allies to bomb the town repeatedly during World War II.

Although none of its medieval features remain, the town was rebuilt along its medieval lines, with winding roads that follow the contours of the riverbank. The modern town hall is built on the foundations of the original medieval castle, and Via Ghiberti, the bustling, central commercial road, connects it with the medieval Sieve bridge as in days past. Today, Pontassieve is a hub for artisanal leather, Chianti wine, olive oil, handmade glass, and ceramics.

🔺 **Leonardo's Rooms B&B** Pr R Br Dr Cr S 7/14, €-/55/65/85, Via Piave 7, info@leonardosrooms.it, tel 360 923824, tel 055 8368192. Open Feb–Oct. €5 breakfast not included. Leonardo is your host.

🔺 **Toscani da Sempre** O Pr R Br Cr 7/14, €-/80/80/110, Via Fratelli Monzecchi13/15, info@toscanidasempre.it, tel 055 8392952.

## THE EARLY YEARS OF FRANCIS

When Pietro and his French wife, Pica, celebrated the birth of their son Giovanni, in about 1181, they undoubtedly expected him to take up the family's prosperous cloth business in Assisi. The boy came to be called Francis (Italian: Francesco) because of his mother's influence on this life. Already he was beginning to stray from the family's expectations when, as an adolescent, Francis preferred perfecting his skills as a horseman, archer, and warrior rather than as a merchant.

In 1202, war broke out between Assisi and neighboring Perugia. Dressed in fine battle gear, Francis boldly joined his countrymen to fight the Perugians, but the tragic result of the brief but bloody conflict was a heavy loss of life and many casualties. The Perugian victors sorted the conquered soldiers into peasants, who were killed, and aristocrats, who were imprisoned for ransom. As a result, Francis spent nearly a year in the dungeons of Perugia while his ransom was arranged. He came back to Assisi in 1203 a very different man.

# STAGE 2
*Pontassieve to Consuma*

| | |
|---|---|
| **Start** | Piazza Vittorio Emanuele II, Pontassieve |
| **Finish** | SR70 at Via Poggio Tesoro, Consuma |
| **Duration** | 5½hr |
| **Distance** | 16.8km |
| **Total ascent** | 999m |
| **Total descent** | 74m |
| **Difficulty** | Moderate |
| **Percentage paved** | 64% |
| **Lodgings** | Diacceto 5.9km, Ferrano (turn-off) 9.5km, Consuma 16.8km |

This constant and demanding uphill stage takes you from scenic vineyards into the first of the quiet forests that will be your setting for the next five days. Today's climb is to the pass at the top of the saddle of mountains around which the Arno River makes a grand loop. Water and services are available only at Diacceto.

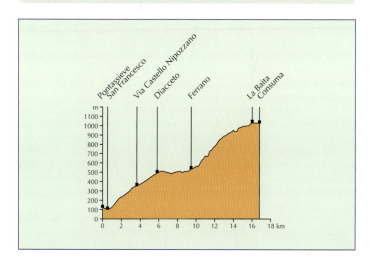

## THE WAY OF ST FRANCIS — VIA DI FRANCESCO

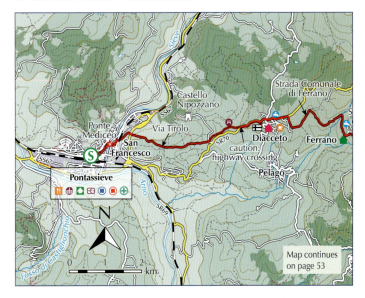

Continue past Piazza Vittorio Emanuele II and walk under the clock tower arch. The road veers left and becomes Via Ghiberti (grocery stores, bakeries). In 500 meters the road heads downhill, turns right and crosses the Sieve River on a stout, medieval bridge. Sometimes called the Medici Bridge (Ponte Mediceo), this two-arched structure was commissioned by Cosimo I in 1555 to replace an earlier structure. After the crossing, continue along the road, now in the village of **San Francesco** (**0.5km**, groceries, café), passing on the right the lovely Chiesa San Francesco, once a Franciscan convent.

One block later, turn left on Via Bettini. Turn right at Via Farulla and in one block come to the Via Forlivese, the main road up and down the Sieve Valley. Just across the street is the barely visible **Via Tirolo**, which you take steeply uphill, first crossing a **railroad bridge**. Climb uphill on this pleasant asphalt lane for the next nearly 3km, with views of the Sieve Valley, vineyards, and the 10th-c. **Castello di Nipozzano**, now a prosperous winery of the historic Frescobaldi company. The asphalt road ends among olive orchards near the top of the hill at the castle's access road (**3.1km**).

Cross the intersection and continue on the gravel road between two stone walls as it heads uphill. In 800 meters, cross an asphalt road and continue straight, enjoying the views of mountains and vineyards and passing a shaded **rest area**.

## Stage 2 – Pontassieve to Consuma

Cross the highway after a couple of hundred meters and continue uphill on the gravel vineyard road on the other side, leading uphill into the village of **Diacceto** (**2.2km**, café, lodging at ⌂ **Locanda Tinti** http://locandatinti.blogspot.com). The bar on the left side at the turn-off for Pelago is the last place for services until the end of the day's walk.

Continue uphill on the highway to the turn-off for Ferrano. Turn right here to follow this forested, quiet and fairly level asphalt road with views on the right of Pelago. Pass the 19th-c. Castello di Ferrano on your right and then come to the hamlet of **Ferrano** (**3.6km**, ⌂ **Santa Maria di Ferrano** Pr Do R Br 1/1 €25/person, Località Ferrano Colle, 68santamariaferrano@gmail.com, tel 338 6901122. Thomas Muller, sculptor and artist, generously welcomes pilgrims. By reservation only. Dinner by reservation, €5 linens).

In about 20min the road surface turns to gravel. Pass an abandoned chapel on the right, cross a bridge, and just afterward come to a **trailhead** on the left. Now turn left and follow the trail marked CAI 11 'Consuma 1.45.' You are now in the forest, which will shade your walk almost to Consuma. To find your way, look continually for the red/white painted waymarks of the official trail.

*Fishermen cast their lines into the Sieve River at Pontassieve*

## THE WAY OF ST FRANCIS — VIA DI FRANCESCO

The pathways lead to **Via La Catena**, a paved road leading left toward Consuma. Turn left and follow this road for 700 meters to an intersection, where you go right on CAI SM (Sentiero della Memoria, commemorating Nazi massacres in the area between 1943 and 1945), toward Consuma. This quiet road heads uphill and curves to the right, then in 400 meters comes to an asphalt road and the **abandoned restaurant** Il Laghetto Nil Bosco. Turn left onto the asphalt road, following signs for CAI 6.

Follow the asphalt road for 900 meters until, after a left bend in the road, the CAI markings point you onto a small trail on the right side that offers a shortcut into Consuma. Turn right and go uphill. Follow the road at the top to the right, through scattered vacation homes, to **La Baita Ristorante** (**6.6km**). Just afterward, turn right onto the **SR70 highway** and follow its left shoulder into the heart of **Consuma** (**0.7km**) with its restaurants and shops.

Vineyards of Sangiovese cover the hillsides on the way to Diacceto

## STAGE 2 – PONTASSIEVE TO CONSUMA

**16.8KM CONSUMA** (ELEV 1050M, POP 150) 🍴 ⛪ 🏨 ⓘ (238.9/482.4KM)
The hamlet of Consuma sits on the Florence side of Passo della Consuma, the main crossing over a spine of the Central Apennines that separates two parts of the Arno River drainage. The town traces its roots to the 15th c., when it is first noted as a village serving travelers between Arezzo and Florence. It now serves vacationers visiting the Casentino National Park on two-lane SR70. A central feature of the settlement is its church, built in 1932 over the foundations of a 16th-c. chapel. The friar Francesco da Menabbio records a miracle performed by St Francis at the Church of Madonna dei Fossi, near Consuma, where Francis created a spring of clear water for the local inhabitants.

⛺ **Ospitale di San Domenico** O Pr Do R K Dr W S 5/14, €25/41/61/75, Via Casentinese 355, elenac71@yahoo.it, www.viadifrancescofirenzelaverna.it, tel 347 1993121, tel 333 5037757. Elena and Luca are your hosts.

⛺ **Albergo Ristorante Miramonti** O Pr Do R Br Dr Cr S Z 20/45, €32/-/80/95, Via Consuma 61 (1km past town and near the path on the next stage), info@hotelmiramonti-ar.com, tel 351 5321130. Pilgrim price with guidebook listed. Breakfast included, dinner and sack lunch available.

53

## FRANCIS AND NATURE

As this stage of the Way of St Francis leads into the forests and mountains, it is fitting to consider the first verses of Francis' 'Canticle of the Sun,' which are a song of praise for the natural world. The piece is widely recognized as both artistic and theological, proposing a form of equality between humans and nature based on their commonality as creations of God. It is the earliest-known literature written in the Umbrian dialect of Italian, the words recorded by Thomas of Celano in 1228.

Most High, all powerful, good Lord,
Yours are the praises, the glory, the honour, and all blessing.
To You alone, Most High, do they belong,
and no man is worthy to mention Your name.
Be praised, my Lord, through all your creatures,
especially Sir Brother Sun,
who brings the day; and you give light through him.
And he is beautiful and radiant in all his splendour!
Of you, Most High, he bears the likeness.
Praised be You, my Lord, through Sister Moon and the stars,
in heaven you formed them clear and precious and beautiful.
Praised be You, my Lord, through Brother Wind,
and through the air, cloudy and serene,
and every kind of weather through which you give sustenance to Your creatures.
Praised be You, my Lord, through Sister Water,
which is very useful and humble and precious and chaste.
Praised be You, my Lord, through Brother Fire,
through whom you light the night and he is beautiful
and playful and robust and strong.
Praised be You, my Lord, through Sister Mother Earth,
who sustains us and governs us and who produces
varied fruits with coloured flowers and herbs.

*Translation by the Franciscan Friars Third Order Regular*

# STAGE 3
## *Consuma to Stia*

| | |
|---|---|
| **Start** | SR70 at Via Poggio Tesoro, Consuma |
| **Finish** | Church of Santa Maria Assunta, Stia |
| **Duration** | 6hr (5¾hr via Campolombardo) |
| **Distance** | 14.6km (18.2km via Campolombardo) |
| **Total ascent** | 640m (393m via Campolombardo) |
| **Total descent** | 829m (976m via Campolombardo) |
| **Difficulty** | Moderately hard (moderate via Campolombardo) |
| **Percentage paved** | 26% (7% via Campolombardo) |
| **Lodgings** | Gualdo 2.8km, Villa turn-off 7.1km, Stia 14.6km |

The elevation gained yesterday is mostly lost in this long, gradual, downhill hike on forested mountain paths and quiet farm roads. A 600-meter shorter option through Campolombardo avoids the highway walking required on the official route. At stage end we meet the Arno River again, this time closer to its source above the historic town of Stia, which with neighboring Pratavecchio forms the largest settlement in the remote Casentino region.

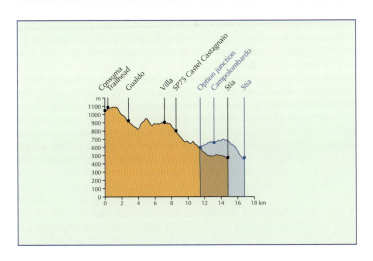

55

*THE WAY OF ST FRANCIS — VIA DI FRANCESCO*

On the sidewalk of the SR70, head uphill to the top of the pass, where across from the bar built of logs you will find the **trailhead** marked 'So.F.T. Trekking, Anello Principale' (**0.4km**). Take this trail as it leads gently uphill under beech and pine trees and away from the highway.

Soon you arrive at a **confusing intersection** with a gravel road heading downhill toward Il Gualdo horse ranch; at this intersection, follow a path marked 'Stia 00' just after the road. You come to a fence and follow it toward a group of houses and finally reach an asphalt road where you turn left. Shortly afterward, go right at the road sign for Gualdo, following the plentiful markers downhill on the asphalt road through the tiny town toward a house marked '25' in **Gualdo** (**2.5km**, ▲ **B&B Il Gualdo** Loc. Gualdo 44, info@ilgualdo.net, tel 0575 554057. 10% discount with credential). The road ends here at a T-junction.

Turn left, take the first right, and follow signs onto a dirt path leading into the woods. If you plan to stay at Villa, watch for signs marking the **Villa turn-off** (**4.2km**). (From the turn-off, the path to Villa leads steeply downhill through the forest to the roadway, where you turn left to find the lodging: ▲ **Ospedale San Jacopo** Pr R Br Dr W S 3/5, €-/40/60/70, Località Villa 2a, elenac71@yahoo.it,

56

## Stage 3 – Consuma to Stia

www.viadifrancescofirenzelaverna.it, tel 347 1993121, 333 5037577, Dinner by request. Linen not included. Elena speaks English.)

If not heading for Villa, continue on the forest path past a pump house operated by a solar cell and then come to the asphalt **SP75** (**1.4km**), where you turn right. A left turn here leads to the settlement of **Castel Castagnaio** about 1km off track.

*Pilgrims walk through a deciduous forest after Gualdo*

> Prior to the 10th c., when a castle was built here by the Guidi counts, the site of **Castel Castagnaio** was host first to an Etruscan temple and later to one built by the Romans. The castle has been in ruins since the 15th c., but there is a small 16th-c. church on the site that perhaps was once the castle's chapel.

Stay on the roadway briefly, and in 100 meters veer left following marking onto another forest path, this one descending for the next several hundred meters. If you plan to take the Campolombardo option (see below), it can be accessed from here via a short, steep, unmarked climb off the wooded trail. The path continues to a gravel road, which you follow past **Gli Amici dell'Asino** donkey farm (see Stia below for details of lodging at La Terrazza in Foresta). As it descends, the roadway turns to asphalt and you come to the wide loop of a switchback on the quiet **SS Stia–Londa road** (**2.8km**). Here you have the option to turn right for the 2.8km longer but much quieter walk into Stia via Campolombardo or to continue left onto the official route that crosses the Arno and follows the highway into Stia.

### Campolombardo option

Although this option adds 2.8km to the journey, it avoids a long stretch of asphalt. Turn right after Gli Amici dell'Asino and follow the quiet and well-groomed gravel roads of the sparse Campolombardo agricultural and residential settlement all the way to Stia.

On the official route, continue downhill on switchbacks. Views to the left include the Convent of Santa Maria delle Grazie, built in 1432 to mark an apparition of the Virgin Mary, and the 13th-c. Castello di Porciano. At a bridge with low stone walls, cross the Arno River, in summer quite diminutive near its mountain source. At the stop sign, turn right and follow signs downhill into the picturesque historic center filled with restaurants, cafés, and shops to arrive at the Church of Santa Maria Assunta in **Stia** (**3.3km**).

---

**14.6KM STIA (ELEV 441M, POP 2413)** 🄷 🛆 🅲 🅾 🅾 ⊕ ✚ Ⓗ 🛈 (224.4/467.8KM)
Stia and its sister city, Pratovecchio, immediately to the south, combine to serve as the economic hub of the Upper Arno Valley. Originally a market town for Porciano Castle to the northwest, Stia became a textile manufacturing center during the Industrial Revolution. In 1838 its largest wool mill employed over 500 people and produced 700,000 meters of cloth per year. The wool industry is celebrated at the Museo della Lana (Via Giovanni Sartori 2, www.museodellalana.it, €5), and shops in the historic center sell high-quality, handcrafted wool garments.

At the heart of Stia's central piazza is the 12th-c. **Church of Santa Maria Assunta**, whose dark and tranquil interior features stone columns decorated with plants, animals, and human figures in the Romanesque and early Gothic styles. The church's terracotta Madonna and child are typical of the work of Andrea della Robbia (born 1435), which we will see throughout the region. Two grates in the apse allow viewing of Etruscan stones found in a 20th-c. restoration of the church.

🛖 **La Terrazza in Foresta** R K W S 2/6 in tents, €30 per person, Loc. Campolombardo 37, amicidellasino@gmail.com, tel 320 0676766. Open May–July. Breakfast included. Space for hiking tents. Your host is Marta Signi.

🛖 **La Piazza Uno** Pr R W S 2/3, €-/30/50/60, Piazza Tanucci 24, olgafiorini1947@gmail.com, tel 335 7242405. Breakfast available nearby. Olga is your host.

🛖 **La Guardia B&B** O Pr R Br Cr S Z 2/4, €-/60/70/75, Piazza Tanucci 59, laguardiabb@gmail.com, www.bblaguardia.it, tel 347 0180074. Contact Federica directly for pilgrim discount. English speaking.

🛖 **The Pilgrim's Lodge** O Pr R K 3/5, €35 per person, Via Fiorentina 29, ivana-grofi@gmail.com, tel 380 4520062. €5 linens. Ivana is your host.

## STAGE 3 – CONSUMA TO STIA

*Pilgrim walkers make their way through a narrow street in Stia*

### FRANCIS AND THE LEPER

While the cold and damp dungeon had taken a toll on his health, it was more likely the traumatic experience of human cruelty in warfare that changed Francis' outlook. He had decided to go to war again, but turned back on his way to Spoleto. On his way back to Assisi, he came across a leper, begging for food. The old Francis would have been horrified at such a sight and would have kept his distance, but this time he subdued his revulsion and, out of a newfound compassion, gently kissed the man. Francis was living into a new worldview that accepted each person as worthy of love in spite of their condition.

## STAGE 4
*Stia to Badia Prataglia*

| | |
|---|---|
| **Start** | Church of Santa Maria Assunta, Stia |
| **Finish** | Church of Santa Maria Assunta, Badia Prataglia |
| **Duration** | 7¾hr |
| **Distance** | 23.8km |
| **Total ascent** | 1116m |
| **Total descent** | 718m |
| **Difficulty** | Hard |
| **Percentage paved** | 31% |
| **Lodgings** | Lonnano 4.7km, Valagnesi 7.9km, Asqua 11.1km, Camaldoli 16.3km, Rifugio Cotozzo 18.1km, Badia Prataglia 23.8km |

The undulating terrain makes this a difficult stage, and an overnight at Camaldoli is a smart idea. After a moderately steep uphill to Lonnano the stage becomes tranquil for a time on paved and unpaved roads in the Casentino National Forest. With a reservation it's possible to enjoy lunch at Rifugio Asqua. A must-see is the Camaldoli Benedictine Monastery, which has exuded deep and genuine calm since the 11th c. After an hour's steep climb from Camaldoli up Poggio Brogli, the remainder of the stage is a very agreeable and restful stroll along the forested footpaths to the mountain resort town of Badia Prataglia.

Pass the waterfall at the center of town on your left, then pass Piazza Mazzini and one block afterward head left and uphill on the SS310. In two blocks come to the steps of the **Planetario del Parco Nazionale**. Head uphill through the planetarium grounds to find Viale Caduti di Montelungo, which you follow uphill among apartment homes until it ends in four blocks.

Turn left on Viale 17 Partigiani, which soon curves right, traversing the mountainside. Take a shortcut path while the road switches back over longer loops, and return to the road before it ends at Via di Pancaldi (**2.3km**). Cross the road onto a pathway to shortcut another switchback and after returning to the road veer left on another path leading through the woods. In a few minutes see signs on the right that mark the **Masseto Etruscan archeological site** (**0.7km**).

### STAGE 4 – STIA TO BADIA PRATAGLIA

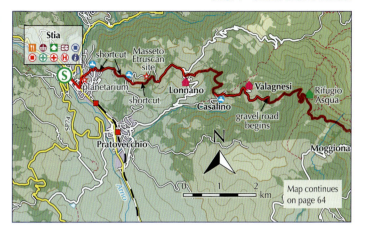

Excavated in 1985–2001, the **Masseto** dig uncovered four buildings that date to the Etruscan era (8th–3rd c. BC), including the only Etruscan chamber tomb in the Casentino area.

Continue on the path as it heads downhill then steeply uphill before meeting the Strada Vicinale della Madonnina asphalt road. Turn left, following the waymarks and enjoying the beautiful vistas of Stia behind you. The road ends at SP72, where you turn right to arrive in the village of **Lonnano** (**1.7km**, 🔺 **La Casina di Lonnano** Pr R K 2/5 €60/person, Loc il Casato, 43, mcparigi@gmail.com, tel 340 7418991. Maria Cristina is your host).

Just 150 meters later, fork left to arrive in the upper part of Lonnano at its historic Chiesa dei Santi Vito e Modesto a Lonnano. The 10th–12th-c. church includes two 17th-c. paintings of its namesake saints. Pass the church to the left and walk downhill just after the parking area. Soon there is a triple-fork intersection where you go straight ahead toward three tall pine trees. Following signage, continue past a barn onto forest pathways that link Lonnano to an asphalt road leading to its hillside neighbor, **Casalino** (**2.1km**).

Turn left, going uphill. At a **fork** (**1.0km**), either go right to continue on the route, or go left for lodging at **Valagnesi** (🔺 **La Capannina** O Pr Do R K Br Dr Gr W S Z 10/25, €-/35/-/-, Valagnesi 39, ivanagrofi@gmail.com, tel 380 4520062. 🔺 **B&B Borgo Valagnesi** O Pr R Br Dr W S Z from €39, or from €45 with half board, Loc. Valagnesi 28, info@borgovalagnesi.com, tel 333 5278965).

Fork right here, pass Agriturismo Casa Pallino, and continue on the gentle gravel road until coming to **Asqua** (**3.3km**, 🔺 **Rifugio Asqua** O Pr Do R Br Dr W S 6/25, €55 per person (includes breakfast and dinner), €68 full board, Via Asqua 12, asqua@asqua.it, www.asqua.it, tel 339 5644292, tel 337 7176235. Host is Sabrina). Continue gradually uphill on the gravel road until it heads downhill and ends at the SP124 (**3.5km**). Turn right and in 200 meters come to the SP67, where you turn left on this quiet, asphalt road that leads past **Camping Camaldoli** (▲ **Camping Camaldoli** Pr R Br Dr Gr 10/36, €45 per person bungalow, Via Camaldoli 12, www.campingcamaldoli.it, tel 0575 556202, tel 390 35527. Bag transfer to La Verna available) and then to the tiny village of **Camaldoli** (**1.7km**).

*Hermits reside in individual hermitages behind a gate at Eremo di Camaldoli*

## 16.3KM CAMALDOLI (ELEV 840M, POP 35) 🍴 🛖 ⓘ (208.1/451.6KM)

Nestled in an ancient forest high above Stia, the Camaldoli community is known in monastic circles for its rigorous interpretation of the monastic Rule of St Benedict. Since its establishment in the 11th c., the remote monastery and its hermitage have produced four cardinals, countless bishops, and many artists, including Guido d'Arezzo, the inventor of modern musical notation.

Established by St Romuald in about 1023, the site was a field (*campus* in Latin) donated by a patron, Maldolus – hence 'Campus Maldolus' or Camaldoli. The local community encompasses the upper Hermitage (Eremo) of Camaldoli, 4km above the monastery and village of the same name. The monastery's solid buildings, built of stone and timber, date from the 16th–18th c. The Camaldesi Order includes another 14 hermitages and monasteries in Italy, Poland, Brazil and the U.S.

The upper complex, the hermitage, is divided between semi-public spaces that include a guest hall and chapel, and 20 individual hermitages sequestered behind a locked gate. In the village, the monastery complex includes a public chapel and guesthouse. Both facilities include pharmacy stores that offer artisanal herbal products. The monastery is open for visits throughout the day, while the hermitage is closed except during specified visiting hours that change with the season (www.monasterodicamaldoli.it; hermitage: eremo@camaldoli.it, tel 0575 556021; monastery: monastero@camaldoli.it, tel 0575 556012).

🔺 **La Foresteria guesthouse of the Monastero Camaldoli** Pr R Br Dr Cr 76/154 €70/person, Loc Camaldoli 14, foresteria@camaldoli.it, www.camaldoli.it, tel 0575 556013. Price includes half-board. By reservation only. The hermitage also welcomes individual guests. See www.camaldoli.it/ospitalita-sacro-eremo for more information.

🔺 **Locanda dei Baroni** Pr R Br Dr Cr W S 12/34, €-/70/78/92, Via Camaldoli 5, locanda@itrebaroni.it, www.alberghicamaldoli.it, tel 0575 556015, tel 393 9035527. €19 half board available, restaurant open 9:00am–8:30pm, sack lunch available. Camping nearby at Camping Camaldoli (see details in route description above). Taxi and transfer services possible.

From the front door of the monastery turn right, walk downhill, round the corner on the main road and cross the stone bridge over the noisy Fosso di Camaldoli stream. Look immediately to the left for a trailhead with several markers, then follow signs uphill on the forested pathway. Soon come to **Rifugio Cotozzo** (**1.8km**), a stone hut with off-the-grid conveniences aimed at hardy souls with cooking gear and sleeping bags.

At a three-way trail junction after the hut, take the middle option to continue uphill toward the first of the day's summits, along the slopes of 1187m **Poggio Brogli**. After a brief descent, find yourself in an undulating area of high ground. Cross the Colia and Tre Confini streams, separated by two small meadows. After

## The Way of St Francis — Via di Francesco

*The route crosses the Casentino National Forest, which spans hundreds of hectares of remote, mountainous territory*

the Acqua Fredda stream, begin the last, easy climb of the day on an arm of 1330m **Poggio alle Capre** (**2.7km**).

The sometimes-steep descent through a forest of oak and pine now begins. Come to a green gate and in 100 meters see a white chalet-style building with

*Stage 4 – Stia to Badia Prataglia*

green shutters. This is **Rifugio Casanova** (**2.3km**, ⌂ Rifugio Casanova [Pr] [R] [K] [Br] [Dr] [Cr] [S] [Z] 19/52 €55/person includes half board, Via Casanova 3, Casanova@rifugionelcasentino.it, www.rifugionelcasentino.it, tel 0575 559897, 335 7361375. Primarily for groups, linens included). Turn into the parking lot and, keeping the hostel on the right, pass the brown gate. Here a wide path leads downhill on a shortcut into Badia Prataglia, with peek-a-boo views toward the red roofs of the resort village on the right side. Head downhill until you connect with Via Vetriceta Bassa, where you turn right to another asphalt road, the Via Vetriceta. Turn right again and come shortly to the main street of **Badia Prataglia**, finding the Church of Santa Maria Assunta near its center (**0.8km**).

---

**7.6KM BADIA PRATAGLIA** (ELEV 835M, POP 901)
(200.5/444.0KM)

This mountain resort town, as its name suggests, was once home to a monastery, and documentary evidence verifies the existence of a major monastic community here as early as the 10th c. A 20th-c. restoration of the town's Church of Santa Maria Assunta and St Bartholomew revealed the abbey's forgotten 11th–12th-c. crypt, complete with Romanesque columns and capitals. Today, Badia Prataglia is filled with vacation homes and tourist lodgings serving part-time residents and visitors who want to enjoy the beauty of the Casentino National Forest.

⌂ **La Casa di Gloria** [O] [Pr] [R] [K] [Br] [Dr] [Cr] [W] [S] 3/15, €-/55/90/120/140, Via Nazionale 47/B, barvittoria56@gmail.com, www.lacasadigloria.it, tel 342 0252538, tel 370 1579449. Breakfast included, dinner available for €25 each.

⌂ **Albergo La Foresta** [O] [Pr] [R] [Br] [Dr] [Cr] [W] [S] [Z] 20/50, €-/45/70/100, Via Nazionale 13, info@albergolaforesta.eu, www.albergolaforesta.eu, tel 339 6197427, tel 0575 559009.

⌂ **Pensione Ristorante Giardino** [O] [Pr] [R] [Br] [Dr] [Cr] [S] 30/80, €-/40/68/85/94, Via Nazionale 15, hotelgiardino@virgilio.it, tel 0575 559016, tel 339 2301632. Pilgrim price includes breakfast.

---

### FRANCIS HEARS 'REBUILD MY CHURCH'

On his return to Assisi after imprisonment in Perugia and after making the decision to renounce the life of a soldier, Francis began to spend time alone in study, deep contemplation, and prayer. He encouraged his friends to do the same. One day in 1206, from the crucifix of the ruined Church of San Damiano just outside Assisi's walls, he heard these words: 'Francis, rebuild my church.'

## STAGE 5
*Badia Prataglia to Santuario della Verna*

| | |
|---|---|
| **Start** | Church of Santa Maria Assunta, Badia Prataglia |
| **Finish** | Convento, Santuario della Verna |
| **Duration** | 6hr |
| **Distance** | 15.9km |
| **Total ascent** | 1084m |
| **Total descent** | 791m |
| **Difficulty** | Hard |
| **Percentage paved** | 6% |
| **Lodgings** | Santicchio turn-off 7.7km, Biforco turn-off 10.1km, Santuario della Verna 15.9km, Chiusi della Verna 17km |

This most challenging day of the entire Way of St Francis sends you steeply up and down the mountain trails of the Casentino National Forest and Foreste Sacre. It is an inspirational, unforgettable, and heart-pumping jaunt, featuring sweeping vistas of green and lush Apennine mountains and valleys. Nestled in the two valleys between the day's three climbs are the tiny villages of Frassineta (no services) and Rimbocchi (bar/café, pizzeria, bakery).

After the final, stair-like ascent, steepest of all, you arrive at the beloved and beautiful mountaintop convent of Santuario della Verna, a Franciscan Shangri-La that is steeped in the contemplative spirit of Francis. A stroll through the corridors and chapels of this lofty retreat helps you understand why this site is one of Italy's most revered holy places. People not ready for the cardio challenge should consider splitting the stage with an overnight off the trail at either Rifugio Casa Santicchio or in nearby Biforco.

Facing the Santa Maria Assunta Church, go left between the church and the grocery store on Via Eden, walking down the asphalt road rather than up onto the highway, to leave town. Continue to the bottom of the valley and cross the Torrente Archiano on the auto bridge. The road now becomes gravel, with a hayfield on the left, and the first climb of the stage begins.

Follow signs to fork right off the road onto a dirt trail, which you follow as it leads steeply uphill on bedrock and loose gravel to a point near the summit of 1113m **Poggio della Cesta**, marked by a clearing and power lines

## Stage 5 – Badia Prataglia to Santuario della Verna

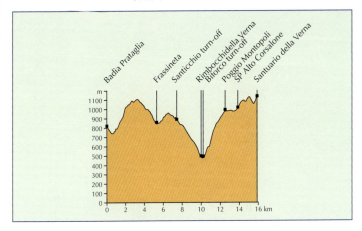

with a concrete utility post. After a short descent among oak trees, continue to the 1134m summit of **Poggio Aguzzo**. The long and pleasant descent now begins on the arm of a ridge among oak forests, with wide vistas to the right. Come to the Chapel of Madonna delle Sette Spade e Dei Sette Dolori (Seven Swords and Seven Pains) and then the Church of Sant'Egidio in the hamlet of **Frassineta** (**5.2km**, bus).

In the 12th c., the quiet hamlet of **Frassineta** was an urban agglomeration with stone walls and watchtower. It stood guard over the medieval Via Romea Germanica, which was frequented by pilgrims to Rome as well as invading armies. The lawn in front of the Church of Sant'Egidio makes a pleasant and quiet rest stop.

Pass the church on the asphalt road to the uphill side of town. Shortly the asphalt turns to a two-track gravel road, which then begins to ascend. Pass to the left of a green gate and continue, coming to a summit. Turn left onto a path leading into the forest to begin the longest descent of the day, with wide views of the surrounding countryside opening on the right. Soon see a sign showing you are halfway between Frassineta and Rimbocchi.

If your choice is to stay overnight at Santicchio, follow **CAI 070A** to the right for **Rifugio Casa Santicchio** (**2.5km** to turn-off, ♦ **Rifugio Casa Santicchio** Pr Do R Br Dr Cr S 8/25, €60/65/120/180, Loc. Casa Santicchio 15, info@santicchio.org, www.santicchio.org, tel 347 7694688, tel 0575 1787586. Price includes breakfast, dinner, linens).

## The Way of St Francis — Via di Francesco

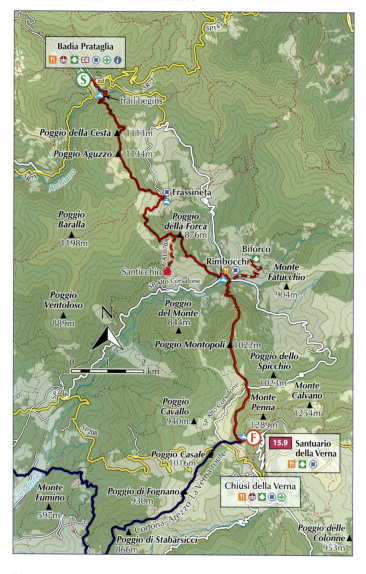

68

## Stage 5 – Badia Prataglia to Santuario della Verna

If you are not heading for Santicchio, in 100 meters come to the summit of 876m **Poggio della Forca**. Continue heading along the ridge, with sparse oak trees and wide vistas to the right and left as a steep descent begins. Some 600 meters later there is a large, abandoned microwave reflector on the right. Soon after passing this odd relic is a meadow with 180-degree views of the surrounding mountains and valleys. Continue carefully down the hill on the eroded and sometimes slippery path, enjoying constant views ahead and to the left and right. Finally come to power lines which guide you downhill toward the town of Rimbocchi, which you can now see below. Continue down and arrive at the paved **SP Alto Corsalone** and then the village of **Rimbocchi** (**2.3km**, bar/café, pizzeria, bakery, bus). At a small park there are picnic tables and kiosks with maps, and nearby is Panificio Rimbocchi (www.panificiorimbocchi.it, open daily). Rimbocchi, like Frassineta, was once a stop on the medieval Via Romea Germanica.

Continue on the narrow lane through the middle of town (water fountain), coming back to the SP Alto Corsalone (**0.2km**). Here you have the option of turning left to find the village of **Biforco** (uphill 600 meters, 🔺 **La Casa di Nonna Menicca** Pr R K W S 3/8, €-/30/55/70, Loc. Biforco, rossana.mazzieri@gmail.com, tel 331 9667967. €7 linens. 🔺 **Affittacamere Silvia Franci** O Pr R Br Dr W S 5/12, €-/50/70/90, Loc. Biforco, silviafranci77@gmail.com, tel 366 2283864, tel 0575 912869).

To remain on the route and bypass Biforco, cross the road, cross the stream, and take the steep uphill path marked CAI 053, which you will follow the rest of the day. The climb soon becomes very strenuous but you are rewarded with majestic views over the mountainous countryside. After a time, come to the summit of 1022m **Poggio Montopoli**. Nearing the top of the climb, you will see a small pond on the right, then just afterward once again is the **SP Alto Corsalone** roadway (**3.6km**). Cross the road and return to the trail, noting the optimistic sign that reads 'La Verna: .50 hrs.'

Now enter a fairytale forest, a quiet and shaded woodland of ancient trees, boulders covered in green moss, and sunlight filtered through layers of birch leaves. Remain on the route, now also called Anello Basso (Lower Ring), identifying it as one of the network of trails of the Foreste Sacre. Note the many roomy cracks and openings among the large boulders – undoubtedly at some point used by Francis and his followers for solitude and prayer. Watch carefully for trail markers as you weave through this gentle and cool woodland. Soon you see the massive rock promontory that forms the foundation of the convent buildings above. Follow the trail up and over the left side of a gate and then circle to the front entry and reception desk of the convent of **Santuario della Verna** (**2.1km**).

## 15.9KM SANTUARIO DELLA VERNA (ELEV 1126M, POP <50) 🍴 🏪 ⓘ
### (184.6/428.1KM)

A self-guided tour of the convent complex begins at the central piazza, framed on one side by a dramatic viewpoint with a tall, wooden cross and on the other side by the 14th–15th-c. Basilica di San Francesco. The basilica houses relics of St Francis, including one of his simple cloth robes, and features white terracotta bas-relief sculptures by the 15th-c. sculptor Andrea della Robbia. The bones of Count Orlando are interred in the adjacent 13th-c. Church of Santa Maria degli Angeli, accessible from the sacristy of the basilica. Returning to the piazza from the basilica, continue along the ambulatory to view its series of murals depicting the life of Francis, then linger in the diverse chapels leading at the far end to the 13th-c. Chapel of the Stigmata, which includes another terracotta by della Robbia, this one of the Crucifixion. Along the way is a small cave remembered as the sleeping place of St Francis, where a person can spend a few moments in a spot that most certainly was once graced by the humble man of Assisi.

Twice daily, the friars lead a procession from the Santa Maria Church to the Chapel of the Stigmata. Legends say that once, when the snow was too deep to make the procession, the friars canceled the observance. When they awoke the next day, the friars saw animal tracks in the snow covering the course and came to believe that the forest animals, on their own, had made the procession in honor of the saint.

On 17 September each year, pilgrims from neighboring parishes come to La Verna to worship, remember the bestowal of the stigmata, and celebrate Italy's patron saint.

⛺ **Dormitorio Pellegrini a Piedi** Do R Br Dr Cr 1/16, €16 per person + €11 takeaway meal or €22 half board, Via del Santuario della Verna 45, santuario-verna@gmail.com, www.laverna.it, tel 0575 5341, tel 0575 534210. Linens not included. Breakfast 8:00–9:00am, dinner 7:30pm.

⛺ **La Foresteria** O Pr R Br Dr Cr S 72/105, €64 per person, Via del Santuario della Verna 45, santuarioverna@gmail.com, tel 0575 534210. Half board included.

**Lodgings in Chiusi della Verna (1.1km on path below La Verna):**

⛺ **Hotel Ristorante Bellavista** Pr R Br Dr Cr S Z 24/50, €-/65/120/-, Viale San Francesco 17, gilbertogabelli@gmail.com, www.ristorantealbergo-bellavista.it, tel 0575 599029, 339 7024754. Breakfast included.

⛺ **Albergo Letizia** Pr R Br Dr Cr W S Z 9/22, €-/50/85/95, Via Roma 26, info@albergo-letizia.it, tel 0575 599020, tel 334 3209082. Open Easter–Oct. Breakfast included, half board available.

⛺ **Casa Ortensia** Pr R K Br W S 3/6, €ask for pilgrim price, Via 25 Aprile 5A, sara-minelli30@gmail.com, tel 339 1478526. Supermarket nearby, Sara is your host.

A Franciscan friar talks to a group of pilgrims above the Chapel of the Stigmata at Santuario della Verna

*A cozy jumble of buildings form the oldest portions of the Santuario della Verna complex*

### FRANCIS RECEIVES THE STIGMATA AT LA VERNA

Here among the ancient trees and rocky crags on the south side of Monte Penna (1289m), St Francis found solitude for meditation and prayer. On 8 May 1213, Count Orlando of Chiusi spontaneously made Francis a gift of this remote mountaintop site, writing that the gift was 'for the health of my soul.' Francis loved the retreat and journeyed here often. According to tradition, in the autumn of the following year, Francis discovered sharp, nail-like protrusions on his hands and an open wound on his side. He shared the presence of this Christ-like 'stigmata' with only his closest friends, but, at the examination of his body after his death at Santa Maria degli Angeli near Assisi in 1226, more than a dozen sworn witnesses confirmed the presence of these marks of the crucifixion.

# SECTION 1A: VARIANT ROUTES TO SANTUARIO DELLA VERNA

*Cortona's 16th-c. Church of Santa Maria Nuova was built after a vision of the Madonna by a group of workers returning from Eremo Le Celle (Variant 1.2)*

## VARIANT 1.1
*Florence to Santuario della Verna – southern route*

| | |
|---|---|
| **Start** | Basilica Santa Croce, Florence |
| **Finish** | Convento, Santuario della Verna |
| **Duration** | 28hr (4 days) |
| **Distance** | 89.2km |
| **Total ascent** | 3243m |
| **Total descent** | 2234m |
| **Difficulty** | Hard |
| **Percentage paved** | 51% |
| **Lodgings** | Bigallo 10.6km, Bombone 19.4km, Vallombrosa 35.6km, Strada in Casentino 53.3km, Poppi 62.6km, Bibbiena 73.2km, Santuario della Verna 89.2km |

As an option for walking from Florence to Santuario della Verna, the southern route has a lot going for it on paper. It has only two climbs above 1000m, versus three on the main route, and it goes through the scenic towns of Poppi and Bibbiena on its way to La Verna. The route encompasses the historic Via Ghibellina (www.unapasseggiata.org/via-ghibellina). However, a shortage of accommodations and lack of trail maintenance make it a difficult itinerary.

This itinerary was documented as a route used by the Guidi counts to protect their properties, and the presence of pilgrim hospitals in Bigallo, Rignano sull'Arno, Vallombrosa, Montemignaio, and Strumi is testament to the importance of the route. The Abbey at Vallombrosa was very influential in its time, and Dante Alighieri was hosted by the Guidi counts in 1310 at their castle in Poppi, where he was believed to have written Canticle XXXIII of his *Inferno*.

Today, the walking route is challenged by lack of maintenance over long, forested paths, and a general shortage of accommodation options. It is quite remote between Rignano sull'Arno and Rifiglio, then again after Strada in Casentino until coming into the Arno Valley just before Poppi. Bring ample food and supplies as well as leather gloves and garden snippers for overgrown paths along the way. The route is well marked with yellow arrows and stickers.

## Variant 1.1 – Florence to Santuario della Verna – southern route

Staging could be:

### Stage 1: Florence to Bigallo (10.6KM)
This allows an overnight at the atmospheric and historic lodging ▲ **Antico Spedale del Bigallo** Pr Do R Br Dr Cr W S Z 3/-, €Ask, Via del Bigallo e Apparita 14, Bagno a Ripoli, ostello@anticospedalebigallo.it, www.anticospedalebigallo.it, tel 055 630907.

### Stage 2: Bigallo to Vallombrosa (25.0KM)
While there are ample tourist lodgings in this secluded valley, best for pilgrims is accommodation at the abbey itself: ▲ **Abbazia di Vallombrosa** O Do R K S 2/25, €Donation, Via San Benedetto 2, Vallombrosa, infomonaci@gmail.com, www.monaci.org, tel 055 862251.

### Stage 3: Vallombrosa to Poppi (26.9KM)
Tourist accommodations.

### Stage 4: Poppi to Santuario della Verna (27.0KM)
See Stage 5 for lodging information.

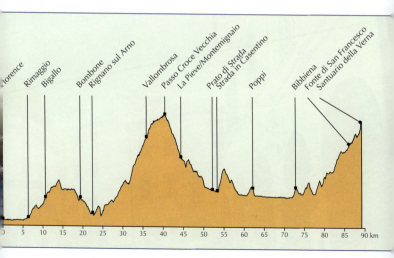

## THE WAY OF ST FRANCIS — VIA DI FRANCESCO

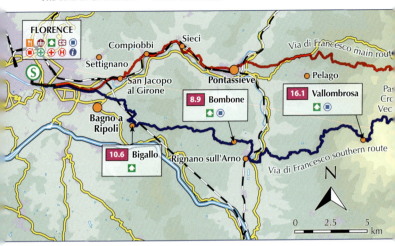

*The hexagonal Chiesa della Madonna del Morbo was built in the 17th c. by residents of Poppi after they were spared from the plague*

## Variant 1.1 – Florence to Santuario della Verna – southern route

*Eremo Le Celle near Cortona was founded by St Francis in 1211*

# VARIANT 1.2
*Cortona and Arezzo to Santuario della Verna*

| | |
|---|---|
| **Start** | Piazza della Repubblica, Cortona |
| **Finish** | Convento, Santuario della Verna |
| **Duration** | 33hr (5 days) |
| **Distance** | 106.4km |
| **Total ascent** | 3608m |
| **Total descent** | 2991m |
| **Difficulty** | Hard |
| **Percentage paved** | 48% |
| **Lodgings** | Eremo Le Celle 3.5km, Castiglion Fiorentino 16.9km, Arezzo 41.9km, Anghiari 66.0km, Caprese Michelangelo 88.8km, Lama 90.4km, Chiusi della Verna 105.3km, Santuario della Verna 106.4km |

A secluded route through Tuscan mountains, rich with history. Much of this route is shared with the Via Romea Germanica, and where there are no signs for the Via di Francesco there are usually signs for the Via Romea.

Cortona has a close connection to St Francis, with a historic church there and nearby the Eremo Le Celle, which, although secluded, is warm and friendly with a resident monastic community. (🏠 **Eremo Le Celle** O Pr R 1/2, €Donation, Via delle Case Sparse 73, Cortona, info@lecelledicortona.it, www.lecelledicortona.it, tel 0575 601017).

Potential staging could be:

### Stage 1: Cortona (Le Celle) to Rigutino (26.2KM)
Castiglion Fiorentino is a beautiful and well-preserved hill town. The itinerary is shared in a south-to-north direction with the Via Romea Germanica, and a special highlight is the parochial hostel in Rigutino. (🏠 **Rifugio La Sassaia** O Do R K Br Dr W S 3/30, €Donation, Pieve La Sassaia 47, Rigutino, gallorobinson@libero.it, www.rifugiolasassaia.org, tel 340 9812896. Giovanni Roberto is the amiable and passionate host in the tradition of the Knights Templar.)

## THE WAY OF ST FRANCIS — VIA DI FRANCESCO

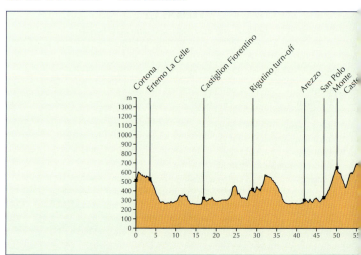

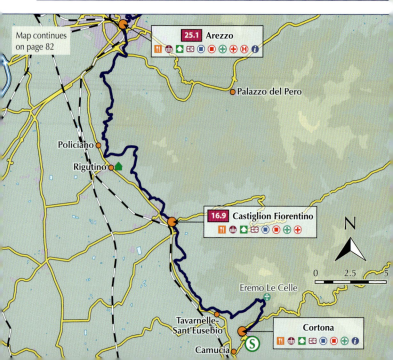

## Variant 1.2 – Cortona and Arezzo to Santuario della Verna

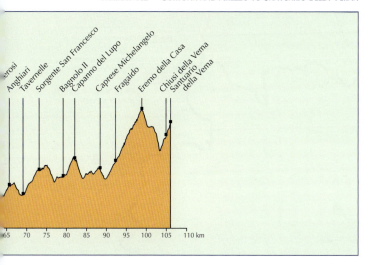

### Stage 2: Rigutino to Arezzo (15.8km)
The route includes some steep climbs in remote areas. Arezzo's Church of San Francesco has famous 15th-c. frescoes of the *Legend of the True Cross* by Piero della Francesca, as well as other artworks on the theme of St Francis. (Tourist accommodations.)

### Stage 3: Arezzo to Anghiari (24.0km)
Via di Francesco markings are rare on this stage, which begins in flatlands north of Arezzo and ends in farmland south of Anghiari. In between are two tall ridges with difficult backcountry walking. The view back to Arezzo, into the Valdichiana, and the north portions of the Valtiberina are often spectacular. A special treat in Anghiari is a visit to the factory of the Busatti family which has made fine textiles here since 1842 (www.busatti.com/en). (Tourist accommodations.)

### Stage 4: Anghiari to Caprese Michelangelo (22.8km)
Michelangelo Buonarroti, one of the greatest artists of all time, was born at Caprese on 6 March 1475. A special treat is the Casa Natale Michelangelo (www.casanatalemichelangelo.it). (Tourist accommodations.)

### Stage 5: Caprese Michelangelo to Santuario della Verna (17.6km)
See Stage 5 for lodging information.

# THE WAY OF ST FRANCIS — VIA DI FRANCESCO

# SECTION 2: SANTUARIO DELLA VERNA TO ASSISI

*The view down to the Basilica di San Francesco from Rocca Maggiore, Assisi's mountaintop fortress (Stage 15)*

## THE WAY OF ST FRANCIS — VIA DI FRANCESCO

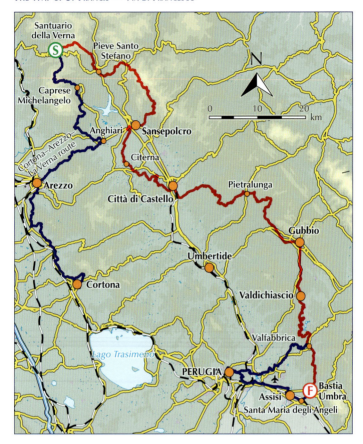

With the descent from La Verna, the route enters the valley of the Tiber (Tevere) River, which skirts Assisi and then flows through Rome on its way to the Tyrrhenian Sea at Ostia. The rich soil of this valley has made it an agricultural center of the Italian peninsula for centuries. Pilgrims pass through farms of wheat, barley, rye, and sunflowers in the lowlands. On the hillsides, vineyards give way to olive groves and pastures, then are replaced by forests of beech, oak, and pine on the higher slopes of the rugged Central Apennine range.

# STAGE 6
*Santuario della Verna to Pieve Santo Stefano*

| | |
|---|---|
| **Start** | Convento, Santuario della Verna |
| **Finish** | Piazza Santo Stefano, Pieve Santo Stefano |
| **Duration** | 4¾hr |
| **Distance** | 14.6km |
| **Total ascent** | 236m |
| **Total descent** | 930m |
| **Difficulty** | Moderate |
| **Percentage paved** | 22% |
| **Lodgings** | Pieve Santo Stefano 14.6km |

Bid a fond farewell to beautiful La Verna on this mountainous, mostly downhill stage enveloped in calm and quiet forests. Come to the town of Pieve Santo Stefano, tucked into a narrow valley of the Tiber (Tevere) River. After two uphill stretches, the remainder is a long descent with excellent trail markings as the Via di Francesco shares paths with the Sentiero Frassati and CAI trails 050, 066 and 075.

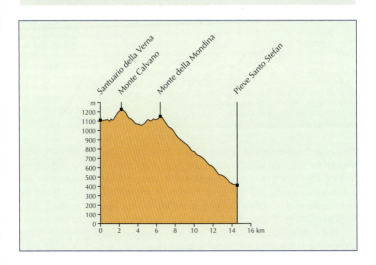

# THE WAY OF ST FRANCIS — VIA DI FRANCESCO

Starting at the Portineria of Santuario della Verna, head down the flagstone path, through the gate, and past the statue of St Francis and the dove seller. See 'Francis and the dove seller' story. Continue downhill, passing the lower parking lot and 100 meters later the tiny Ristorante Piadina. In another 100 meters, at a sharp curve in the road, a trailhead appears on the left. Among the many markings is the Francesco/Sentiero Frassati, the day's first path. Turn left here, onto the **gravel road**.

In a couple of hundred meters, turn left onto a gravel path going uphill, and soon arrive at a summit with a tall **wooden cross** and a triple fork in the road.

## STAGE 6 – SANTUARIO DELLA VERNA TO PIEVE SANTO STEFANO

*Pilgrims celebrate the day as they descend from Santuario della Verna to Pieve Santo Stefano*

Go to the right on the Francesco/CAI/GEA 050 trail, which heads uphill steeply on a now-narrower path for 800 meters to 1254m **Monte Calvano** (**2.2km**). After passing through a gate, come to the wide expanse of a mountain meadow with wide views of the countryside. After the brow of the meadow's ridge, begin your descent, returning to the forest on the narrow path of the Francesco/CAI 050.

Follow signs through a series of gates and cross a gravel road to join CAI 066, where the path begins going uphill again. In 1km the path follows the Francesco/CAI 075, soon reaching the summit of 1182m **Monte della Modina** (**4.2km**). After

## The Way of St Francis — Via di Francesco

this, the long downhill stretch begins. Pass a section of charred trees remaining from a forest fire and continue past a **cell phone tower**. In another 2km the road is joined by a driveway on the left and makes a sharp right turn. From here you can look down and see Pieve Santo Stefano tucked into the narrow Tiber Valley.

Pass the **Asvanara equestrian school**, after which the road turns to asphalt and continues downhill. Pieve Santo Stefano is clearly visible below, and you follow signs leading you to cross the **SS3bis freeway** on an overpass. Turn right on the Strada Provinciale 208, which you follow into town. Just after the tall stone church, turn left, go one block, and turn left again onto the Piazza Santo Stefano, the heart of **Pieve Santo Stefano** (**8.2km**).

---

**14.6KM PIEVE SANTO STEFANO** (ELEV 431M, POP 2970) 
(170.0/413.5KM)

Pieve Santo Stefano sits between mountains in a narrow valley drained by the Tiber River. As the Germans retreated from Italy in August 1944, they bombed the town, depriving it of its historic and charming medieval character. Today it is known as the 'City of the Diary' for the archive of over 10,000 journals and diaries gathered by journalist Saverio Tutino at the **Piccolo Museo del Diario**, as a sort of memorial to the daily lives of ordinary people. The fascinating and poignant treasury of stories is well worth a visit and is a highlight of the entire walk for many (€5 guided visit, reservations recommended, open daily, closed afternoons, Piazza Pellegrini Plinio 1, www.piccolomuseodeldiario.it).

The lead-domed 17th-c. church on the south side of town, Madonna dei Lumi, is the starting point for the town's annual Palio dei Lumi, a celebration of light held in early September each year since 1631. This tradition of burning haystacks and illuminating the town with candles began when the town's vicar, Pietro Strozzi, promised to celebrate the Blessed Virgin annually if the town would be free from plague.

🔺 **B&B Il Castellare** O Pr Do R Br Dr Cr W S Z 4/13, €20/35/50/75, Strada La Verna 20, info@ilcastellare.eu, tel 0575 799393, 339 3463117. Breakfast included, €25 with linens. €10 dinner available. Domestic animals are allowed.

🔺 **Hotel Santo Stefano** O Pr Do R Br Dr Cr S Z 24/50, €30/65/95/120, Via Tiberina 95, info@hotelsantostefanoarezzo.it, www.hotelsantostefanoarezzo.it, tel 0575 797129, 339 7024754. Ask for pilgrim price, breakfast included.

🔺 **La Torre di Pieve** O Pr R K Br S 2/5, €-/-/70/80, Via delle Oche 5, paolo-gennaioli@gmail.com, https://www.facebook.com/la.torre.di.pieve.pieve.santo.stefano/, tel 331 3075005.

*Stage 6 – Santuario della Verna to Pieve Santo Stefano*

▲ **Camping la Civetta** O Pr R K Br Dr Cf S 4/16, €28/person, Via la Civetta 11 (on the Sansepolcro road, with van service by request to city center), info@lacivetta.it, tel +44 746 3121916, 331 331 6073725. Ask for pilgrim price. Beds in bungalows and tents, linens available. Seasonal pricing, e-bike charging.

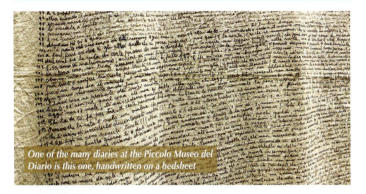

*One of the many diaries at the Piccolo Museo del Diario is this one, handwritten on a bedsheet*

## FRANCIS AND THE DOVE SELLER

The story is told that Francis was at a village marketplace when he met a boy selling doves he had snared. Francis saw them trapped in the boy's small cage and asked the boy for the doves, so he could spare them being killed for food. The boy obliged, and Francis built nests for the doves at the Porziuncola, where they lived as tamed pets. The boy later became a follower of Francis, devoting his life to prayer and respect for creation.

*The story of St Francis and the dove seller is remembered in this sculpture outside Santuario della Verna. Francis accepted the doves as a gift and made nests for them at the Porziuncola*

# STAGE 7
## Pieve Santo Stefano to Montagna

| | |
|---|---|
| **Start** | Piazza Santo Stefano, Pieve Santo Stefano |
| **Finish** | Montagna |
| **Duration** | 7¼hr (7¾hr via Strazzanella) |
| **Distance** | 22.6km (23.0km via Strazzanella option; the Monte Verde wet weather option adds 4.2km to the route) |
| **Total ascent** | 838m (992m via Strazzanella option) |
| **Total descent** | 591m (750m via Strazzanella option) |
| **Difficulty** | Moderately hard (hard via Strazzanella option) |
| **Percentage paved** | 16% (5% via Strazzanella option) |
| **Lodgings** | Pian della Capanna 16.1km, Il Palazzo 21.6km, Montagna 22.6km |

The *autostrada* (freeway) has consumed the traditional passage through the Tiber Valley between Pieve Santo Stefano and Sansepolcro (which today is just a 15-minute drive), so the official Via di Francesco track instead goes east and over the mountains in a challenging 33.8km course, here divided into Stages 7 and 8. This mountainous route allows visits to two Franciscan locations tucked up in the hills, the first of which is found on this stage – the Hermitage of Cerbaiolo. There are two options for getting to Cerbaiolo: the official route goes first alongside the highway and then onto quiet gravel roads, while the recommended option misses the highway and opts for the forest pathways, albeit steep, into the Strazzanella drainage.

After Cerbaiolo, come to a café/bar at Passo Viamaggio where there is an important, weather-dependent choice to make regarding the hike up Monte Verde. The quiet, forested hamlet of Montagna offers options for overnight lodging, although the hardiest of hikers may choose to continue on to Sansepolcro, one of the most atmospheric and memorable towns of the Upper Valtiberina.

Facing the church in Piazza Santo Stefano, turn left, walk a short block, turn left again and cross the Tiber (Tevere) on a modern, steel bridge. A right turn leads to the official route to Cerbaiolo after 1.2km of highway walking, while a left turn takes you to the Strazzanella mountain trail option.

## STAGE 7 – PIEVE SANTO STEFANO TO MONTAGNA

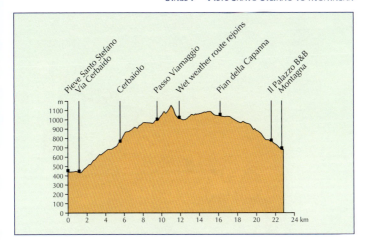

### Official route: road option to Cerbaiolo

Turn right at the SP50 and follow it past the striking silver dome of the 16th–17th-c. Santuario della Madonna dei Lumi. The mid-16th-c. fresco of the Madonna dei Lumi stands out among the mostly baroque and neoclassical adornments inside this tall and slender church. At the roundabout, the SP50 becomes the SP77 main highway, which you follow without benefit of sidewalk. On the right are the Tiber River and *autostrada*. After the Tratos Cavi distribution warehouse, turn left off the highway and onto Via Cerbaiolo (**1.5 km**).

Follow this road along several switchbacks and curves, on asphalt at first, then continuing as it turns to gravel. At a right fork onto the Cerbaiolo driveway, the official route continues up the hill, bypassing Cerbaiolo; alternatively, fork right at the driveway (**3.7km**) to arrive in 500 meters at the **Hermitage of Cerbaiolo** (Eremo di Cerbaiolo) (**0.5km**).

### Strazzanella mountain trail option to Cerbaiolo

Turn left after the bridge and follow the SP50 for three blocks, turning right on Via Alberto Camaiti where you begin to climb. A right turn onto Via Gioiello after a curve leads to a dirt path on the left, which this Francesco variant shares with the E1/GEA trail. The E1 (Europe 1) trail leads 8000km from the Arctic Circle in Norway to the southernmost tip of Sicily, while the GEA (Grande Escursione Appenninica) is the portion of it that runs through the Apennines in Emilia-Romagna and Tuscany.

## THE WAY OF ST FRANCIS — VIA DI FRANCESCO

## STAGE 7 – PIEVE SANTO STEFANO TO MONTAGNA

The path becomes a narrow, gravel road as it snakes steeply uphill. Continue past the Quercia Tonda (round oak) **rest area**, pass through a metal gate, and after a left onto another path begin a pleasant mountainside traverse in and out of the shaded forest. Soon on a farm track, circle around a large hayfield with wide views of surrounding mountains. The path crosses alongside a second and then third hayfield and once again begins to climb, now into the drainage of the Strazzanella Creek. Continue up the heavily eroded path of jagged rocks, following red-and-white markings shared by the three trails.

At the first summit, merge with a gravel road going downhill that leads to another traverse of the mountainside. Pass through a barbed wire gate, after which the path ends in a T-junction at a gravel road. It is tempting to maintain the hard-fought elevation gain and go left on the E1/GEA to Passo Viamaggio, skipping Cerbaiolo, but a right turn saves 1.1km and features a visit to lovely and serene Cerbaiolo. Turn right and in 450 meters come to the Cerbaiolo driveway, where a left turn brings you to the historic and scenic **Hermitage of Cerbaiolo** (Eremo di Cerbaiolo) (**5.9km**).

### THE HERMITAGE OF CERBAIOLO

Formed by Benedictine monks in the 8th c. and later serving as a local parish, the site of Cerbaiolo was offered by its priests to Francis of Assisi in 1217, after his third visit to La Verna. Francis happily accepted the donation and installed a community of friars to tend the facility, which stands against a dramatic, tall, granite bluff on the mountainside and features vast views toward the Valtiberina and surrounding mountains. While there is no official record of Francis visiting the site, St Anthony of Padua's stay here is well documented and his stone bed can be viewed within the site.

After heavy damage in World War II, the buildings were slowly restored by resident hermits and local volunteers from nearby towns. Since 2019, the site has been overseen by Father Claudio, a Camaldolese monk. Due to lack of staffing, overnight accommodation is limited to clergy and nuns, but all are welcome to enjoy a tour of the site and a coffee and simple snack in return for a donation (https://eremodicerbaiolo.org, tel 338 8589482).

⌂ **Eremo di Cerbaiolo** Pr R Br Dr 3/4, €36/person, Via Cerbaiolo, claudio-marcello1963@libero.it, www.fraternitasandamiano.it, tel 338 85 89482. Reservation 2+ days in advance, no animals, available only Monday, Wednesday, Friday 16–17:45, no weekends. Father Claudio is your host.

*A wooden cross stands atop a peak above Eremo di Cerbaiolo*

### Main route
From the main hermitage entrance, shortcut back to the trail by following markings across the lawn to a path leading up the mountain. In 100 meters come to a tall **cross** with spectacular 270-degree views from above the hermitage. From the cross, a narrow path continues along the ridge. Turn right after the barbed wire fence and come to an intersection where you go straight up the hill.

Pass through an electrified gate and then a second electrified gate. An **old farmhouse** appears on the left. Pass through two green gates and come to another **farmhouse** where the path ends at a T-junction with the Via Cerbaiolo. Turn left and uphill, arriving in 400 meters at the SP Nuova Sestinese highway. Turn right and come to the **SP258** where you find the Bar L'Alpe (breakfast, snacks, closed Tuesdays) and rest area at **Passo di Viamaggio** (**3.7km** ⌂ **La Casetta di Ca La Fonte** Pr Do R K S 5/35, €25/person, Via Alpe 11, Frazione Passo di Viamaggio, via Alpe 11 at 200m from the trail, calafonteimperatore@gmail.com, www.calafonte.it, tel 339 3028614, 575 736152. Reservation required).

### Monte Verde fair weather option
This route is muddy in wet weather, while in fair weather its steepness and lack of footing require patience and determination. Pass the bar and immediately afterward turn left onto a dirt path that circles behind the bar's buildings as it climbs the hill. After a series of wooden gates, begin a steep climb and come to a summit. Continue on and very soon join a gravel road to the right. You now see straight ahead a ridiculously steep bank of loose dirt and scrub plants that leads to the summit of 1149m **Monte Verde**. There is no way up other than climbing the 50m bank, and tackling it in wet weather is not advised.

Once at the top, find the hidden gate within the barbed wire fence and continue toward a sometimes-overgrown path that leads down Monte Verde on the

## STAGE 7 – PIEVE SANTO STEFANO TO MONTAGNA

opposite side. After a wooden gate, turn left at a **gravel road** (**2.4km**) where you join the wet weather route.

### Monte Verde wet weather option
From Passo Viamaggio, follow the asphalt SP258 in the direction of Sansepolcro. In 3.5km watch for a green metal gate on the left, where a gravel road begins. Take the road, following it past a gravel quarry and continuing on to where the fair weather option rejoins the route from the left in 6.5km.

### Main route
This very well-graded and pleasant gravel road leads several kilometers along the mountainside, reaching a summit at Passo dello Spugnolo and entering the beautiful **Alpe della Luna Nature Reserve**. This nature preserve of 1540 hectares protects the flora and fauna of the Alpe della Luna range of the Central Apennines, which separates the Tiber–Tyrrhenian drainage from the Adriatic. Continue along the quiet gravel road to the forest refuge of **Pian della Capanna** (**4.4km**, ▲ **Rifugio Pian della Capanna** Strada Proviciale Marecchiese,

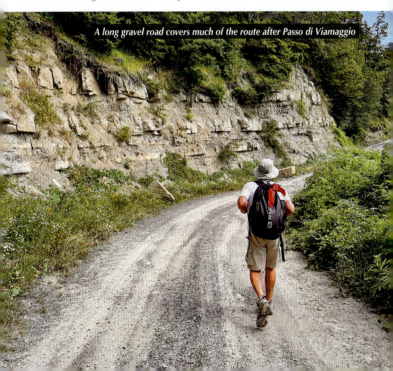

*A long gravel road covers much of the route after Passo di Viamaggio*

*The Way of St Francis — Via di Francesco*

prenotazioni@fattoriadigermagnano.it, www.fattoriadigermagnano.it, tel 333 5956500. Shaded outdoor rest area).

Continue on the road, watching carefully for a path on the left in 2km which will connect you with the road to Montagna. If you arrive at Rifugio La Spinella, you have missed the turn. Take the path of rounded stones downhill and afterward enjoy the comfortable traverse under oak trees, realizing you have crossed into the next valley over from your original route. The path becomes a gravel road, passing **Il Palazzo B&B** (**5.5km**), and turns to asphalt just before arriving in **Montagna** (**1.1km**).

---

**22.6KM MONTAGNA (ELEV 682M, POP 70)** 🍴 🛏 **(147.4/390.9KM)**
A tiny hamlet in two clusters of buildings from at least the 11th c. The northern cluster, Prato, has an 18th-c. chapel dedicated to Blessed Ranieri, a 13th-c. lay Capuchin friar from here. After a miracle story in which he raised two children from the dead, Ranieri has been invoked by local women in labor. His tomb is at San Francesco Church in Sansepolcro, whose bell is rung to announce the town's newborn children. The other cluster of homes, La Villa, includes the 13th–14th-c. Church of San Michele Arcangelo.

🔺 **Il Palazzo B&B** O Pr R K Br Dr Gr W S Z 4/8, €40 per person, Fraz. Montagna 55, ilpalazzobb@gmail.com, tel 347 7817173. Giovanna is your host.

🔺 **Alla Battuta B&B** O Pr R Br W S 3/8, €25 per person, Fraz. Montagna 46, a.puleri@gmail.com, tel 349 3829435, tel 0575 749352. Breakfast included.

---

### A TEST OF OBEDIENCE

At nearby Montecasale, and wanting to test two potential followers, Francis instructed the two to plant cabbages upside down in the garden. One followed instructions to the letter, planting his cabbages upside down. The other planted the cabbages right side up, as he thought best. Francis welcomed into the order the one who had followed directions, and bade the other farewell. Most important to Francis was not independence or common sense, but obedience to instruction, even when it might seem hard to understand.

# STAGE 8
## Montagna to Sansepolcro

| | |
|---|---|
| **Start** | Montagna |
| **Finish** | Piazza Torre di Berta, Sansepolcro |
| **Duration** | 3½hr |
| **Distance** | 11.2km |
| **Total ascent** | 149m |
| **Total descent** | 502m |
| **Difficulty** | Moderate due to footing on trail |
| **Percentage paved** | 42% |
| **Lodgings** | San Martino Val d'Afra 7.0km, Sansepolcro 11.2km |

The first portion of this short stage is a descent on forest paths that includes a stop at the fascinating Sasso Spico cave formation. The second part of the stage is a humdrum and gradual descent on the roadway into the fabulous Upper Tiberina town of Sansepolcro, which is surely one of the urban highlights of the Via di Francesco. The short stage allows a full afternoon to enjoy the services and sights of this scenic town. For those in a hurry, it's possible to continue to Citerna for the overnight.

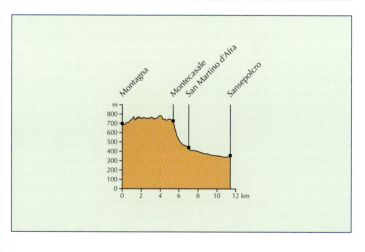

*The Way of St Francis — Via di Francesco*

Pass the small monument and welcome sign to Montagna and fork left, heading uphill, at first on asphalt. The road turns to gravel, crosses a bridge, and ends at a farmhouse (water spigot). Descend to the right immediately after the farmhouse on a wet dirt path, and cross a stream on stones. Head uphill on the opposite side, climbing steeply to a limestone bluff with a view back to Montagna.

Now enjoy a beautiful transit among and atop rocky bluffs featuring vast views over the green mountains. Follow Francesco signs to remain on the route, avoiding the many hiking trails that crisscross this scenic area. The signs lead you around the bluffs on a mostly flat, comfortable, and scenic dirt path. After a time, come to a large meadow with sweeping views to the south. Take a right fork onto the trail leading to a ridge and turn left onto a gravel road. Remain on the gravel road, which leads downhill to a white gate, then several buildings, a statue of St Francis, and, on the right, the **Eremo di Montecasale** (**5.4km**).

From the main terrace, follow the patio past the restrooms and find the trail marked 'Sasso Spicco.' Take this delightful trail as it leads downhill on one side or

*STAGE 8 – MONTAGNA TO SANSEPOLCRO*

### THE HERMITAGE OF MONTECASALE

This former Camaldolese hermitage was given to St Francis after his visit in 1213, and he prized it enough to establish a small community of his Friars Minor here. The chapel includes a treasured medieval statue of the Madonna and Child.

Capuchin monks have inhabited the hermitage for the last few centuries and an active community exists here today. The buildings center on a small cloister, and the chapel and oratory are open daily for self-guided tours. A west-facing terrace features an iconic statue of St Francis sitting on the low wall, gazing down the valley. (Prayer services are offered five times daily, four times on Sunday: https://sites.google.com/view/eremomontecasale.

🔺 **Eremo di Montecasale** O Do R K 2/10, €Donation, Fraz. Basilica 59, cappuccini.montecasale@gmail.com, www.eremomontecasale.it, tel 0575 733695. Pilgrim's salon has room for sleeping bags on the floor; male pilgrims may stay overnight in the hermitage by reservation. No food or hotel services are available at Montecasale.

### THE BANDITS OF MONTECASALE

One of the many stories about Francis and Montecasale is of robbers who were camped near the monastery. The friars debated what to do, pondering whether they should take up arms to protect themselves and their meager possessions. Instead, Francis counseled them to take food to the robbers and speak words of grace and welcome. Surprised to receive such good treatment, the bandits soon were carrying firewood to the monastery to return the brothers' kindness. Not long afterward, they gave up their brutish ways and two of them later became friars themselves. Two skulls of the redeemed criminals are mounted inside in a small cavity of the walls of the oratory.

another of the San Martino Creek. In wet weather it is wise simply to follow the hermitage driveway down to the highway, avoiding mud on the path. From the path, follow signs to the right to visit the **Sasso Spicco** cave formation (just a few meters from the trail).

The **Sasso Spicco** (protruding stone) is a marvel of geology in the form of a long, open cave set under a roof-like abutment of stone. In season, a small stream splashes over the stone from above, adding a twinkling melody to this welcoming and dry chamber.

*Hikers pause under the cover of Sasso Spicco near Montecasale*

Return to the trail to continue downhill and out of the forest to the confluence of the San Martino and Afra streams, coming to the pilgrim lodging of **San Martino Val d'Afra** (**1.6km**, 🔺 San Martino Val d'Afra O Pr R Br Cr W S 4/13, €-/65/80/100/110, Loc San Martino Val D'Afra Fraz Montagna 100, info@sanmartinovaldafra.com, tel 0575 749364, 349 7834112. WhatsApp best contact, dinner available for small groups. Paul is your host). Just beyond the chapel and other buildings is the **Via della Montagna**, where you turn left, following this road to the outskirts of Sansepolcro. Cross the Via dei Montefeltro, and turn right on the Via Anconetana, coming soon to Piazza Torre di Berta in **Sansepolcro** (**4.2km**).

*'Resurrection,' by Piero della Francesca, is remembered as the 'painting that saved a city' (image source: Wikimedia Commons)*

## STAGE 8 – MONTAGNA TO SANSEPOLCRO

### 11.2KM SANSEPOLCRO (ELEV 330M, POP 16,109)
(136.2/379.7KM)

Nestled at the foothills of the Apennine mountains, Sansepolcro is a precious treasure among Tuscan towns and one of the urban gems of the Via di Francesco. Its medieval appellation of 'Borgo San Sepolcro' derives from the name of a 9th-c. monastery founded here and points to the town's deeply religious roots. Today, Sansepolcro is much more than an economic hub for the Upper Valtiberina: it also serves as a reminder of the human-scale virtues of the medieval small town, where every necessity can be found in a short walk and where everyone knows the life story of their neighbors. To stroll among the cafés, shops, churches, and restaurants of Sansepolcro is to step back to a gentler and more communal time.

Among the stucco-covered, wood-framed buildings of its core are two major artistic treasures. The oldest and most legendary is the Volto Santo (Holy Face – not to be confused with the cross of the same name in Lucca), an evocative, 270cm-tall wooden crucifix that has been a subject of wonder for centuries. Held originally in the Pieve Vecchia and then the Parish of Santa Maria, it was moved to the Cathedral of Sansepolcro in the late 18th c., where it is now housed in a dedicated side chapel. While documents trace its presence in Sansepolcro to at least the 14th c., recent carbon dating puts its production to as early as the 8th–9th c.

The Palazzo della Residenza (Via Aggiunti 65, www.museocivicosansepolcro.it) contains another treasure, an early-Renaissance wall mural, *The Resurrection*. Painted in the 1460s by Piero della Francesca, it played a role in the town's modern history. As the Germans retreated from the Tiber Valley in 1944, the Allies planned to shell Sansepolcro to clear out any remaining soldiers. The British troop commander, Lt. Anthony Clarke, remembered an essay by Aldous Huxley that described the painting as 'the greatest picture in the world.' Clarke ordered an early end to the bombardment, which ended up being unnecessary as the Germans had already departed the town. So not only was the painting saved, but the preservation of this medieval Tuscan jewel was assured as well.

🔺 **Camere Mazzini 49** ◎ Pr R 3/6, €35 per room, Via Mazzini 49, cestellim@gmail.com, tel 348 6040941.

🔺 **Locanda Guidi** ◎ Pr R Br Dr Cr S 6/12, €-/65/95/120, Via Luca Pacioli 46, info@enotecaguidi.com, www.enotecaguidi.com, tel 0575 736587, tel 393 8101964. Family run with a restaurant downstairs. In city center.

🔺 **Relais Oroscopo** ◎ Pr R Br Cr S 10/22, €-/70/90/120, Via Togliatti 68, info@relaisoroscopo.com, www.relaisoroscopo.com, tel 393 6921513.

🔺 **Convent of Santa Maria dei Servi** ◎ Pr Do R S 4/22, €20 or donation, Piazza Dotti 2, info@santamariadeiservi.it, www.santamariadeiservi.it, tel 0575 742347, 339 6246194. Open, but no heat in winter.

THE WAY OF ST FRANCIS — VIA DI FRANCESCO

## STAGE 9
*Sansepolcro to Citerna*

| | |
|---|---|
| **Start** | Piazza Torre di Berta, Sansepolcro |
| **Finish** | Piazza Scipioni, Citerna |
| **Duration** | 3½hr |
| **Distance** | 12.2km |
| **Total ascent** | 229m |
| **Total descent** | 84m |
| **Difficulty** | Easy |
| **Percentage paved** | 97% |
| **Lodgings** | Gricignano 5.8km, Mancino 7.5km, Convento Zoccolanti 11.3km, Citerna 12.2km |

Until a final climb, this is a short and very flat stage through urban streets, warehouse districts, and farms, on the way to the tiny but very charming hill town of Citerna. It may be best to consider Citerna a pleasant lunch and provisioning stop, because the town presently has no lodging in its boundaries. However, just 1km before is the spartan Convento Zoccolanti, and 1–2km afterward are Poggio Villa Fano apartments. Another possibility entirely is to have a relaxed lunch in Citerna and continue on 4.9km to Agriturismo Le Burgne.

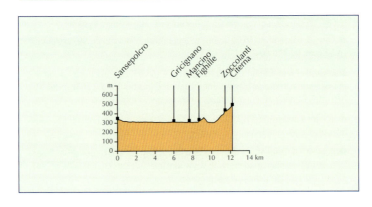

## STAGE 9 – SANSEPOLCRO TO CITERNA

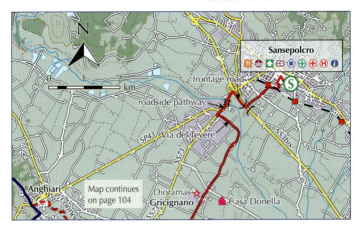

With the tourist information office in Piazza Torre di Berta on your right, go straight ahead onto Via della Fraternità, turning right when it ends and then left one block later onto Via San Gregorio. After the roundabout and **train tracks**, turn right onto Via della Santucce, which leads you out of town and under the **SS3bis highway** via a tunnel. Turn right and continue on the frontage road until it ends at the Via Senese Aretina, where you turn left. Continue along this busy road and cross the Tiber River on the auto bridge.

In two blocks, after the commercial district, turn left onto Via del Tevere (Way of the Tiber). Follow this long, flat road, first along the river and then through a mixture of warehouses, factories, and farms; note the factory and world headquarters of Buitoni pasta on the right. Continue along the road through the town of **Gricignano (5.8km, ♦ Casa Donella B&B** ⊙ Pr R Br Gr S 4/8, €-/35/50/-, Via San Marino 2, casadonella.bnb@gmail.com, www.casadonella.it, tel 339 1358039).

Intricate **dioramas of the Nativity and Resurrection of Jesus**, created by local craftsmen, are available here for viewing (Via di Vittorio 63, www.prolocogricignano.org).

Go straight at the next intersection, where you enter the region of Umbria. Named after the Umbri people, an ancient, rural civilization that inhabited the Apennine area north of the Tiber, Umbria is often called 'the green heart of Italy.' Citerna now becomes visible on the hilltop straight ahead, and in a few hundred meters you come to the tiny settlement of **Mancino** and its posh but pilgrim-friendly ♦ **Relais Antonella** (www.relaisantonella.com, tel 075 8592838,

## THE WAY OF ST FRANCIS — VIA DI FRANCESCO

*Pilgrims walk among farm roads before the final climb to Citerna on the hill ahead*

from €70). After leaving Mancino, go left briefly on the SP100 toward the town of **Fighille** (**2.8km**). In just 100 meters, turn right on Via Gabriotti and left onto Via del Pozzo. Wind your way up toward the café/bar, which serves the Centro Sportico swimming pool and sports complex behind it.

After the sports complex, continue uphill and veer left toward the cemetery at the next fork, with Stations of the Cross guiding the way. A right turn at the next street after the cemetery allows a connection to Anghiari and the Cortona route to Santuario della Verna. Come to the gate of a villa and go to the left of it, heading downhill along a green chain-link fence on a narrow path until it ends at Via del Mulino, which you take straight ahead as it climbs the hill. Continue on this road and partway up find signs leading

104

## Stage 9 – Sansepolcro to Citerna

onto a dirt pathway that ends, along with the road, at the Monastero del Santissimo Crocifisso e Santa Maria, also known as **Convento Zoccolanti** (**2.7km**, see Citerna below for lodging information).

Turn left now and continue the ascent as you come to the first homes of Citerna and a view of the valley through trees to the left. Continue with the fortification wall on your right and come to the tiny Piazza Scipioni of **Citerna** (**0.9km**), with its panoramic view on the left. Behind is the town's clock tower, the Chiesa di San Michele Arcangel, and beyond is a bar and upscale restaurant that shares the epic view.

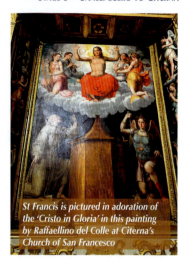
*St Francis is pictured in adoration of the 'Cristo in Gloria' in this painting by Raffaellino del Colle at Citerna's Church of San Francesco*

**12.2KM CITERNA** (ELEV 480M, POP 3332) 🍴 🏛 🏠 🅒 🄬 (124.0/367.5KM)
With its commanding position over the Upper Valtiberina, it's little wonder that Citerna was a prized fortress as early as the 13th and 14th c. Perched at the top of the village is a citadel that still houses a system of defensive walkways and underground cisterns. The Church of San Francesco is festooned with depictions of St Francis, who visited the area twice, according to tradition, on his way to La Verna. The church also features a Madonna and Child by Donatello, while the Monastero di Santa Elisabetta, at the far end of town, features a 14th-c. German pietà. Above the town square is a clock tower with wooden workings from the 16th c.

While all these are notable, it is the view from the main piazza that attracts the most attention. From here you can see back to Sansepolcro and as far to the northwest as the high peak of Monte Penna, home to Santuario della Verna.

🏠 **Monastero Santissimo Crocifisso e Santa Maria** O Pr Do R K Br Dr S 4/8, €Donation, Loc. Zoccolanti 8, benedetticiterna@gmail.com, www.benedettiniciterna.wordpress.com, tel 366 2969218. Sleeping bag or linens required. Arrive by 6:00pm to respect prayers of the community. Possibility of participating in communal prayer.

🏠 **Poggio Villa Fano apartments** O Pr R K W S 4/8, €-/70/80/100, Località Villa Fano, info@poggiodivillafano.it, tel 347 083 4295. Swimming pool. Rosella is your host.

## THE WAY OF ST FRANCIS — VIA DI FRANCESCO

🏠 **Fonte Degna Affittacamere** O Pr Do R K Br W S 4/12, €-/25/40/60 + €15 linens, Via degli Eroi 15, manudicre@gmail.com, www.facebook.com/lafontedegnadeipellegrini, tel 331 7431965.

🏠 **Casa degli Artisti** O Pr R K Br W S 3/9, €-/60/80/120, Corso Garibaldi 24, casadegliartisti.umbria@gmail.com, tel 331 7431965. English speaking. Manuela is your host.

### FRANCIS RENOUNCES HIS EARTHLY POSSESSIONS

Angered once he discovered Francis had sold his cloth at the Foligno marketplace, Francis' father Pietro Bernardone imprisoned his son in the basement of the family home. His mother appealed to Bishop Guido to mediate a solution. He agreed, and scheduled a public trial to be held in front of the cathedral. The bishop confronted him, explaining that he had hurt his father and that God would not want him to use stolen money to rebuild a church. The bishop said, 'Have confidence in the Lord and act courageously. God will be your help and will abundantly provide you with whatever is necessary.'

These words struck Francis in a deep way. Standing before his father, the bishop, and the crowd, Francis stripped off his clothes and handed them to his father. He said, 'Listen, everyone. From now on, I can say with complete freedom, "Our Father who art in heaven." Pietro Bernardone is no longer my father.'

The stunned bishop wrapped his cloak around the naked man. Bernardone left, defeated. Francis left, freed from the expectations of his family and from any attachment to possessions.

*The view from Citerna takes in the many fields and forests lying in the direction of Arezzo.*

# STAGE 10
*Citerna to Città di Castello*

| | |
|---|---|
| **Start** | Piazza Scipioni, Citerna |
| **Finish** | Cattedrale di San Florido, Città di Castello |
| **Duration** | 6¼hr |
| **Distance** | 19.1km |
| **Total ascent** | 621m |
| **Total descent** | 799m |
| **Difficulty** | Moderate |
| **Percentage paved** | 70% |
| **Lodgings** | Agriturismo Le Burgne 4.9km, Borgo di Celle 6.4km, Lerchi 10.5km, Città di Castello 19.1km |

Today's beautiful but deceptively challenging stage crosses three tall ridges that separate fertile valleys before finishing in a long downhill walk to beautiful Città di Castello. The stage can be shortened via the highway from Lerchi, either by a treacherous walk along the highway or by taking the bus, but that would involve missing a Franciscan landmark, the Eremo del Buonriposo, a private property that can be visited by reservation.

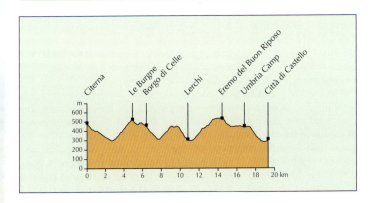

Standing in Piazza Scipioni of Citerna with the panoramic view at your back, turn left on Corso Garibaldi and head downhill, walking under the arch and past the

107

*The Way of St Francis — Via di Francesco*

Municipio and Monastero di Santa Elisabetta. After going through the city gate, turn left and follow the winding SP100 downhill. In 400 meters, fork right to a quiet road heading past the soccer pitch and to the valley floor at the **SS221**. Stay on the highway for just 60 meters and then turn right onto a gravel road, where you make your first climb of the day.

Follow the gravel road across a creek and 175 meters later turn left, beginning an ascent that becomes steeper in a few hundred meters. The curvy road continues between hayfields and along woods as it makes its way to the top of the hill. Following signs to the top of the hill, turn left on the gravel road. From this height you can see back to Citerna, Sansepolcro, and beyond. In a few meters is the entrance to **Agriturismo Le Burgne (4.9km)**, where you may want to enjoy a sumptuous breakfast or stay the night (⌂ **Agriturismo Le Burgne** Pr Do R K Br Dr Gt W S Z 10/38, €35/70/100/135 (including breakfast), Voc. Le Burgne 12, info@agriturismoleburgne.it, www.agriturismoleburgne.it, tel 329 0192923. Open end Mar–end Oct. Swimming pool. Your host is Patrizia).

## Stage 10 – Citerna to Città di Castello

Continue on the same gravel road along the ridge, as the road goes gently downhill then uphill once again. Come to a summit and 300 meters later the gravel road ends at the Vocabolo Sant Pietro asphalt road (**1.5km**); just ahead is a stylish hotel in a historic hilltop village property, the **Borgo di Celle Relais and Spa** (www.borgodicelle.com). Turn right, heading downhill, and follow the asphalt road, passing the Casa da Maria pilgrim accommodation (⌂ **Da Maria, Casa del Pellegrino** Pr R K Br Dr W S Z 2/7, €35 per person (including breakfast and dinner), Voc. Caldese 14, faelalla@alice.it, www.facebook.com/damariacasa, tel 338 9035947, tel 075 8510144. Open 15 Mar–30 Nov. Laura is your host) on your way to the valley floor. As you descend, you can see among peaks to the right the lofty 11th-c. Monte Santa Maria Tiberina castle, home to the Bourbon *marchesi* from 1250 to 1815 (www.montesantamariatiberina.org).

At the valley bottom, turn left on the asphalt **SP102** and 100 meters later turn right onto a gravel road. Cross a small stream and begin your second climb of the day, following signs to fork left in 200 meters to another gravel road. After the summit, the road turns to asphalt and you make your way downhill to the Via Toscana highway in **Lerchi** (**4.1km**).

---

**10.5KM LERCHI** (ELEV 293M, POP 508) 🍴 🛏 ⊙ (113.4/356.9KM)
The village is bisected by the SS221 highway, which serves as the primary western access for Città di Castello.

⌂ **Agriturismo La Rosa** O Pr R K Br Gr S Z 2/22, €-/60/70/-, Voc Pulcino, Fraz. Lerchi, info@agriturismolarosa.it, www.agriturismolarosa.it, tel 339 8440298, 339 7779866.

---

### Shortcut by bus to Città di Castello
If you are tempted to shorten your day via the highway from Lerchi to Città di Castello, the safest option is to take the SI381 bus, which runs every couple of hours. If you choose to walk along the highway, bear in mind that, with speeding cars and no sidewalks, it can make for an unpleasant and dangerous walking experience, so great care should be taken.

To follow the official, recommended route, turn right. In 200 meters, the waymarks point you toward the right – for your third uphill climb of the day. Soon the asphalt ends on a well-graded gravel road, which at first climbs steeply. At the iron gate of a large villa, turn right onto a two-track gravel road that continues uphill. Soon you come to a fork, where you turn left and begin a gradual downhill past a small shrine. In 5min leave a gate to the right and follow a stone wall next to the gate around the left side of the **Eremo del Buonriposo** (**3.7km**).

*Sunflowers fill the fields between Citerna and Monterchi, shown in the distance*

*The Way of St Francis — Via di Francesco*

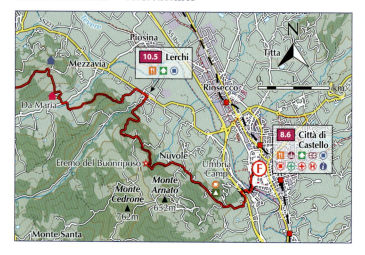

Originally called Santa Croce di Nuvole, the place took on the name **Eremo del Buonriposo** after St Francis visited here and said 'Oh, what a good rest.' The caves served as habitats for hermits for many centuries and sheltered displaced local residents during World War II. Francis is documented to have traveled here in 1213 and again in 1224, after receiving the stigmata. A cloister and chapel are among the buildings. (Although privately owned, it is possible to visit by contacting Andrea Coltellini: tel 333 5407782, andreacoltellini@hotmail.it.)

Wind down through the driveway toward the left and then continue downhill. Patches of asphalt begin to appear and then you reach an intersection with an asphalt road. Turn right, then go straight at the next fork, where soon you can look down to Città di Castello. On your way downhill, pass **Umbria Camp** (2.3km, restaurant, mini-market, bar, ▲ Umbria Camp Via Alice Hallgarten Franchetti 3, www.umbriacamp.it, tel 333 2477794), where you can stop for a welcome refreshment or tent overnight.

Continue along the asphalt road to a fork and go left for 400 meters on the **SP103**, before forking right on the Via Carbini. Follow this road downhill and under the freeway until it ends in a T-junction with the Via Arentina. Jog right 100 meters and then left as the road crosses the Tiber River to enter town.

At the roundabout, go left, and in 200 meters fork right to walk uphill and inside the city walls. At the end of this lane is a small staircase leading to a Vittorio

112

*Stage 10 – Citerna to Città di Castello*

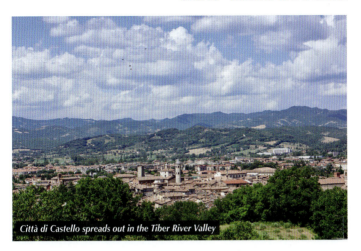

*Città di Castello spreads out in the Tiber River Valley*

Emmanuel statue in a park, across from the lovely 11th-c. Cattedrale dei Santi Florido e Amanzio of **Città di Castello** (**2.5km**).

### 8.6KM CITTÀ DI CASTELLO (ELEV 288M, POP 38,181) 🍴 🌐 🏠 💶 ⓞ 🔴 ✚ ⓗ ⓘ (104.9/348.4KM)

The Umbrian people established Città di Castello on the banks of the Tiber River over 2500 years ago. Continuously occupied since then, the town was rebuilt and fortified by its bishop, Floridus, around a new castle, ultimately earning it the name Città di Castello. Its medieval walls, many of which survive, date to the 14th and 15th c.

Towering above the town's buildings are the 11th-c. Torre Comunale and the cathedral's 12th-c. Campanile Cilindrico. The town is a center for medieval and Renaissance art, and its Pinacoteca Comunale art gallery has significant works from Ghiberti, Signorelli, Raphael, and della Robbia. The cathedral's museum houses a collection of Christian art, including a display of 25 rare objects from the 6th c. used for Eucharistic liturgy, which were found while plowing a nearby field in 1935. The cathedral crypt houses the 'Dragon's Bone,' found in nearby Pietralunga and transported here as evidence of dragons – or at least of dinosaurs.

It is hard to imagine powerful demons and embarrassed saints among the warm brick-and-umber tones of today's Città di Castello. The town has a lively street life among its cafés, bars, and restaurants. The local bread, cooked below the ashes of the oven, is called *ciaccia* (pronounced 'cha-cha'), and is used to make handheld pizza-like sandwiches.

🏠 **Albergo Ristorante Umbria** Pr R Br Dr Cr S Z 25/45, €-/45/65/85, Via dei Galanti, umbria@hotelumbria.net, www.hotelumbria.net, tel 075 8554925, tel 075 8520911. Open 31 Mar–10 Dec. Restaurant open only for groups of 6+ by reservation. In center of city.

🏠 **Hotel Tiferno** O Pr R Br Dr Cr S Z 40/85, €-/80/140/180 (range of prices), Piazza R Sanzio 13, www.hoteltiferno.it/en, tel 075 8550331. 4-star hotel. Laundry service, spa, Turkish bath, gym.

🏠 **Residenze Antica Canonica** O Pr R K Br W S 3/9, €-/60/80/120, Via San Florido 25, info@anticacanonica.it, www.anticacanonica.it, tel 347 1564910. Vacation apartment/hotel.

🏠 **Residence San Bartolomeo** O Pr R K Cr 5/20, €-/-/50/75, Via San Bartolomeo 4, residence.sanbartolomeo@gmail.com, tel 327 1111363. Autonomous apartments.

🏠 **Monastero delle Clarisse Urbaniste di Santa Cecilia** O Pr Do R Br Dr S Z Via dell Fraternita 1, info@lerosedigerico.it, www.lerosedigerico.it/monastero-santa-cecilia.html, tel 075 8553066, 371 188674. Breakfast included, dinner by reservation. Sister Carmela is your host.

---

### FRANCIS EXPERIENCES FAILURE

Thomas of Celano reports in his biography of Francis that a woman possessed by a devil lived in Città di Castello and caused a great deal of disturbance to the inhabitants. While Francis was visiting town, the inhabitants implored him to call on this woman and cast out her demon. Francis sent one of the brothers instead and, on meeting the woman, the demon began to mock the brother, knowing he was not Francis. After hearing this, Francis himself came to the woman, who immediately upon seeing him began to tremble violently. Francis shouted to the demon to come out – but no change to her behavior took place. Francis' embarrassment was so great that he immediately left town, ashamed for his failure.

However, the next time he came to town, the cured woman sought him out and thanked him for saving her life. She threw herself at his feet and kissed his footprints until she finally was able to reassure him that his earlier ministry to her had been a success. Celano reports that the momentary embarrassment helped Francis accept the gift of humility, reminding him that it was a power beyond his which enabled any miracles.

*The dual clocks of the Mayor's Palace in Città di Castello show hours and minutes, while a third face above shows the direction of the wind*

*THE WAY OF ST FRANCIS — VIA DI FRANCESCO*

## STAGE 11
*Città di Castello to Pietralunga*

| | |
|---|---|
| **Start** | Cattedrale di San Florido, Città di Castello |
| **Finish** | Piazza 7 Maggio, Pietralunga |
| **Duration** | 8½hr |
| **Distance** | 28.7km |
| **Total ascent** | 834m |
| **Total descent** | 566m |
| **Difficulty** | Moderately hard due to distance |
| **Percentage paved** | 71% |
| **Lodgings** | Candeggio 13.5km, Pieve de' Saddi 19.3km, Pietralunga 28.7km |

Start early for this long but scenic stage that climbs among pastures and pine forests to the atmospheric medieval village of Pietralunga, first stop in the transit to the Chiascio River drainage. A stay at the hostels of Candeggio (13.5km) or Pieve de' Saddi (19.3km) can shorten this quiet and rural day.

Watch for online updates to this route, as Via di Francesco stewards plan to announce a new, forested walking route between Città di Castello and Candeggio.

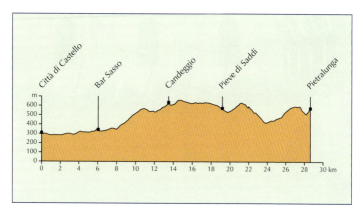

*Stage 11 – Città di Castello to Pietralunga*

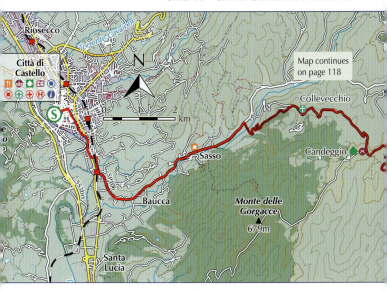

Facing the front door of the cathedral, follow its left side along Corso Cavour. In a few blocks, at Piazza Matteotti, make a right turn onto Corso Vittorio Emanuele. Head outside the city walls at Porta Santa Maria Maggiore and go straight ahead. The road now becomes Via Rignaldello, which you follow until the roundabout at Viale Orlando. The official route goes straight onto Via Pierucci here, but it is just as easy to turn right onto Via Roma (supermarket). In 500 meters take a left turn, and three blocks later, after the railroad tracks, turn right onto the **SP106**.

Follow this quiet paved road as it begins a gentle climb toward the mountains. At **Baucca** take the left fork, which briefly leads around a narrow section that is somewhat dangerous for pedestrians. Arrive at **Bar Sasso** (**6.0km**), which is the last bar until Pietralunga. Across the street you may enjoy the park and its gentle cascade of water over bedrock.

Continue on the SP106, following signs to a right turn on a gravel road in about 1.5km. Soon cross a creek and at the following fork go left and uphill. The gravel road now climbs, first through fields and then through woods on a series of switchbacks. On your way uphill come to an asphalt road, turn right and pass the tiny settlement of **Collevecchio**. Stay on the road and arrive at a small and hospitable rest area with log benches and drinking water on the right at the turn-off to

*The Way of St Francis — Via di Francesco*

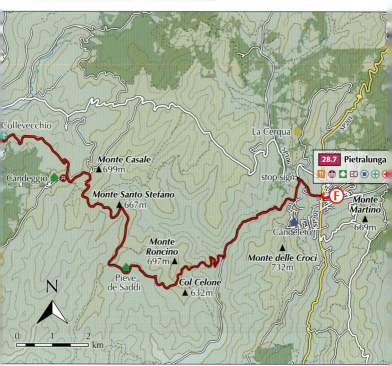

**Candeggio** (**7.5km**, ▲ **Rifugio Candeggio** O Do R K Br Dr S 7/28, €Donation, Loc. Candeggio 1b, rifugiocandeggio@gmail.com, tel 329 5620677).

Continue on the asphalt road and in about 15min come to the highest point of elevation of the stage, at 632m on the slope of 667m **Monte Santo Stefano**. Turn left at a fork, and come to the 4th-c. church of **Pieve de' Saddi** (**5.7km**) with its adjoining pilgrim hostel (▲ **Pieve de' Saddi Accoglienza Religiosa** Do R K Br Dr S 3/16, €Donation, Loc. Pieve de' Saddi, pievedesaddi@gmail.com, www.facebook.com/pievedesaddi, tel 329 5620677 (Federico). Open 25 Apr–10 Oct).

Even if you choose not to stay at **Pieve de' Saddi**, it is still worth a knock on the door to investigate the ancient church's frescoes, and a volunteer *hospitalero* (host) may offer you a *caffè* while you relax on the back lawn.

*Stage 11 – Città di Castello to Pietralunga*

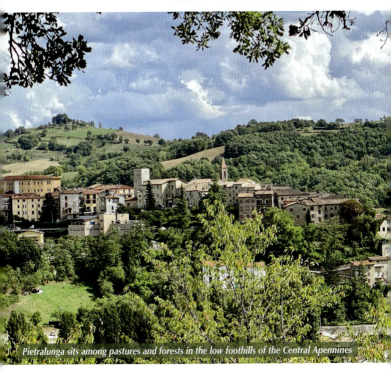

*Pietralunga sits among pastures and forests in the low foothills of the Central Apennines*

Return to the asphalt road, where you briefly descend and then begin another climb to a forested summit where paths branch to the left and right. Go straight ahead and begin a long descent until the road ends at a T-junction. Following signs to the left, remain on this road until it meets the **SP106** at a **stop sign**. While it's possible to follow this road to the SP201 into town, it's shorter and easier to turn right onto Via Vincenzo to descend more directly to the SP201. Continue right and enjoy views of Pietralunga ahead.

Come to the **SP201**, which you reach after a stairway. Cross the road and immediately turn right (uphill) onto a narrow lane that takes you on switchbacks and stairways through the narrow streets of the old village and up to the Piazza 7 Maggio of **Pietralunga** (**9.5km**). Enjoy views over the countryside to the right, and behind you to the historic buildings of this friendly village that has been animated by Via di Francesco pilgrims.

**28.7KM PIETRALUNGA** (ELEV 566M, POP 1980) 🔲 ⊕ 🔺 🔲 ⊙ ⊕ ⊕ (76.2/319.6KM)
A settlement here has been traced back to prehistory, and the ancient Umbrian settlement was called Tufi or Tufiernu. The Romans called it Forum Julii Concupiensium, and it was home to villas, aqueducts, and paved Roman roads. Completely destroyed by the Goths in the 6th c., it was reconstructed in the Lombard era. It came to be called Pratalonga (long grass) for the extensive pastures that surround it.

More than 100 soldiers from Pietralunga perished in World War I, and in World War II Pietralunga was a center of the anti-Fascist Resistance movement, earning the town the Bronze Medal for Military Valor. The Piazza 7 Maggio remembers the date in 1944 when seven boys were executed by the Nazis and Fascists in reprisal for their armed resistance. Below the piazza is a monument: 'Al Partigiano Umbro' ('To the Umbrian Partisan').

Adjacent to the piazza is the 8th–10th-c. Church of Santa Maria and remnants of the 8th-c. citadel gate and tower. Crowded into the narrow streets are the 18th-c. former hospital, 15th-c. Captain's Palace, and 12th-c. convent, all worthy of a contemplative stroll to absorb the quiet of this ancient village.

🏠 **La Locanda del Borgo** O Pr K Br Gr S Z 8/18, €-/65/85/120, Via Roma 139, info@locandadelborgo.com, www.locandadelborgo.com, tel 075 9460798.

🏠 **Bio Agriturismo La Cerqua** O Pr R Br Dr Gr W S Z 10/25, €-/52/80/105, Voc. San Salvatore 27, info@cerqua.it, www.cerqua.it, tel 075 9460283, tel 340 5160633. 3km off trail. Breakfast included, dinner available. Possibility of free transport to Pietralunga. Summer swimming pool.

🏠 **Casa Biron B&B** O Pr R K Br Dr Gr W S 4/8, €-/30/50/65, Via Molino Sant'Anna 32, info@casabiron.com, www.casabiron.com, tel 075 5454588, 379 2935202 (WhatsApp only). 3km off route with transport available from owner by request. Stable available. Ask for pilgrim price.

🏠 **Agriturismo Borgo di Cortolla** O Pr R K Br Dr Gr W S Z 4/15, €20/45/65/90 + €10 breakfast, Voc. Cortolla 105, info@cortolla.it, www.cortolla.it, tel 349 7483897, tel 340 4098910. Located off the trail before the turn-off down into Pietralunga. Group discount and private pool. Your host, Gianluca, also has a grocery in the main square for sandwiches and supplies.

🏠 **Parrocchia di Santa Maria 'Rifugio Betania'** O Do R S 4/30, €Donation, Via della Pieve 2, donfranci@gmail.com, tel 328 0338261 (Fr. Francesco). Call at least one day before.

*Stage 11 – Città di Castello to Pietralunga*

🏠 **Hotel Aldo Tinca** Pr R Br Cr W S 9/25, €40/person including breakfast, Via Guglielmo Marconi 5, info@hotel-tinca.com, www.hotel-tinca.com, tel 333 8049985, 075 9460057. Elevator.

🏠 **Loc Ale Guest House** O Pr R Cr 2/4, €-/60/80/-, Piazza VII Maggio 2a, tel 333 2359304, tel 333 6179532. Center of town, above restaurant.

🏠 **B&B Villa Ginevra** Pr R K Br Dr W S 3/8, €35 per person, Via Falani 3, bebginevra@gmail.com, tel 333 6179532, tel 335 5743249. Abundant breakfast, swimming pool, bag transport available.

*The archway and tower are remnants of Pietralunga's 8th-c. fortifications*

## ST FRANCIS AND LADY POVERTY

Francis took literally the New Testament prescription 'blessed are the poor,' and saw it as the most important step in following Jesus Christ. He came to call his renunciation of possessions 'Lady Poverty,' and taught his followers to renounce their belongings in the same way. His order, called the Friars Minor, set to make their living by hard work, but when they were unable to grow enough crops, they would ask for alms to support their work. By not focusing on cares about the source of the next day's food, Francis hoped to put the focus instead on service of God. St Bonaventure wrote: 'When there seemed to be no way for them to get the food they needed, God's providence immediately came to their aid. For suddenly a man appeared carrying bread.'

# STAGE 12
*Pietralunga to Gubbio*

| | |
|---|---|
| **Start** | Piazza 7 Maggio, Pietralunga |
| **Finish** | Chiesa di San Francesco, Gubbio |
| **Duration** | 7¾hr |
| **Distance** | 26.2km |
| **Total ascent** | 623m |
| **Total descent** | 694m |
| **Difficulty** | Moderately hard due to distance |
| **Percentage paved** | 52% |
| **Lodgings** | Agriturismo Borgo San Benedetto 3.7km, Loreto 15.8km, Gubbio 26.2km |

The first half of the day is on quiet roads and sometimes-steep paths in the forested mountains, while the second half is along fields of hay and sunflowers as you approach the picturesque and ancient town of Gubbio. An early start to the day allows more time to enjoy this popular and historic town, which really deserves a full day for exploration.

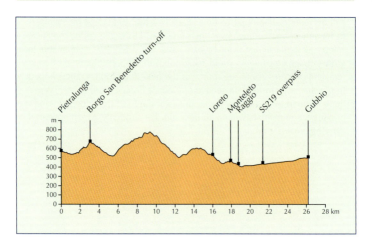

*Stage 12 – Pietralunga to Gubbio*

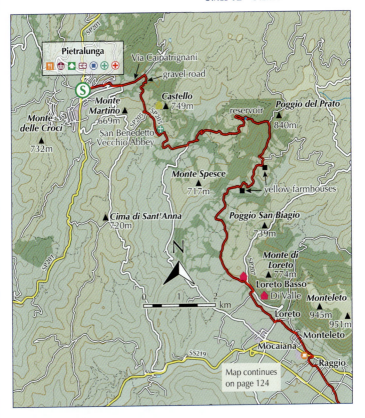

From the main piazza of Pietralunga follow Via Roma east, between the pizzeria and grocery, heading downhill and out of town. In 1km, instead of joining the SP204 at a fork, go straight, following the Francesco sign indicating 14.8km to Loreto and 23.2km to Gubbio. This puts you on the **Via Caipatrignani** in the direction of Salceto Lame and Morena.

Turn right in 700 meters at a **gravel road** that appears on the right. This climb connects you to a loop in the asphalt **SP205** (**3.1km**). (Just before you connect to the SP205, a left turn leads to 🏠 **Borgo San Benedetto** Pr R K Br Dr Gr W S Z 5/14, €-/80/80/105, Loc. San Benedetto Vecchio, sanbenedettovecchio@gmail.

com, www.sanbenedettovecchio.com, tel 349 3215695, tel 075 59241002. Closed Jan–Mar. Dinner and sack lunch by reservation.)

On joining the SP205, veer left to proceed downhill on the quiet roadway. In 700 meters come on your left to the restored but silent monastery buildings of **San Benedetto Vecchio**. The abbey flourished in the 11th–15th c., and in 1451 was transformed into a parish church. The oldest portion of the remaining structures is the 12th-c. church apse.

Continue past the monastery on the SP205 and in about 20min, after crossing a bridge over a small stream, follow signs left on a gravel road leading uphill with a pasture on its right. Follow this road for the biggest climb of the day, spanning nearly 4km while gaining an elevation of about 260m on the southern slope of 840m Poggio del Prato. Near the top, see a sign welcoming you into this area, the Alto di Chiascio, and soon afterward pass a small **reservoir** as you near the steepest part of the climb. Once at the summit, instead of going left with the road, follow signs that lead straight ahead onto another gravel road, which goes in a southerly direction through a logging area to connect to the SP207 at Loreto. A long descent begins here and leftward vistas open over hayfields to the valley below.

In 500 meters the signs lead you right at a fork and you pass a **yellow farmhouse** that you've seen from above for some time. Walk past the farmhouse and continue downhill to a second **yellow farmhouse**, where you walk between the

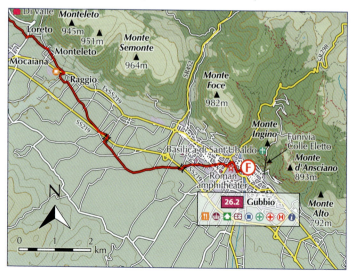

## STAGE 12 – PIETRALUNGA TO GUBBIO

house and its accompanying barn, now near the valley floor. Once at the valley floor, another climb awaits, this one taking you over the hill among pastures and scattered woods toward Loreto. After a summit, the wide Chiascio Valley floor can be seen ahead. Soon the road levels out and begins to hug the sheer mountainside of pinkish orange stone, traversing the slope as the road gently descends to the valley floor below (🏠 **B&B Di Valle** Pr R K Br Dr W 5/15, €-/50/70/85, Frazione Loreto 27, annalisasantolin@libero.it, www.bbdivalle.it, tel 347 9768879. From 15 Mar to 7 Jan).

In a few hundred meters, just as you sense the presence of the SP207 above, the route takes a sharp right turn, passing the Pieve San Giovanni Battista in Loreto (**12.7km**, church open daily 9:00am–5:00pm. An extensive renovation of the historic parish church of San Giovanni Battista in Loreto was completed in 2023, including restoration of the 9th-c. crypt, which had recently been used as a chicken coop.)

After the church, the road plunges right and down a steep hill between two houses, leading to **Loreto Basso** and then the SP207. Follow signs leading you across the roadway, and 40 meters later turn right into **Loreto** proper and take a short climb back up the hill, where you come to the neighborhood of **Monteleto** (no services), with its parish church on the left. Continue downhill and, before crossing the Via dell'Assino **ExSS219**, note the very welcome Bomboletti bar/café/tobacco shop 50 meters on the right in **Raggio** (**2.7km**).

*A pilgrim makes their way down a rutted road near Pietralunga*

*The Way of St Francis — Via di Francesco*

A left turn here would take you directly to Gubbio on the highway, but to spare the highway walking, you now cross the road and head across the valley floor. Follow signs that lead you across the **SS219** *autostrada* (freeway) on an **overpass bridge** (**2.5km**) and then turn left onto the same road that you were on before crossing the freeway; this road (the Via delle Sette Strade) would have continued straight if not for being bisected by the freeway. Gubbio now appears visible on the mountainside to the left.

The road gradually curves around to again cross the **SS219**. Continue after the freeway bridge, now in a busy commercial suburb of Gubbio with a supermarket, hospital, and bars. Stay on the Via dell'Arboreto as it crosses the Via Leonardo da Vinci arterial and in four blocks come to Viale Umberto Paruccini. Straight ahead is the park that holds Gubbio's impressive 1st-c. **Roman amphitheater**. If you are able, this is a good time to visit this treasure since otherwise it is inconvenient to the center of Gubbio. Veering left toward the city walls, follow the Viale Teatro Romano to the right and alongside them, turning left at the next automobile portal

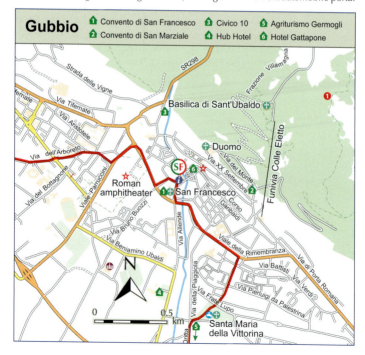

## STAGE 12 – PIETRALUNGA TO GUBBIO

into the city walls, the Via Repubblica. In one block you arrive on the left at Chiesa di San Francesco of **Gubbio** (**5.2km**), finding yourself now at the base of this striking town, spread out in all its medieval glory on the hillside above.

*A pilgrim loads onto the Funivia Colle Eletto for a scenic ride up the mountain*

### 26.2KM GUBBIO (ELEV 522M, POP 32,998)
(50.0/293.5KM)

Gubbio is one of Umbria's most beloved municipalities and is emblematic of the historic hill towns that cling to the mountainsides of Central Italy. Its rich and long history, its scenic beauty, and its unique architectural character make it a highlight for Way of St Francis pilgrims.

Gubbio traces its roots to the ancient Umbrian people, and its Civic Museum in Palazzo dei Consoli holds some priceless relics of its Umbrian past. In 1444 a set of seven 3rd–1st-c. BC bronze tablets inscribed in Umbrian and Latin were discovered nearby. The tablets are the most important source of information about the Umbrian language, civilization, and religious practices.

By the 2nd c. BC, Gubbio (Roman Iguvium) was a prosperous Roman settlement, and its large Roman amphitheater attests to its importance in Roman times. In the Middle Ages, Gubbio sent 1000 knights to fight in the First Crusade and, according to local legend, these knights were the first to enter the Church of the Holy Sepulcher when Jerusalem was captured in 1099.

Many buildings in the old town come from the 14th–15th c., giving Gubbio a distinctly medieval aspect, although it may seem somewhat austere due to the grayish color of the local stone used in construction. North–south streets in the hillside town are notoriously steep, and a series of pedestrian escalators and elevators allow easier access from the lower town to the main piazza, and above it to the cathedral.

A tour of Gubbio from bottom to top should include at least the **Roman amphitheater**, the 13th-c. **Church of San Francesco**, the 14th-c. **Palazzo dei Consoli** with its museum on the **Piazza Grande** (€5 entrance fee), and the 12th-c. cathedral, the **Duomo**, with its many works of sacred art and stunning rose window. While in the upper town, a stop at the **Church of San Francesco della Pace** allows a visit to the crypt where the wolf of Gubbio is remembered. Not to be missed is the **Funivia Colle Eletto**, an open-air funicular that takes you, standing in a metal basket, to the **Basilica di Sant'Ubaldo** and its lovely gardens and restaurant (www.funiviagubbio.it).

All Italy knows of the Corsa dei Ceri (Candle Race), held in Gubbio each year on 15 May. On that day, three large corps of colorfully clad locals race up the city streets from Piazza Grande to the Basilica di Sant'Ubaldo, carrying a trio of 4m-tall, 280kg columns. Each heavy column has at its crown a statue of one of the town's favorite saints. Tourists from throughout Italy and beyond fill the streets to cheer on the teams.

🛖 **Istituto Maestre Pie Filippini** O Pr R Br W S Z 9/25, €40 including breakfast, Corso Giuseppe Garibaldi 100, maestrepiefgubbio@virgilio.it, tel 075 9273768. Elevator.

🛖 **Accoglienza Convento di San Francesco** Pr Do R K S Z 8/30, €Donation, Piazza Quaranta Martiri 2, accoglienzasanfrancescogubbio@gmail.com, tel 370 3490485. Easter–mid Oct.

🛖 **Accoglienza Sorelle** O Pr R K Br S 3/7, €Donation, Via XX Settembre 111, pictestn1@gmail.com, tel 329 7199958. Please contact by email or WhatsApp. Ask for Sister Daniela.

🛖 **Civico10** O Pr R Br Cr S 3/8, €-/45/60/80, Via del Camignano 10, info@civico10.it, www.civico10.it, tel 333 1229144, tel 347 6511520. Maria Teresa.

🛖 **Hub Hotel** O Pr R Br Dr Cr S Z 51/120, €-/76/84/104, Via Perugina 74, info@hubhotel.net, www.hubhotel.net, tel 075 6700040. Dinner available €30.

🛖 **Tenuta di Fassia** O Pr R Br Dr Cr S Z -/78, €-/80/100/130, Via Santa Maria Maddalena 46, info@tenutadifassia.it, www.tenutadifassia.it, tel 353 3124481.

## STAGE 12 – PIETRALUNGA TO GUBBIO

🏠 **Hotel Gattapone** O Pr R Br Gr W S Z 17/43, €-/70/85/100, Via Beni 11, info@hotelgattapone.net, www.hotelgattapone.net, tel 075 9272489. Possible sack lunch and early breakfast.

### FRANCIS AND THE WOLF OF GUBBIO

A marauding wolf was terrorizing the countryside around Gubbio, at first targeting livestock, but then humans. The town and surrounding residents were terrified of the wolf and implored Francis to come to town and intervene. Francis approached the wolf's refuge, with a small crowd following from a safe distance.

Upon seeing Francis, the wolf lunged with bared teeth, but when Francis made the sign of the cross the wolf stopped and listened. With the crowd watching in amazement, Francis spoke quietly with the wolf, which sat patiently at his feet. At the end of their talk the animal placed his paw in Francis' hand, as though to confirm an agreement.

*The famous interaction between St Francis and the wolf is memorialized in this statue near Chiesa della Vittorina*

Francis and the wolf then walked together into town, and the wolf laid at his feet while Francis announced to the village that an agreement had been made. In exchange for daily food provided by the village residents, the wolf would no longer harm any humans. Affirming the agreement in the presence of the villagers, the wolf once again placed his paw in Francis' hand. The townspeople complied with the pact, and each day the wolf went from house to house to receive food.

The wolf lived in peace with the village until its death two years later. When it passed away, residents buried its body with honor at the Church of San Francesco. In the renovation of the church in 1872, a wolf's skeleton was found under a slab outside the building. It was brought inside the church and placed under the altar of a side chapel, in memory of its transformation by the beloved saint.

## STAGE 13
*Gubbio to Valdichiascio*

| | |
|---|---|
| **Start** | Chiesa di San Francesco, Gubbio |
| **Finish** | San Pietro in Vigneto, Valdichiascio |
| **Duration** | 4¾hr |
| **Distance** | 15.9km |
| **Total ascent** | 354m |
| **Total descent** | 390m |
| **Difficulty** | Moderate due to long climb |
| **Percentage paved** | 64% |
| **Lodgings** | Ponte di Riocchio 8.8km, La Brocca di Valdichiascio 11.0km, Casalotto Francescano 11.4km, Il Beccafico 12.8km, San Pietro in Vigneto 15.9km |

In one large climb of about 250m you leave Gubbio behind and embrace the quiet green of the Umbrian countryside. St Francis knew this territory well, having walked from Assisi to Gubbio in 1206–1207 after his estrangement from his family. The undulating topography of the Chiascio Valley leads to many vistas of neighboring green hills, populated by small farms and *agriturismi*, which offer several options for overnight stays, although people on a budget or wanting pilgrim camaraderie will choose the *ostello* at San Pietro in Vigneto for their overnight.

Go downhill from the Piazza San Giovanni in the heart of Gubbio on the Via Repubblica, past the **San Francesco Church** and then turn left at the stoplight just after the city walls onto Via Matteotti. Cross toward the gas station to get onto the gravel walk, following this road opposite the city walls. Soon you see a bank, and a Saldi Sport store (selling hiking gear and other items that might be useful for hikers). In four long blocks, turn right onto Via Manzoni and follow the gravel walk downhill. In 300 meters, arrive at Via Frate Lupo and a sculpture remembering Francis and the wolf of Gubbio, with **Chiesa Santa Maria della Vittorina** (**1.1km**, water) across the road.

After a visit to the chapel, cross straight ahead in front of the church onto the pedestrian walk through the park. Cross the oblong traffic circle and follow the **Via Piaggiola** with its convenient supermarket, continuing first under the Strada

## STAGE 13 – GUBBIO TO VALDICHIASCIO

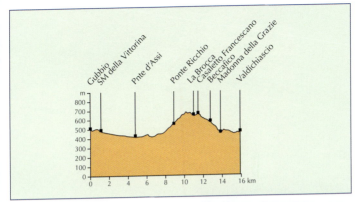

Statale della Contessa (**SS219**), then past a 12th-c. former leper hospital, along fields, past a soccer field, and into the town of **Ponte d'Assi** (**3.7km**). A block from the route, on the SR298, is a café, gas station, and small grocery, which is the last place to stock up on supplies until Valfabbrica.

This road finally merges with the **SR298** highway, the main route through the valley, and you walk on its shoulder for the next 1.1km. Continue uphill to the road to San Ciprignano, which takes off to the right and gives a brief respite from the highway. Soon you fork left, returning downhill to the highway, which you follow for another 300 meters.

Soon say goodbye to the busy road. Carefully cross it and immediately fork right to begin the day's long uphill jaunt. Come to **Agriturismo Ponte di Riocchio** (**4.1km**, **Agriturismo Ponte di Riocchio** Pr R Br G Z 5/17, €44/person including breakfast, Loc Colonnata,

*Looking back on the town of Gubbio on the way to Valdichiascio*

## THE WAY OF ST FRANCIS — VIA DI FRANCESCO

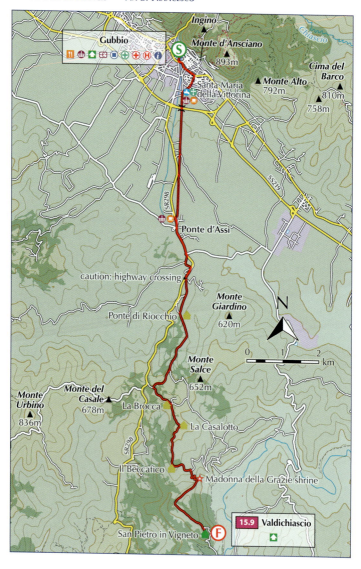

## STAGE 13 – GUBBIO TO VALDICHIASCIO

Voc Riocchio, info@pontediriocchio.com, www.pontediriocchio.com, tel 350 1862707. Elisabetta is your host): this is the first option for your overnight and, with advance notice to the owners, a potential coffee break. Continue uphill and take a moment to look back for the first of many sweeping views of Gubbio. In the winters since 1981, Gubbio has adorned the hillside behind the town with colored lights in the shape of a 750m-tall Christmas tree, earning a Guinness World Record for the largest in the world.

The road continues up a long and sometimes-steep hill for the next 2km until it ends at an asphalt road in a T-junction. Turn left and in just 100m finally come to the summit of your climb, where you fork right onto a gravel road at *agriturismo* **La Brocca di Valdichiascio** (**2.1km**, 🏠 La Brocca di Valdichiascio Pr R Br Dr W S 5/12, €-/65/90/120, Via Valdichiascio 1, info@labroccadivaldichiascio.it, www.valdichiascio.net, tel 353 4313124). Remain on this gravel road through the rest of the stage, passing a series of *agriturismi* as you descend on the long downhill; these include **Casalotto Francescano** (**0.5km**, 🏠 Casalotto Francescano O Pr R K Br Cr W S Z 5/13, €-/55/70/90, Fraz. Valdichiascio 3, info@casalottofrancescano.it, www.casalottofrancescano.it, tel 347 3643807, tel 075 9227010) and **Il Beccafico** (**1.3km**, 🏠 Agriturismo Il Beccafico O Pr Do R K Br Dr Cr W S Z 9/21, €-/60/95/130, Fraz. Vallingegno 18, info@agriturismoilbeccafico.it, tel 380 3037587. Breakfast included).

Follow signs through a series of intersections for the next 2km to arrive at the **Madonna delle Grazie** shrine (**1.1km**) with its large lawn, suitable for a rest or picnic. Begin a brief climb upward from here and come to the pilgrim *ostello* at the 15th-c. **Eremo di San Pietro in Vigneto** (**2.1km**).

*The Madonna delle Grazie shrine collects mementoes of pilgrims on their travels*

## 15.9KM VALDICHIASCIO (ELEV 455M, POP <50) 🏕 (34.0/277.5KM)

This stretch of backcountry in the Valdichiascio (Chiascio Valley) between Ponte d'Assi and Valfabbrica contains scattered farms and lodgings, but no villages or towns except those on the SR298, west of the route. The first of two notable historic sites on the way, Eremo di San Pietro in Vigneto (the other being Castello di Biscina), is mentioned in historical documents as early as 1131, although traces of a Roman temple have been found at the site by archeologists.

At one time this road linked Le Marche to the east with the Via Flaminia, making it a prime location for the hospitality offered by a community of monks at this location. By the 16th c., other routes gained prominence, and the buildings fell into disrepair. Earthquakes in 1979 and 1984 further damaged the facilities. The entire complex was restored in the 1990s and was dedicated to pilgrims on the Via di Francesco and the Sentiero Francescano della Pace, which also follows this route.

🏠 **Eremo San Pietro in Vigneto** Do R K Br Dr S 2/50, €Donation, Loc. Eremo di San Pietro in Vigneto, ospedaleconfraternitasanjacopo@gmail.com, www.confraternitasanjacopo.it, tel 334 9450501. From Apr to Sep. Tent space available. Confraternity of San Jacopo is your host.

### FRANCIS RETREATS TO GUBBIO

After his estrangement from his parents, Francis left Assisi with only a rude robe given him by Bishop Guido. Although the weather was cold and the ground was covered in snow, Francis was singing happily to himself in French. When local bandits caught sight of him, they stopped him and asked his business in the area. Francis replied: 'I am the herald of the Great King. What is it to you?' Their response was to beat him, strip him, and search him for valuables. Finding none, they threw him into the snowy ditch and left him for dead.

Finally arriving at Gubbio, Francis was taken in at the home of his friend, Giacomo Spadalunga, whose home is now the site of Gubbio's Church of San Francesco. Here, Francis began a ministry to a nearby leper colony, and service like this became a key theme of his life.

# STAGE 14
*Valdichiascio to Valfabbrica*

| | |
|---|---|
| **Start** | San Pietro in Vigneto, Valdichiascio |
| **Finish** | Piazza Mazzini, Valfabbrica |
| **Duration** | 6½hr (5¾hr via shortcut) |
| **Distance** | 20.8km (18.6km via shortcut) |
| **Total ascent** | 570m (436m via shortcut) |
| **Total descent** | 732m (599m via shortcut) |
| **Difficulty** | Moderate (moderate via shortcut) |
| **Percentage paved** | 29% (33% via shortcut) |
| **Lodgings** | Tenuta di Biscina 5.2km, Borgo Sambuco 12.5km, Valfabbrica 20.8km |

In this stage on forest paths and quiet country roads the route makes many twists and turns in order to pass around Lago di Valfabbrica. In theory, hardy walkers could combine this with the following stage and walk directly to Assisi in one 31.8km day, factoring in the 2.2km shortcut before Valfabbrica.

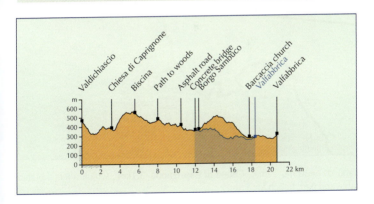

Continue on the road past the hermitage and head downhill toward the valley of a creek. On the way, follow signs onto a path that begins to the right. Make your way on the path to a creek crossing, which can be done on concrete pylons with a rope to steady you as you cross. Follow signs leading back to a gravel road and

*The Way of St Francis — Via di Francesco*

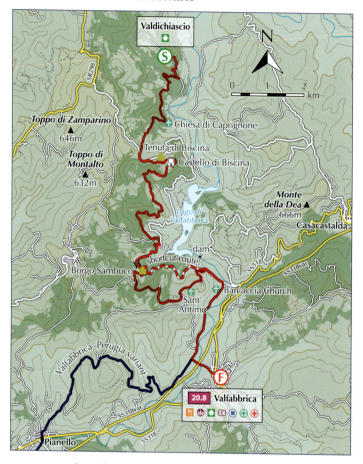

soon come to the 14th-c. **Chiesa di Caprignone** (**3.1km**), which offers a picnic table and park bench for a rest.

Traces of Roman settlement were found at **Chiesa di Caprignone**, but the earliest record of the church and monastery here is from the late 11th c. The construction suggests a later remodel in the Franciscan style, and according to legends this site hosted the first meeting of a Franciscan society outside Assisi.

Continue on the path to the right, which narrows as it goes through the woods. Come to a pasture with farm buildings above. Follow the fence up past the shepherd's quarters onto a driveway, and then continue up past the house and garden to find an asphalt road where you turn left. Soon see signs for **Agriturismo Tenuta di Biscina** (**2.0km**, 🔶 Tenuta di Biscina P R K C Z 12/30, €Seasonal, Località Biscina, info@biscina.it, www.agriturismotenutadibiscina.com, tel 331 3003021). Continue on the road a few hundred meters to come to the **Castello di Biscina**.

Situated equidistant between the rival powers of Gubbio, Assisi, and Perugia, 14th–16th-c. **Castello di Biscina** holds a commanding position over the Chiascio Valley. Its name, similar to the word *biscia* – Italian for 'snake' – may evoke the snake-like tendrils of the many mountainous arms of the region. At its height, the castle had a moat and drawbridge as defensive structures, along with the high tower still partly in existence today, giving it a view over many miles.

Follow the road as it circles down and around the castle and enjoy the wide views of the dam below on the Chiascio River. In 1.5km come to the bottom of the valley opposite the castle and begin walking uphill. After a low rise, fork left on a path through the woods (**2.9km**) that will return you in 2.5km to the paved road you have just left. Once at the road (**2.5 km**), continue south and cross the

*The Lago di Valfabbrica has long been in the works as an agricultural and flood-control reservoir for the area*

## THE WAY OF ST FRANCIS — VIA DI FRANCESCO

**concrete bridge** that spans a west arm of the reservoir. In a further 500 meters, a series of signs instruct you to turn right and go uphill, passing **Agriturismo Borgo Sambuco** (**1.9km**). Now you have a choice between turning right to the official route, which takes a wide loop south before returning to this road and adding 2.2km to the day's journey, or remaining on the road (recommended) to cut the loop off and save time and elevation gain.

### Official route
Follow the road uphill, and after the first switchback look for a path on the left which you take on a gradual ascent along the forested hillside. Watch for thick mud on the path in wet weather. The path ends at an asphalt road, where you turn right and follow it on a wide, curving traverse with views over sloping fields to the lake below. At the end of the road, turn right onto a gravel track leading to the historic **Church of Sant'Antimo**.

> The ancient **Church of Sant'Antimo** at the now-vanished town of Coccorano replaced the castle church at Biscina when the castle was decommissioned. An elaborately carved altar stone from the castle church, dated AD1157, was placed here in the 15th c.

Continue downhill on the steep and sometimes-slippery gravel road until it meets the shortcut route at the paved road.

### Recommended shortcut
Stay on the road, which passes the earthen **Lago di Valfabbrica dam**. Just after the dam, the official route rejoins from the right.

Continue downhill along the now-untamed Chiascio River and in 600 meters turn right before a bridge onto an asphalt road. Remain on this tractor road, passing first the **Benedictine Church of Barcaccia** (**5.4km**) and then among the buildings of a small farm.

> The **Barcaccia Church** is believed to have been built by the Lord of Biscina, in part to assist pilgrims coming to

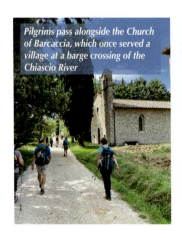
*Pilgrims pass alongside the Church of Barcaccia, which once served a village at a barge crossing of the Chiascio River*

138

## STAGE 14 – VALDICHIASCIO TO VALFABBRICA

Assisi and Rome. The name derives from the use of barges to cross the Chiascio. There is also evidence nearby of bridges built for the same purpose.

In 1.5km the tractor road comes to an end at an asphalt road. Turn left, following this road for 150 meters before taking another left that leads under the SS318 roadway and up the hill, directly to Piazza Mazzini in the heart of **Valfabbrica** (**2.9km**).

### 20.8KM VALFABBRICA (ELEV 289M, POP 3250)
(13.2/256.7KM)

The treasure of the tiny medieval quarter of Valfabbrica is the 12th-c. Church of Santa Maria with its frescoes, perhaps painted by the famous artist Cimabue in the 14th c. Valfabbrica was established around the prominent Monastery of Santa Maria Assunta, likely founded in the 11th c. by Benedictines. A chapel of the monastery still exists today at the town's cemetery, adjoining former monastery buildings that today serve as private residences. Inside the chapel are several frescoes, the most important of which perhaps is attributable to Cimabue and shows Christ wrapped in a burial shroud.

🏠 **Camere Villa Verde** O Pr R Br Cr S 7/13, €40/person including breakfast, Via Roma 26, info@camerevillaverde.it, www.camerevillaverde.it, tel 339 7019998, 075 9029013).

🏠 **Locanda Francescana** O Pr Do R Br Dr Cr Z 10/40, €20–40 per person depending on season, Via Piave 3, info@locandafrancescana.it, www.locanda-francescana.it, tel 351 6837673

🏠 **Affittacamere Sui Passi di Francesco** O Pr R S 4/20, €18/person pilgrim price, Via Castellana 23, suipassidifrancesco@tiscali.it, tel 338 5824259, 346 6156189.

🏠 **Terra Media** Do R Cr 1/9, €20/person, Via Castellana 11/a, terra.media20@gmail.co, tel 371 4876048. Paola is your host.

### FRANCIS LEARNS A LESSON IN HUMILITY

After Francis left Assisi in his self-exile from his family, he walked north toward Gubbio in the Valdichiascio. Coming to the Monastery of Santa Maria in Valfabbrica he asked for help. Although known for its charity, the monks at the monastery offered little comfort and no warm clothes, thinking Francis was simply a beggar taking advantage of their hospitality. They received him reluctantly and set him to work in the scullery in return for some thin soup without bread. Years later, he met the abbot of the monastery, who remembered the incident and apologized with great shame.

*The route to Valfabbrica touches on asphalt roads built to serve the Lago di Valfabbrica reservoir*

*The Way of St Francis — Via di Francesco*

# STAGE 15
*Valfabbrica to Assisi*

| | |
|---|---|
| **Start** | Piazza Mazzini, Valfabbrica |
| **Finish** | Basilica di San Francesco, Assisi |
| **Duration** | 4½hr |
| **Distance** | 13.2km |
| **Total ascent** | 568m |
| **Total descent** | 497m |
| **Difficulty** | Moderate due to climb |
| **Percentage paved** | 61% |
| **Lodgings** | Il Pioppo 1.8km, Assisi 13.2km |

Ending at one of the best-preserved and best-loved towns in Italy, this short stage travels among farms and then up into forests as it crosses a ridge to make its way to the hometown of St Francis. An option at the end avoids a car-choked hill and instead offers a walk through the shaded and serene Bosco San Francesco. Start early so you have more time to enjoy Assisi and its many spiritual and scenic delights.

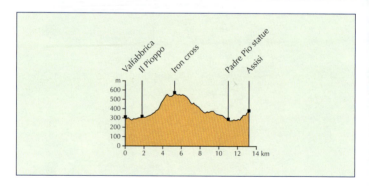

With the piazza and clock tower of Valfabbrica in front of you, go left and at the first street, Via Castellana, turn right. Cross the Via Roma and continue upward as the road now becomes Via Osteria, which climbs a small rise before descending

*Stage 15 – Valfabbrica to Assisi*

to the valley floor below. Enjoy the artful spray-painted graffiti of the life of St Francis on the left as the road descends. The houses now spread out and you see the high ridge ahead that you will cross.

*THE WAY OF ST FRANCIS — VIA DI FRANCESCO*

# Assisi

1. Basilica di San Francesco
2. Santa Maria Minerva
3. Chiesa Nuova
4. Santa Maria Maggiore
5. Basilica di Santa Chiara
6. San Damiano
7. Cattedrale di San Rufino
8. Rocca Maggiore castle
9. Santa Maria degli Angeli
10. Porta Nuova
11. Palazzo del Cardinale

Continue on this quiet lane until you pass between two closely spaced commercial buildings that house **Agriturismo Il Pioppo** (**1.8km**). Cross a bridge and follow the road uphill and to the right, following signs to turn right on a gravel road, where you pass a bench and fountain (drinking water) for pilgrims.

Remain on this path as it climbs the ridge, finally coming out of the forest to a pasture and **stucco house** where you join a gravel road. Continue onto a paved road in the same direction, and just afterward reach a summit, where to the right is your first glimpse of Assisi in the distance. Here, a 2m-tall **iron cross** (**3.4km**), **viewpoint**, and cairn of stones recall Monte do Gozo on the Camino de Santiago.

## STAGE 15 – VALFABBRICA TO ASSISI

The road and the ridge climb end at a T-junction (picnic table). Turn right, going downhill and enjoying views of the Rocco Maggiore fortress and the bare, rounded top of Monte Subasio, the lower slopes of which are home to the town of Assisi. Just before a group of farm buildings, turn left onto a gravel road going downhill, sometimes steeply, to connect to another asphalt road, the Via Padre Pio, below. Making its way downhill among olive groves, the road ends at a **statue of Padre Pio** (**5.8km**) at the bottom of the hill.

Turn left on Via Vittorino at the base of Monte Subasio and continue around a curve to the right, passing a parking lot. Take the right fork and cross the stone bridge next to the historic mill. For a slightly shorter option, go left of the tiny Santa Croce chapel and head uphill on the Via Ponte dei Galli to arrive at Porta San Giacomo above the Basilica di San Francesco. A right fork before the church leads to the Visitors Center of the **Bosco San Francesco** (bookstore, restroom). Here, pilgrims with a valid credential are entitled to reduced price entry to the forest below the city walls of Assisi; this lovely forested walk leads to a small door immediately adjacent to the Basilica di San Francesco, and makes a serene entry into St Francis' hometown of **Assisi**.

Once inside the walls, if you would like to make an application for a *testimonium* certificate that documents your completion, go to the lower piazza, down the steps from the main level, and look for the Statio Peregrinorum (Pilgrim Office) adjacent to the Lower Basilica entry. Congratulations, you've arrived at one of Italy's most beloved and sacred places, the birthplace and resting place of St Francis of Assisi (**2.2km**). Note that there is a daily mass at 6:00pm for pilgrims in the Lower Basilica.

---

**13.2KM ASSISI** (ELEV 603M, POP 27,683) (243.5KM)
The town of Assisi is steeped in the spirit of its most prominent and most humble resident, even nearly 800 years after his death. For the last decades its wise city fathers and mothers, knowing its importance as a pilgrim and tourism destination, have carefully preserved the town's medieval character. The result is a warm and scenic, if perhaps kitschy, taste of medieval life.

### Walking tour of Assisi
To tour Assisi's main sites, begin with its most prominent and iconic building, the **Basilica di San Francesco** (1). The church, begun just two years after Francis' death, is situated on a rocky projection from Monte Subasio, affording it dramatic views of the Spoleto Valley and ensuring it can be seen for many miles around. The oldest part of the basilica is the Romanesque lower level, which contains the tomb of St Francis, along with those of his four closest followers – Rufino, Leone,

*THE WAY OF ST FRANCIS — VIA DI FRANCESCO*

Masseo, and Angelo. His patroness, Lady Jacoba (or Brother Jacoba, as he lovingly called her), is interred at the entrance stairway to this level, facing the altar. To the right of the main altar and down some stairs is the Chapel of the Relics, which contains the sandals and tunic of Francis, among other historic items.

In the Upper Basilica is a high altar, directly over Francis' tomb. Frescoes by Giotto, Cimabue, Cavallini and others adorn the walls of the early Gothic nave. While these cherished artworks were damaged in the 1997 earthquake, their careful restoration allows them still to tell the story of Francis' life. The entire basilica is well worth a long and meditative visit.

Continue the tour by walking out the main door of the basilica's upper level to the Upper Piazza of San Francesco, then follow the road straight ahead, the Via San Francesco, which becomes the Via Fortini and Via Portica before arriving at the **Piazza del Comune**. In the piazza is **Santa Maria Minerva** (2) with its ancient Roman columns. Here, Francis and his friends first opened the Bible and found the call to poverty. Little remains of the church of Francis' day but the ancient columns.

Back in the piazza, make a hard right before the fountain to see the **Chiesa Nuova** (3), built over the traditional site of Francis' parents' home, where his father imprisoned Francis after his well-intentioned theft of precious cloth.

Downhill, past the Church of San Antonio, is **Santa Maria Maggiore** (4), which was the cathedral church of Assisi until the 11th c. This is the site of the trial by the bishop in which Francis renounced his parents and returned his

*The bronze statue 'Return of Francis' sits before the Basilica di San Francesco in Assisi*

## STAGE 15 – VALFABBRICA TO ASSISI

clothes to them. In this square, note the fountain, old enough to have been witness to this event. From the door of the church, turn right and follow Via Santa Agnese past the **Palazzo del Cardinale** (11), home to Francis' friend and protector, Bishop Guido.

Now turn toward the right and come to the spacious Piazza Santa Chiara and the grand **Basilica di Santa Chiara** (5), built on the site of San Giorgio, where Clare first heard her friend Francis preach. Inspired by his example, Clare founded the Order of the Poor Clares, and became a holy woman in her own right, revered by bishops and popes. Her body is kept in the crypt downstairs, along with relics that include her hair, a breviary of Francis, and many other articles from her life. The cross that spoke to Francis at San Damiano is now in a small chapel to the right of the altar on the main floor.

After touring the church, turn right from the front doors and walk around the building, through the archways and along Via Santa Chiara. After the **Porta Nuova** (10), you can turn right and follow the steps and narrow road steeply downhill to **San Damiano** (6). Although it is a fair walk down (and back up), this church is filled with history. Here, Francis heard the words 'Rebuild my church,' and devoted himself to restoring the crumbling structure, not realizing his life would help rebuild the entire Church of his day. Here also Clare was cloistered with her disciples, and here St Francis completed his immortal 'Canticle of the Sun.'

If you have time, a visit to Assisi's **Cattedrale di San Rufino** (7), site of the baptisms of Francis and Clare, is in order. While in the upper part of town, it is also worthwhile to tour the **Rocca Maggiore castle** (8), which dominates the town and the valley below.

A very pleasant couple of hours can be spent walking down the brick-lined path to **Santa Maria degli Angeli** (9) on the valley floor below town. At the transept crossing inside this grand baroque church is the Porziuncola – a church within a church. This tiny chapel is the place where Francis began his order and where, surrounded by his devoted followers, he breathed his last breath. Buses leave every few minutes for the return trip to Assisi; or simply walk uphill for 30min along the brick sidewalk and enjoy the excellent views of Assisi and the Basilica di San Francesco.

🛖 **Hospitale Laudata Si** Do R Br Cr S Z 4/18, €Donation, Viale Albornoz, adjacent to the Cimitero Storico, info@hospitalelaudatosi.it, tel 331 1224691, tel 075 5094588. Associazione di Promozione Sociale Hospitale Laudato Si. Easter–Oct.

🛖 **Hotel Properzio** O Pr R Br Cr S 9/22, €-/65/119/139, Via San Francesco 38, info@hotelproperzioassisi.it, www.hotelproperzioassisi.it, tel 075 815198.

🛖 **Camere Martini** O Pr R Cr W S 6/14, €-/30/27/53/66, Via San Gregorio 6, cameremartini@libero.it, tel 075 813536, 347 9085212. Villelma is your host.

## THE WAY OF ST FRANCIS — VIA DI FRANCESCO

🏠 **Green Village Hotel** Pr R K Br Dr Cr W S 40/150, €Seasonal, Via Campiglione 110, prenotazioni@greenvillageassisi.it, www.greenvillageassisi.it, tel 075 816816, 391 3271130 Cristiano. From 15 June to 2 Nov. Swimming pool.

🏠 **La Casa di Famiglia** O Pr R K Cr W S 3/9, €25–35 per person, Via Santureggio 6, bazzoffiangela@live.it, tel 347 9065606, tel 075 8155207. Minimum 2 nights. Angela is your host.

▲ **Hotel & Camping Fontemaggio** Pr R K Br Cr W Z 32/100, €-/-/50/92, Via Eremo Carceri 24, info@fontemaggio.it, www.fontemaggio.it, tel 075 812317, 758 13636. €7 breakfast, restaurant, bar, and mini-market on site.

### THE DEATH OF FRANCIS

By his mid-forties, Francis was in poor health, suffering from the results of malaria, malnutrition, tuberculosis, and rheumatism. Knowing he would soon die, the people of Assisi sent knights to Nocera Umbra to bring him back to his hometown and ensure that Perugia would not end up with his body, certain to be prized in the coming years as a saintly relic. Francis was brought on a stretcher to the Porziuncola chapel below town. He asked that Jacoba dei Settesoli, a supporter whom he had lovingly come to call Brother Jacoba, be called to his side, and that she bring his favorite almond cakes. Even before word reached her, she had come to Assisi with the almond cakes.

Francis asked that he be stripped of his clothes and that his body be placed naked, directly on the ground. It is said that at the moment of his death, among his weeping and grief-stricken followers, the Porziuncola was bathed in light and church bells began to ring spontaneously.

Francis' words in the second part of the 'Canticle of the Sun' speak to his understanding of death:

> Praised be You, my Lord, through our Sister Bodily Death,
> from whom no living man can escape.
> Woe to those who die in mortal sin.
> Blessed are those who will find Your most holy will,
> for the second death shall do them no harm.
> Praise and bless my Lord,
> and give Him thanks
> and serve Him with great humility.
> *Translation by the Franciscan Friars Third Order Regular*

# SECTION 2A: VARIANT ROUTE TO ASSISI

*The Porziuncola, now covered in frescoes, sits inside the Basilica of Santa Maria degli Angeli (Variant 2.1)*

*The Way of St Francis — Via di Francesco*

## VARIANT 2.1
*Valfabbrica to Assisi via Perugia*

| | |
|---|---|
| **Start** | Piazza Mazzini, Valfabbrica |
| **Finish** | Basilica di San Francesco, Assisi |
| **Duration** | 17½hr |
| **Distance** | 54.7km |
| **Total ascent** | 1056m |
| **Total descent** | 985m |
| **Difficulty** | Moderate |
| **Percentage paved** | 75% |
| **Lodgings** | Monteverde 5.5km, Perugia 29.3km, Bastia Umbra 48.9km, Santa Maria degli Angeli 51.3km, Assisi 54.7km |

Climbs to Monteverde, Perugia, and Assisi punctuate this otherwise flat journey in farmlands and among suburban industrial estates. From Perugia to Assisi there are several towns and ample services, although the route around the airport can feel desolate. While the route adds a day to the walk from Valfabbrica to Assisi, to visit Perugia is to visit Umbria's premier city; to visit Santa Maria degli Angeli is to visit one of the most important places in the life of St Francis.

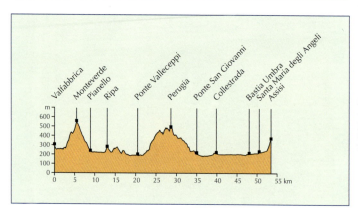

## Variant 2.1 – Valfabbrica to Assisi via Perugia

The Basilica di Santa Maria degli Angeli dominates the skyline of Assisi and holds inside it the Porziuncola chapel, once the home base of St Francis

Cyclists and pedestrians travel between Assisi and Santa Maria degli Angeli on the Pace e Bene brick walkway.

## THE WAY OF ST FRANCIS — VIA DI FRANCESCO

The walk is unspectacular and mostly on paved roads. Staging could be quite simple:

### Stage 1: Valfabbrica to Perugia (29.3KM)
⛺ **Ostello Little Italy** Pr Do R K Br Cr W S 6/32, €33/61/67/69/79, Via della Nespola 1, perugiainfo@littleitalyhostel.it, www.littleitalyhote.it, tel 075 9661997, 375 5290757. Daniele is your host.

### Stage 2: Perugia to Assisi (25.4KM)
⛺ **Casali dell Ghisleria (Casa Vacanze)** O Pr R K Cr W S Z 9/29, €Seasonal, Via San Padre Pio 47/49, Bastia Umbra, info@casalidellaghisleria.com, www.casalidellaghisleria.com, tel 075 6973500, 393 4375728. Swimming pool. Paola is your host. See Stage 15 for additional lodgings in Assisi.

# SECTION 3: ASSISI TO RIETI

*A group of pilgrims walk along the dike of the Velino River before Piediluco (Stage 20)*

# THE WAY OF ST FRANCIS — VIA DI FRANCESCO

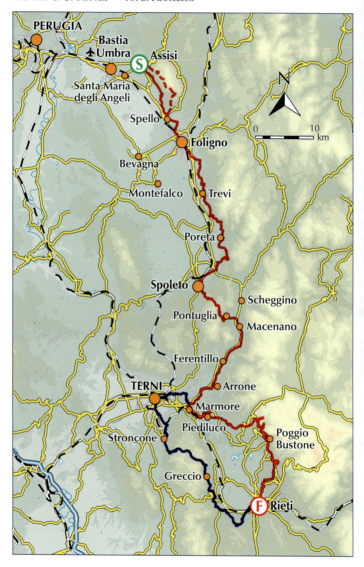

## Section 3 – Assisi to Rieti

Beginning in Assisi and ending 140km later in Rieti, the pathways of this part of the Way of St Francis hug steep mountainsides, giving panoramic views of the fertile valleys below. The first days are spent walking through olive groves while the nights are in historic hill towns like Spello, Trevi, and Spoleto, all well known to Francis. After Spoleto, the route ascends Monte Luco and climbs along the slopes of Monte Pàtrico before descending to the quiet Nera River Valley with its protected forests and recreational nature trails. The walk along the Nera leads to the majestic waterfall at Cascata delle Marmore, a wonder of the Roman Empire, and afterward to the Holy Valley of Rieti. Places in this hilly itinerary important to the story of St Francis include the Faggio San Francesco, Poggio Bustone, and Santuario della Foresta.

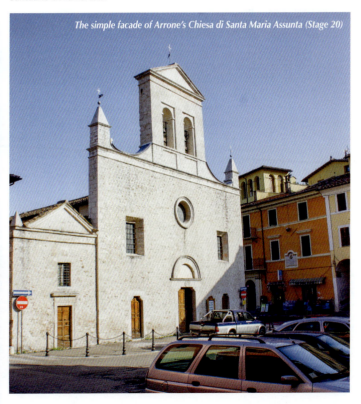

*The simple facade of Arrone's Chiesa di Santa Maria Assunta (Stage 20)*

*THE WAY OF ST FRANCIS — VIA DI FRANCESCO*

# STAGE 16
*Assisi to Spello*

| | |
|---|---|
| **Start** | Basilica di San Francesco, Assisi |
| **Finish** | Piazza della Repubblica, Spello |
| **Duration** | 3¾hr (5¼hr via upper route) |
| **Distance** | 12.9km (15.6km via upper route) |
| **Total ascent** | 234m (716m via upper route) |
| **Total descent** | 322m (867m via upper route) |
| **Difficulty** | Easy (moderately hard via upper route) |
| **Percentage paved** | 63% (31% via upper route) |
| **Lodgings** | Spello 12.9/15.6km |

The lower route of today's two options leads gently through olive orchards toward scenic and touristic Spello, allowing plenty of time to enjoy the shops and restaurants of this justifiably popular Umbrian hill town. The higher option has a steep climb, but not only allows a visit to the Franciscan convent at Eremo delle Carceri but also offers extraordinary and unforgettable views of Assisi and the entire Spoleto Valley from above the tree line of Monte Subasio. While medieval Spello is a very charming overnight, continuing on to the larger town of Foligno adds just 6.4km to the day.

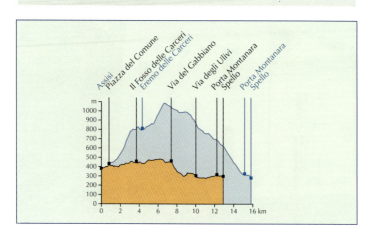

156

## STAGE 16 – ASSISI TO SPELLO

With the front door of the Basilica di San Francesco behind you, go straight ahead, following the right-hand walkway toward the Via San Francesco. Continue on this street gently uphill to the main **Piazza del Comune** (**0.7km**), coming to an important option at the fountain.

### Lower route to Spello

At the fountain ahead, fork right and slightly downhill. Continue along what is now Corso Giuseppe Mazzini, through Portella San Giorgio, and pass the piazza in front of **Basilica di Santa Chiara** with its wide view over the valley. Keep on through the archway after the basilica, and head through **Porta Nuova** at the end of the old city. Go straight along the road, coming to the bottom of a U curve with a parking lot on the right. Take the fork to the right and then go straight at the traffic circle, which puts you briefly on Via della Madonna dell'Olivo. At a small shrine to the Virgin Mary, fork left and go uphill on **Via San Benedetto**; views of the valley and Santa Maria degli Angeli now open up to the right.

After the **Fosso delle Carceri Hotel** (**2.9km**), take the middle of three forks, going straight ahead. Here the road becomes more level while the asphalt becomes patchy and broken. You are in a territory of olive groves, soon with the Parco di Monte Subasio on your left. Continue on this road until the **Via del Gabbiano** (**3.6km**). Turn right here and follow signs that lead you downhill after twists and turns, passing the **Domus Antiqua B&B**. A few hundred meters later, arrive at the Via degli Ulivi (**2.5km**), where the road ends and you turn left.

Continue on this hillside traverse until the road ends at **Via Poeta** (**1.9km**), the road into Spello. Turn left. The street is now lined with tall trees, with a stone wall on the left and beautiful views of stone houses, towers, and churches on the right, leading you to Porta Montanara, the upper gate of **Spello** (**0.3km**).

### Upper route to Spello

Branch left and uphill at the fountain in Piazza del Comune in the direction of San Rufino Cathedral. Follow Via del Torrione from the right side of the piazza, climbing up to **Viale Umberto I** (SR444), across from the parking lot at Piazza Matteotti. Go left for a block then right, in the direction of Eremo delle Carceri, climbing uphill to **Porta dei Cappuccini** (Capuchins Gate) in the old city walls.

The road to Eremo delle Carceri goes straight ahead from here, but for the hiking trail turn left on a footpath that passes by the fortification tower of Rocca Minore and veers west to begin a climb up Monte Subasio; you'll gain about 400m elevation in the next 2km. The path ends at a paved road (picnic table), where you turn right and walk on the road to **Eremo delle Carceri** (**3.5km**, restrooms, kiosk with coffee).

## THE WAY OF ST FRANCIS – VIA DI FRANCESCO

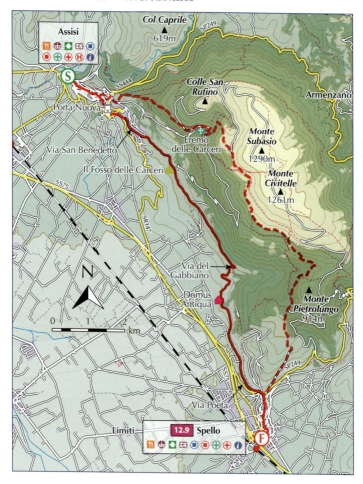

Originally a complex of prison cells (*carceri* is 'prison cells') used by the town of Assisi before becoming a Benedictine monastery, the site of **Eremo delle Carceri** became an important retreat for Francis and his disciples. The nearby caves provided modest shelter, and the quiet pathways of Monte Subasio offered beauty and solitude. Today, the tiny Franciscan convent consists

158

## STAGE 16 – ASSISI TO SPELLO

of 15th-c. buildings completed by St Bernardino of Siena, while the innermost chapel dates back to the time of Francis. It is said that, commanded by Francis, water first gushed from the well that is in the center of the convent.

The entire area has a calm and quiet aura, and it is easy to see how it could have been a place of meditation for Francis and his brothers. (With advance permission, Eremo delle Carceri has basic accommodation available for people who wish to remain for retreats: www.eremodellecarceri.it.)

After your visit, return back up the driveway to the main road. Turn right and take the road as it circles behind the hermitage. Watch for signs that send you onto a path forking left off the asphalt and begin to climb through the woods. In about 800 meters come to the meadows atop Monte Subasio, where you turn right to follow along the top of the woods on a long traverse, with spectacular views over Assisi and the valley below. Having reached this height, you are rewarded with 4km of spectacular and relatively flat hiking among small hills and dales, where you may see signs of wild horses and other livestock.

Follow signs to reenter the woods for the pathway down the hill. Come to Via Bulgarella, where you see Spello clustered ahead at the foot of the mountain. This road ends at **Via Poeta**, where you turn left to come to Porta Montanara, the upper gate of **Spello** (**10.5km**).

### Walking through Spello
Head downhill from Porta Montanara and fork left on Via Giulia. Continue until it ends and turn right onto Via Garibaldi. Come to Piazza della Repubblica on your left at the center of town (**0.9km**).

*Pilgrims spread out as they walk the pastures of Monte Subasio on the upper route to Spello*

## 12.9/15.6KM SPELLO (ELEV 280M, POP 8284) 🍴 ⊕ 🏠 ⓒ ⦿ ⦿ ⊕ ⊕ ⓘ (230.8KM)

Unlike Assisi and other Italian hill towns, Spello's city walls touch the valley floor, and with a train station just a few flat blocks away, Spello is unusually accessible to visitors. In spite of this, the town has retained its medieval characteristics. Its stone palaces, churches, and homes cluster tightly together and exude medieval charm.

Spello is best known for its annual Infiorata Festival – when the streets of the old city are elaborately decorated with intricate carpets of flower petals. The festival, held for over 150 years, is observed annually on the day of Corpus Domini, the ninth Sunday after Easter. Locals spend days planning and creating complicated designs, while visitors throng the streets to admire them. Afterward, the designs pave the way for the Procession of Corpus Christi, led by the local bishop, atop the brilliant and colorful mile-long path.

Founded by the Umbrians and later called Hispellum by the Romans, Spello has ancient roots. Ruins of a Roman amphitheater lie on the north side of town. Spello is renowned for the nearly two-dozen medieval churches within its walls. Among the several 11th- and 12th-c. churches, Santa Maria Maggiore, with its frescoes by Perugino and Pinturicchio, is particularly noteworthy. Although the churches have stood many centuries, older by over a millennium is the town's Porta di Venere, which dates from the 1st c. BC, and the Porta Consolare just a few centuries newer.

Wine connoisseurs will want to take this opportunity to taste the area's unique varietal, Sagrantino di Montefalco, a bold red with high tannin levels that may have been cultivated as communion wine by local Franciscan friars.

🔺 **Convento Piccolo San Damiano of the Franciscan Missionary Sisters** €Donation Via Fontevecchia 22, piccolosandamiano@libero.it, tel 0742 651182.

🔺 **B&B Fratello Sole** Ⓞ Pr R K Br Gf W S 3/7, €-/60/75/85, Via Monterione 6, bebfratellosole@libero.it, www.bedandbreakfastinspello.it, tel 0742 651902.

🔺 **Urbe Apartments** Ⓞ Pr R K Gf W 7/30, €-/60/70/85, via Giulia 97, info@inurbe.it, www.inurbe.com, tel 351 6592282, 0742 301145. Vacation apartment.

### FRANCIS PREACHES TO THE BIRDS

Once, when Francis was walking with his companions at Bevagna, near Spello, a flock of birds settled nearby. To the astonishment of his friends, when Francis approached the birds, they calmly waited for him to join them. When he addressed them, he said, 'My brother and sister birds, you should praise your Creator and always love him: He gave you feathers for clothes, wings to fly and all other things that you need. It is God who made you noble among all creatures, making your home in thin, pure air. Without sowing or reaping, you receive God's guidance and protection.'

When the sermon was done, the birds flew off, singing in joyful song.

*The narrow streets of Spello are framed by buildings in the pinkish limestone of the area*

*The Way of St Francis — Via di Francesco*

# STAGE 17
*Spello to Trevi*

| | |
|---|---|
| **Start** | Piazza della Repubblica, Spello |
| **Finish** | Piazza Garibaldi, Trevi |
| **Duration** | 5¼hr |
| **Distance** | 19.0km |
| **Total ascent** | 329m |
| **Total descent** | 190m |
| **Difficulty** | Easy |
| **Percentage paved** | 79% |
| **Lodgings** | Foligno 6.4km, Trevi 19.0km |

After leaving Spello, there is a quiet hour of walking among farms on the valley floor, but after crossing under the highway you are immersed in the bustle of suburban Foligno. Downtown Foligno is a pedestrian's dream, while afterward it is once again suburban sprawl until crossing under the highway, this time finding a verdant climb among hillside olive groves. Come to hilltop Trevi, unspoiled by tourism and yet appealing for its medieval charm.

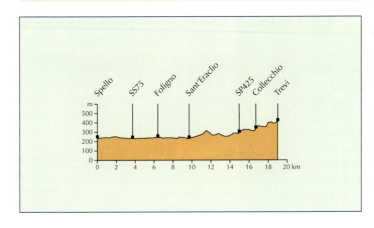

## STAGE 17 – SPELLO TO TREVI

Head downhill from Piazza della Repubblica, now on Corso Cavour, passing Collegiata Santa Maria Maggiore.

> The 13th-c. **Collegiata Santa Maria Maggiore** contains a Roman altar, reused as an entry stoop, as well as a 17th-c. Giorgetti painting of the Stigmata of Saint Francis. Most notable, though, is the Baglioni Chapel and its must-see frescoes by Pinturicchio.

At the bottom of the hill, pass through Porta Consolare. This medieval, three-portal gate stands on Roman foundations, which are visible around the pedestrian walkways. Now turn left and follow alongside the walls on Via Sant'Anna, following the road right at a fork just after the Church of Sant'Anna. You are now on Via Brondolini, which ends at a T-junction with Via Rapecchiano, where you turn left. This takes you via the **SS75 highway underpass** (**3.7km**) to the outskirts of Foligno.

After the underpass, turn left on this tiny but busy road, and curve with it across the **railroad tracks** to its end at Viale Firenze, a main arterial into Foligno. Go straight through a traffic circle and continue to a bridge that crosses the **Topino River**. Fork right in two blocks onto Via Venti Settembre and come in a few blocks to Piazza della Repubblica at the historic center of **Foligno** (**2.7km**).

---

**6.4KM FOLIGNO** (ELEV 234M, POP 55,218) (224.2KM)

Although about 80 percent of Foligno was destroyed by Allied bombardment during World War II, the town has heroically recreated its historic center, doing its best to ensure its urban heart would retain its medieval character. The project was largely successful, and on sunny mornings the piazza is filled with local residents enjoying a cup of coffee or strolling among the shops.

The Cattedrale di Santa Feliciano, built in the 12th c., is dedicated to the bishop and martyr of the 2nd and 3rd c. who evangelized in the area. Two blocks south of the piazza is the Church of San Francesco and its tomb of Blessed Angela of Foligno (1248–1309), a Franciscan mystic known for her ecstatic visions and meticulous attention to Francis' way of poverty.

🔺 **City Hotel and Suites** O Pr R Br Ct S Z 87/200, €-/-/90/120, Via Massimo Arcamone 16, info@cityhotelfoligno.com, www.cityhotelfoligno.com, tel 0742 321666.

🔺 **Ostello Palazzo Pierantoni** O Pr Do R Br Ct S Z 37/130, €-/23/40/55, Via Pierantoni 21, info@ostellodifoligno.it, www.ostellodifoligno.it, tel 0742 353776.

## THE WAY OF ST FRANCIS — VIA DI FRANCESCO

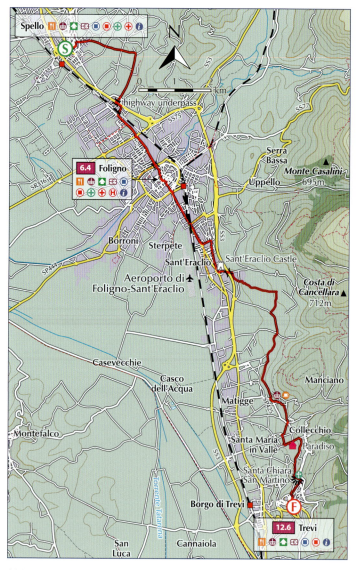

## STAGE 17 – SPELLO TO TREVI

### FRANCIS SELLS HIS FATHER'S CLOTH

After hearing in a vision at San Damiano that he should rebuild the church, Francis set about the task of reconstructing the dilapidated building. Needing funds to buy materials, Francis took cloth from his father's inventory and brought it to the market here at Foligno to sell. Francis' father was understandably irate, and, after an angry confrontation, he locked Francis in the basement of their Assisi home. A plaque on the outer wall of the cathedral here remembers Francis' sale of his father's cloth in the market, which almost certainly would have been held in this same square.

Continue through the square and onto Corso Cavour, the main commercial street of Foligno's pedestrian center. Go through Porta Romana and straight ahead onto the sidewalk of the Viale Roma arterial. Pass a military barracks on your left and walk onto a bridge that crosses the **train tracks** on an elevated traffic circle. Go straight here, but at the next traffic circle go left and uphill for a long block on Via Verona. Turn right on Via Flaminia Vecchia (the original Roman route that connected Rome and Ancona and crossed through this valley), and enter inside the walls of the tiny **Sant'Eraclio Castle** (**3.3km**, bar, bakery, minimart, and pizzeria are within a block just outside the walled enclosure).

The 8th–15th-c. **Sant'Eraclio Castle**, at one time part of a village that has now been subsumed into industrial estates around Foligno, was built to guard this stretch of the Via Flaminia. It is named after Saint Heraclius, a Roman soldier who had converted to Christianity and was martyred near here in 251.

*The route crosses agricultural land after it passes Sant'Eraclio*

*The town hall sits to the left of the tower at Piazza Mazzini in the historic center of Trevi*

Turn left after passing through the castle gate, then turn left and uphill on Via Fontevecchia, which leads under the **SS3** Flaminia highway. After the overpass, turn right onto Via Londra to begin your first ascent of the day. Soon you have your first taste of the vast olive groves of this area. Follow signs that take you up through olive groves and then back down to Via Pozzo Secco, where you turn left. Follow this paved road until it ends, and then continue straight onto gravel, where you descend for a time before once again climbing. Join the asphalt Via San Nicolo to continue the climb until the road ends at the **SP425** (**6.2km**, supermarket, bar).

Turn left and take the next road, the Strada San Clemente, which you follow as it becomes the Strada San Donato and returns to the **SP425**. Cross and continue on gravel, again among olive groves, as signs lead you across the Via dei Giardini to the road's end at Località Collecchio. Turn left for the steepest climb of the day, among the homes of the tiny hamlet of **Collecchio** (**0.8km**, 🔶 **Residenza Paradiso** www.residenzaparadiso.it).

As you climb, follow signs to the right and downhill, which connects you through the woods onto a path that is your last climb of the stage. Now you reach Viale Augusto Ciuffelli, at the base of the walls of the **Monastery of Santa Chiara in San Martino**. Opposite the monastery is a photo-worthy **viewpoint** across the draw to picturesque Trevi. Continue on the sidewalk of Viale Ciuffelli into town, veering left after the park to find Piazza Garibaldi just outside the upper gate of **Trevi** (**2.4km**).

*Stage 17 – Spello to Trevi*

## 12.6KM TREVI (ELEV 412M, POP 8042) (211.6KM)

Trevi is first mentioned in the historical record by Pliny the Elder, who identified it as the Umbrian town named Treviae. The oldest portion of the extant city wall dates to the 1st c. BC, and the inner of two walls that surround the old city are of Roman origin. Trevi has 20 historic churches, and a well-preserved if plain historic center mounted on a dramatic spur of the mountain, giving it a commanding view of the valley. Top among the artistic treasures of Trevi are frescoes by Perugino at the **Madonna delle Lacrime** (15th–16th c.), the last signed works of the 16th-c. master.

Modern Trevi is divided into two halves – historic Trevi above and Borgo Trevi with its train station below. A hilly walk of 3km separates the two. The best way to enjoy Trevi is to walk its quiet streets and catch views of the valley below from the heights of its ancient walls. Afterward it's time to enjoy a coffee or glass of wine in the bar of its Piazza Mazzini, just inside the walls.

⌂ **Residence Sant'Emiliano** O Pr R Cf S 4/12, €-/30/55/70, Via Salvatore Zappelli 24, residences.emiliano@libero.it, www.residencesantemiliano.it, tel 348 2285443. Claudio is your host.

⌂ **Comunità Chemin Neuf** Pr R K 21/50, €Call, Via dei Monasteri 2, santachiara.ccn@gmail.com, www.chemin-neuf.it, tel 0742 78613 Mauro. From 16 Apr to 15 Oct.

⌂ **Antica Dimora alla Rocca** Pr Do R Br Cf S Z 34/50, €-/90/100/-, Piazza della Rocca, info@hotelallarocca.it, tel 0742 38541. Breakfast included.

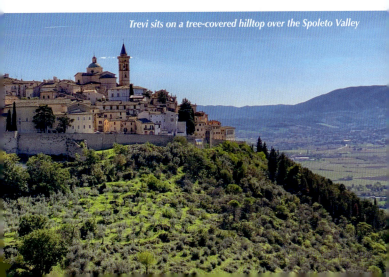

*Trevi sits on a tree-covered hilltop over the Spoleto Valley*

## STAGE 18
*Trevi to Spoleto*

| | |
|---|---|
| **Start** | Piazza Garibaldi, Trevi |
| **Finish** | Piazza del Duomo, Spoleto |
| **Duration** | 8¾hr |
| **Distance** | 27.1km |
| **Total ascent** | 952m |
| **Total descent** | 969m |
| **Difficulty** | Hard due to distance and elevation changes |
| **Percentage paved** | 52% |
| **Lodgings** | Poreta 11.7km, Bazzano Inferiore 19.2km, Spoleto 27.1km |

This hilly and very scenic stage transits olive groves, castles, and monasteries on its way to the wonders of Spoleto, the valley's largest and most sophisticated town. The undulating topography makes it a challenge, but the epic views of the valley make it worthwhile. Since the long stage includes nearly 1000m of up- and downhill climbs, it makes sense to divide the stage with an intermediate overnight at Poreta, for instance, which frees up more time on a second day to enjoy Spoleto.

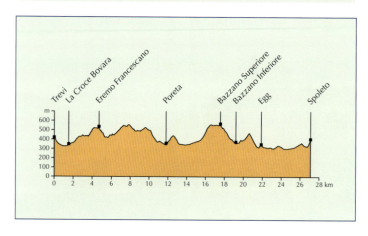

## STAGE 18 – TREVI TO SPOLETO

From Piazza Garibaldi, head south and take the narrow Via delle Fonti road that leads downhill between stone walls. Signs lead you downhill to cross the SP425 above the Chiesa della Madonna delle Lacrime.

In 1483, the owner of a rural home had a painting made of the **Madonna and Child with St Francis**. Two years later, someone saw the painting's Madonna shed tears of blood, and by 1522 the citizens of Trevi had built the Chiesa della Madonna delle Lacrime to house it. Perugino and Lo Spagna added several important frescoes.

Cross the SP425 onto a gravel path that rejoins the SP425 at the bottom of the valley, where you come to an important turn in the hamlet of **Bovara** (**1.5km**, no services). Follow signs to fork left here onto Località La Croce to begin the day's first climb. Follow signs through a cluster of homes and continue uphill. The road turns to gravel and snakes along the hillside until reaching a summit, soon coming to the walls and gate of **Eremo Francescano** (**3.3km**).

In the 11th c. a convent was built here around a cave identified with followers of St Francis. Today the walled complex of **Eremo Francescano** includes a large lawn and scattered buildings, and is inhabited by an order of nuns established in 1920 by Sister Maria, a Franciscan. The nuns are nicknamed *allodole* (larks) and welcome sisters of many Christian denominations.

Pilgrims are welcomed with generosity and grace, and after a visit the sisters may sing a farewell blessing. The hermitage sits nearly 3km above the historic settlement of Campello sul Clitunno, with its oasis-like spring and Roman temple, on the valley floor.

Turn right at the gate of the hermitage and follow a trail that heads downhill, hugging the mountainside below the tan walls of the hermitage. Soon begin your second major climb of the day on this gravel track that heads through olive groves and mountainside forests. After the summit, come to a

*Pilgrims descend on a narrow path above Campello sul Clitunno*

169

## THE WAY OF ST FRANCIS — VIA DI FRANCESCO

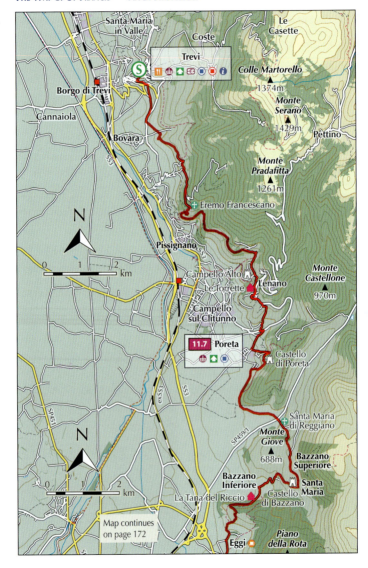

*STAGE 18 – TREVI TO SPOLETO*

paved section and join a road heading downhill at first, which on its uphill takes you near the castle at **Campello Alto**.

The castle at **Campello Alto** traces its roots to a 10th-c. land grant from the Duke of Spoleto to the French knight, Rovero di Champeaux. Today, it is home to a posh boutique hotel (www.borgocampello.com).

The road now leads to a summit at the SP458/1 roadway near **B&B Le Torrette** (see Poreta below for lodging information), where you turn left and follow the road downhill. A gravel road forks right to cut off a long switchback of the road, and when you come back to the road you cross it to arrive at the hamlet of **Poreta** (**7.0km**).

---

**11.7KM PORETA** (ELEV 328M, POP 189) 🍽 🛏 ◉ (199.9KM)
Originally a Roman villa, in the Middle Ages the town fortified itself against frequent raids, and the current walls date from the 13th c. An earthquake in the late 18th c. damaged many of the buildings. The castle was abandoned, but when the Madonna image in the Church of San Cristoforo somehow remained unscathed, the church was renamed Santa Maria della Misericordia.

Poreta's Info Point & Store is hosted by Signora Rosella, an institution on the Via di Francesco; call in advance for lunch or snacks (tel 349 1997232).

🔺 **Le Torrette B&B** O Pr R K Br Dr Cr S 2/9, €40/person including breakfast, Via delle Torrette 85, robertaloretoni@libero.it, tel 339 3766035, 0743 5210124. Mirella is your host.

🔺 **A Casa di Francesco** O Pr R K W 1/5, €38/person, Fraz Poreta 1, acasadifrancescoporeta@gmail.com, tel 349 8309327 (Cinzia) 349 1997232 (Rosa). Bag transport available to Spoleto.

🔺 **Villa del Cardinale B&B** O Pr R K Br Dr W S 5/10, €-/35/70/100, Fraz. Poreta n.8, nazzarosigismondi@gmail.com, www.villadelcardinale.com, tel 338 1632778, tel 0743 778819. Includes a very special breakfast.

---

The route turns left on the uphill side of town to come alongside the **Castello di Poreta**, and from there it heads down the hillside toward the floor of the Torrente Spina valley. Continue uphill and cross first the streambed and then the roadway of the **SP459/1**, passing the **Church of Santa Maria di Reggiano**.

The 12th–13th-c. **Church of Santa Maria di Reggiano** was built partly of recycled materials from a pre-existing Roman building. Inside, it preserves 14th-c. frescoes of Christ, Madonna and Child, and St Sebastian.

*The Way of St Francis — Via di Francesco*

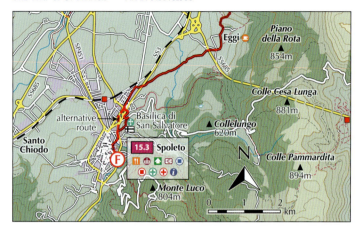

Now begins the steepest climb of the day, from Bazzano up to **Bazzano Superiore** (**5.8km**), the latter capped by **Castello di Bazzano**. In Roman times this settlement stood along the route to Norcia, but the castles here date to the 12th c. Just past the castle, turn right and begin a steep downhill, winding your way to **Bazzano Inferiore** (**1.7km**, ▲ La Tana del Riccio B&B ⓞ Ⓟⓡ Ⓡ Ⓑⓡ Ⓓⓡ Ⓒⓡ Ⓦ Ⓢ 2/7, €-/45/70/90, Via della Semina 10, tanadelriccio1@gmail.com, tel 328 1973251. Chiara is your host).

When the road ends on the far side of town, turn left and continue on Via Semina, first on asphalt and then on gravel; this takes you up and down an arm of the mountain, which is covered first in forests and then in olive groves. The road turns to asphalt as it approaches the fortified town of **Eggi** (**2.6km**, café).

Originally a Roman settlement, **Eggi** reached a climax of prosperity in the 16th–18th c., giving it a rich architectural and artistic patrimony. Most striking is the Church of Santa Maria delle Grazie, whose frescoes are on the theme of protection from the plague. Eggi is most famous today for its springtime Wild Asparagus Festival.

At the center of town, follow signs that lead you to a right turn on Via dei Pini and head downhill, crossing under the **SS685** roadway. This puts you on the asphalt Località Colle Marozzo road and takes you over a low rise to cross under the **SS3** highway. Take the first left, which is the former Via Flaminia, and come to a roundabout, where there is a choice of routes.

*Stage 18 – Trevi to Spoleto*

## Official route

From the roundabout, the official route crosses back to the other side of the SS3 on busy auto roads to reach the historic **Basilica di San Salvatore** in the midst of Spoleto's elaborate and fascinating cemetery. To continue on the official route, cross under the Via Flaminia SS3, turn left, cross the river, and catch the first of a series of escalators up to the Piazza del Duomo of **Spoleto** (**5.3km**).

## Alternative route

An alternative and perhaps safer route continues straight at the roundabout and takes the first left (Via delle Lettere) to catch a bike path that continues toward the city center. The route becomes the Via Ponzianina; after crossing the river, you can either take the escalator uphill or turn left on the next block and walk uphill to Spoleto's Piazza del Duomo.

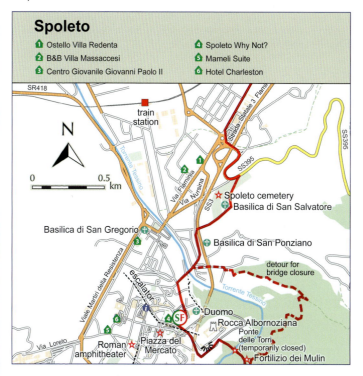

*THE WAY OF ST FRANCIS — VIA DI FRANCESCO*

**15.3KM SPOLETO (ELEV 396M, POP 36,234)** 🍴 ⛪ 🏨 🛒 ⓘ ⏺ ⊕ ✚ ⓘ **(184.6KM)**
Situated at a strategic entry to the Tiber River Valley, the city of Spoleto has ancient roots, tracing its beginnings to the Umbrian people of pre-Roman times. Spoletium, as the Romans called it, is mentioned many times in ancient Roman literature, and its Roman amphitheater, today largely restored, is testament to the prosperity and importance of the town in that period.

In addition to the amphitheater, Spoleto is rich in architectural treasures. Its **Basilica di San Salvatore**, which dates from the late 4th c., is a UNESCO World Heritage site and an important example of early basilica-style church architecture. The **Duomo di Santa Maria Assunta**, which dates from the 12th c., contains the tomb of the 15th-c. painter Filippo Lippi, who painted the beautiful, jewel-toned scenes from the life of the Virgin Mary in the ceiling of the church's 12th-c. apse. The church's mosaic-topped Romanesque facade and tower exude a gentle and warm presence over the Duomo's piazza. Not to be missed is one of its most prized treasures, an original, signed letter from St Francis to Brother Leo. One of only two extant penned notes signed by the saint, the letter can be viewed in the Duomo's Reliquary Chapel off the left aisle.

Looming over the town is the immense 15th-c. **Rocca Albornoziana** fortress, which, after its military uses were not needed, served first as a prison and now as a museum. Constructed in the 13th c., the impressive **Ponte delle Torri** aqueduct spans a deep gorge, standing on huge towers. Now used solely as a pedestrian bridge (and closed to pedestrians since the earthquake of 2016), the enormous structure connects Spoleto to Monteluco to the south, and when reopened will serve again as the beginning of the next stage over the mountain to Ceselli.

Each June to early July, Spoleto's world-famous Due Mondi (Two Worlds) festival attracts classical virtuosi from Europe and the U.S. to perform in its public places and enjoy the town's classic charm. In a bid to make the city more accessible, Spoleto's city elders oversaw construction of an escalator system that reaches some of the loftier parts of the city. The relaxed hub of central Spoleto's social life is the **Piazza del Mercato**, which corresponds with the location of the ancient Roman forum and today is filled with restaurants, cafés, and shops. Ask in a restaurant for the local pasta, *strangozzi alla spoletina*, based on an eggless pasta of semolina flour served with either tomato sauce or a sauce of asparagus gathered from the surrounding hills.

⛺ **Ostello Villa Redenta** O Pr R Br Dr Cf W Z 15/45, €40/person includes breakfast, Via di Villa Redenta 1, info@villaredenta.com, www.villaredenta.com, tel 0743 224936.

⛺ **B&B Villa Massaccesi** O Pr R Br S 2/5, €-/48/76/110, Via XVII Settembre 13, info@villamassaccesi.it, tel 342 9385405, tel 339 4178982. Breakfast included. Fluent English.

*Stage 18 – Trevi to Spoleto*

🟢 **Centro Giovanile Giovanni Paolo II** Do R K Br Dr Cr W S Z €Donation of €8+, Piazza Garibaldi 35, pastoralegiovanile@spoletonorcia.it, tel 331 3407043, 392 5887677. Open Jun to Aug. Near Basilica di San Gregorio. Fr. Pier Luigi, Sister Lorella.

🔴 **Spoleto Why Not?** O Pr R K W S 1/2, €-/30/50/-, Vicolo S. Filippo 29, fegrisan@gmail.com, tel 345 3369641. Felicita is your host.

🟣 **Mameli Suite** O Pr R Br Cr W S 2/4, €Call, Piazzetta Porta San Lorenzo 1, mamelisuite@gmail.com, https://mameli-suite.webnode.it, tel 329 4024676, tel 339 5798984. Price for full apartment.

🔵 **Hotel Charleston** O Pr R Br Dr Cr W S 28/75, €-/59/89/110, Piazza Collicola 10, hotelcharleston@gmail.com, www.hotelcharleston.it, tel 0743 220052. In heart of town, 17th-c. building.

## A LETTER BY FRANCIS

A handwritten letter from Francis, the authenticity of which is not doubted by scholars, is preserved in the Cathedral of Spoleto. In English, it reads:

> Brother Leo,
> Wish your brother Francis health and peace! I say to you: Yes, my son, and as a mother, I say it. In this word and counsel I sum up briefly all the words we said on the way. If, afterwards, you need to come to me for advice, thus I advise you: In whatever way it seems best to you to please the Lord God and to follow His footsteps and poverty, do so with the blessing of the Lord God and in my obedience. And if it is necessary on account of your soul or other consolation that you wish, Leo, then come to me, come!

*A side chapel in Spoleto's Duomo holds this original letter signed by St Francis*

# STAGE 19
*Spoleto to Macenano*

| | |
|---|---|
| **Start** | Piazza del Duomo, Spoleto |
| **Finish** | Vie Cartiera and Carducci, Macenano |
| **Duration** | 6¼hr |
| **Distance** | 19.7km |
| **Total ascent** | 656m |
| **Total descent** | 799m |
| **Difficulty** | Moderately hard due to elevation changes |
| **Percentage paved** | 28% |
| **Lodgings** | Monteluco 2.5km, Ceselli 14.7km, Macenano 19.7km |

After a very steep first hour to the Franciscan convent of Monteluco, this stage crosses a vast, forested ridge, arriving at inspiring viewpoints overlooking the Valnerina (Nera River Valley) and mountains beyond. After a steep downhill path, followed by a long and quiet asphalt road, the stage comes first to Ceselli and then, after a jaunt down the Valnerina Greenway, arrives at Macenano.

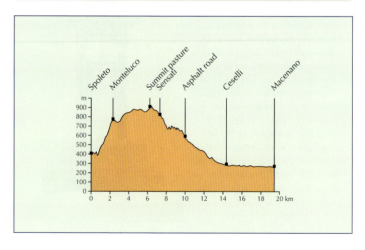

### STAGE 19 – SPOLETO TO MACENANO

In 2016, the Central Italy earthquake caused extensive damage and the loss of nearly 300 lives, particularly at Amatrice and Norcia. Spoleto's 13th–14th-c. masonry bridge, the Ponte delle Torri, which made an easy connection to Monteluco for Via di Francesco pilgrims, was also damaged, and in the intervening years has been closed. Here are walking directions to use if you find the bridge either open or closed.

### When the Ponte delle Torri is open

With the lovely Cathedral of Spoleto at your back, climb the stairway up to Via del Ponte and follow it around the base of **Rocca Albornoziana** fortress to the viewpoint. Take the **Ponte delle Torri** across the gorge, coming to the stone tower on the opposite side, **Fortilizio dei Mulini**.

### When the Ponte delle Torri is closed

Facing the Duomo, retrace your steps from yesterday's stage, heading left and downhill on Via Mura Ciclopiche. Turn right on Via Ponzianina, cross the river, and turn right again onto Via del Tiro a Segno. Turn right in two blocks and immediately left onto CAI path 1. Turn right on CAI path 3 to come to the south end of the **Ponte delle Torri** at **Fortilizio dei Mulini**.

From the south side of the Ponte delle Torri, turn right and continue on switchbacks up this very steep climb toward Monteluco, about 40min ahead, watching carefully for blue-and-yellow Via di Francesco markers. Come to the SP Monteluco roadway and find the path on its opposite side that goes uphill to the left, with a sign that says 'Monteluco: 15 minutes.' Continue uphill and soon see Hotel Feretti straight ahead. Behind it is **Albergo Paradiso** (see Monteluco below for lodging information). Turn right and peer through the trees to see the parking lot and understated entry of the **Convento di Monteluco (2.5km**, kiosk with bar and restrooms).

*A pasture at the summit makes the perfect rest stop for the climb after Monteluco*

*The Way of St Francis — Via di Francesco*

> **2.5KM MONTELUCO** (ELEV 775M, POP 27) 🍴 ⛺ (182.1KM)
> St Francis first arrived in Monteluco in 1218, seeking solitude with his brothers in the caves. A simple *oratorio* (oratory) was built in 1673 over a cave where he lived. Many humble and famous people have taken refuge in the quiet of Monteluco, including St Anthony of Padua, San Bernardino of Siena, St Bonaventure, and Pope Pius IX. In 1556, the 81-year-old artist Michelangelo lived here briefly to rest from his work in Rome. The Franciscan convent has been remodeled and enlarged many times over the years, but an ongoing Franciscan community is still in residence.
>
> ⛺ **Albergo Paradiso** O Pr R Br Dr G W S Z 25/50, €-/40/70/80, Loc. Monteluco 19, info@albergoparadiso.net, www.albergoparadiso.net, tel 0743 223082, tel 0743 223427. Adjacent to the sanctuary.

Go through the parking lot and turn right toward a café/bar in the park below. This café and the restaurant on the opposite side of the field are your last opportunity before the end of this stage for food and indoor plumbing. Walk through the field toward the right, looking for a stone tower, then go to the left of the stone tower onto a gravel road. When the road ends, follow signs that lead you uphill on a dirt path. Come to an asphalt road at a clearing with **picnic tables** and a large outdoor fireplace. Go up the asphalt road toward the left and take the path that goes right. Soon you come to a chain-link fence and then the driveway of a **white house**. At the house, keep the stone wall on your left and head toward a three-story stone house. Open the gate in the fence and go straight ahead through sometimes-tall grass, looking for a stone marker on the right in 20 meters. Follow this path to a large open field with an asphalt road on the left and a fenced pasture on the right.

At a U in the asphalt road, find a **trailhead** across a gravel strip to the left; take the path and begin a traverse under trees. The trail becomes a pleasant, earthen track through beech tree woodlands. In 750 meters come to a **pasture at the summit** (3.9km), the elevation apex of today's walk and the best place nearby for a rest, snack, or lunch.

After the pasture, go straight ahead across the gravel road onto an overgrown and deeply rutted path that leads downhill. In 300 meters, breathtaking vistas of the mountains and the Valnerina (Nera River Valley) open up before you. In a few minutes, arrive at the once-deserted settlement of **Sensati** (1.1km, water. Coffee, snacks by donation).

The tiny hamlet of **Sensati** was abandoned in the early 1960s, but since 2022 Mario Galdini D'Ascenzo has offered hospitality to pilgrim hikers. Ask him to

STAGE 19 – SPOLETO TO MACENANO

show you the frescoes at the small church, the only intact building from the one-time mountain hamlet.

## The Way of St Francis — Via di Francesco

The downhill path now becomes steep and slippery in places until you reach an **asphalt road** (**2.7km**), where you say goodbye to the forest. Turn left here, following the road downhill, first to the village of **Pontuglia** (no services) and then passing Il Ruscello Affittacamere (see Ceselli below for lodging information) to arrive at the community center in the modern portion of tiny **Ceselli** (**4.4km**).

Come to the SP209 highway, the main road through the Valnerina.

---

**12.2KM CESELLI** (ELEV 317M, POP 127)  (170.0KM)

Ceselli's historic district is just to the south, surrounded by trees on a small hill, and includes a Romanesque church dedicated to San Vito and a larger church with an octagonal tower, built in the 16th c. and dedicated to St Michael the Archangel. The sleepy village has an official population of 130 residents.

🏠 **Affittacamere Il Ruscello** Pr R K Br S 3/6, €36/person includes breakfast, Via Contaglia 21, casavacanzeruscello@gmail.com, www.affittacamereilruscello.com, tel 340 2296792. Closed Jan to Mar. Swimming pool and garden. Bring food as no shops in this village.

---

The posh hotel at the 10th-c. Abbazia San Pietro in Valle, set in a remote setting 1km above Macenano, is a favorite overnight splurge for pilgrims

*Stage 19 – Spoleto to Macenano*

The **Nera River** stretches from its headwaters in the Sibylline Mountains 116km to Orte, where it flows into the Tiber. Its valley, the Valnerina, includes the Parco Fluvial del Nera nature park. The narrow valley is a popular region for hiking, mountain biking, canoeing, and kayaking.

The route now follows the **Valnerina Greenway** along the river's east bank, also called Via della Cartiera. Come to the bridge at **Macenano** (**5.1km**) at its intersection with Via Carducci, where you find the village 200 meters uphill along the SP209 highway.

---

**5.1KM MACENANO (ELEV 257M, POP <100)** (164.8KM)
This tiny village within the Ferentillo jurisdiction is clustered along the SP209, which divides it in two – the upper Borghetto and the lower Colleponte. It has long served as the commercial hub for the San Pietro abbey above, and a walk among the stone homes along its labyrinth of streets gives a taste of village life from past centuries.

🏠 **Ai Tre Archi Pizzeria/Ristorante** O Pr R Br Dr Cr 5/13, €-40/75/90, Strada Statale Valnerina 29, ai3archi@libero.it, www.aitrearchi.com, tel 0744 780004, 339 2543731. Cristina is your host.

🏠 **Abbazia San Pietro in Valle** Pr R Br Dr Cr 18/40, €-/-/120/160, Via del Abbazia Macenano (1.2km above Macenano), abbazia@sanpietroinvalle.com, tel 0744 780129, tel 333 8120558. Worth the splurge, but often booked for weddings on weekends.

---

### THE FLAMING CHARIOT

Once, when traveling, Francis left his companions to sleep while he prayed. With Francis gone, the disciples were startled to witness an astonishing sight: a flaming chariot like a globe of light twisted in the air around them. Although Francis was not in the room, his brothers instantly knew that the appearance was part of Francis' powerful prayer nearby.

*The Way of St Francis — Via di Francesco*

## STAGE 20
*Macenano to Piediluco*

| | |
|---|---|
| **Start** | Vie Cartiera and Carducci, Macenano |
| **Finish** | Church of San Francesco, Piediluco |
| **Duration** | 6½hr |
| **Distance** | 23.4km |
| **Total ascent** | 335m |
| **Total descent** | 215m |
| **Difficulty** | Moderate due to distance |
| **Percentage paved** | 37% |
| **Lodgings** | Ferentillo-Precetto 4.8km, Arrone 9.7km, Marmore 17.9km, Piediluco 23.4km |

After a short, flat walk on the Valnerina Greenway bike path, with the small, quiet town of Ferentillo-Precetto offering food and rest, climb 250m to two of the highlights of the route: the unforgettable Cascata delle Marmore (Marmore Falls), and serene Lake Piediluco. While most of the route is on quiet roads, a 400-meter stretch is on the edge of the SS79 highway. After consulting the Marmore Falls website (www.cascatadellemarmore.info), time your departure from Macenano to arrive at Marmore when the park is open and water is cascading down the mountainside.

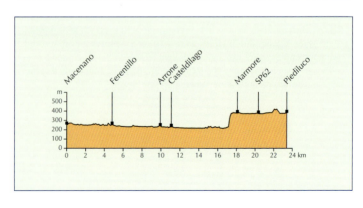

## STAGE 20 – MACENANO TO PIEDILUCO

Leaving the bridge to Macenano on your right, go straight and follow the large concrete sluice pipe to the left, turning right at the top and then continuing straight. The

> **4.8KM FERENTILLO-PRECETTO** (ELEV 260M, POP 1788) 🍴 ⊕ 🛖 © ● ⊕
> ⊕ **(160.0KM)**
> In 740 when the Lombard king Liutprando of Ferento arrived here, he named the town he established Ferentillo (Little Ferento). To protect the abbey upriver and to levy tolls on travelers in the early 12th c., the dukes of Spoleto built fortresses on opposite sides of the gorge, the remnants of which still stand silent watch over the town.
>   In the 19th c. it was discovered that bodies buried in the medieval crypt at the Church of Santo Stefano had been mummified. The result is one of the oddities of the route, the haunting Museum of the Mummies just a block from the piazza (www.mummiediferentillo.it).
>   Across the river is Matterella (supermarket, café, pharmacy), the sister neighborhood of Precetto, and together they make the twin town of Ferentillo.
>
> 🏠 **Il Borgo Agriturismo** Pr R K Br Dr Cr W S 4/9, €-/45/65/80, Vicolo S. Anselmo 1, teresasalvatori@yahoo.it, tel 329 7352101, from 1 Mar to 30 Oct. Dinner and washing machine available by request.

road turns up toward the left, first on broken asphalt and then on gravel. Follow signs along this delightful flat road to the SP74 in the neighborhood of **Ferentillo-Precetto**.

Turn left on the SP74 to come to the piazza of **Precetto** with its café, bar, and convenience store. Cross the highway now and follow signs back to the Greenway del Nera, descending at first among houses. Soon come to a parking lot and then

> **4.9KM ARRONE** (ELEV 239M, POP 2736) 🍴 ⊕ 🛖 © ● ⊕ ⊕ **(155.2KM)**
> A Roman nobleman named Arrone established his namesake town here in the 9th c. At first a castle constructed from wood, it was later rebuilt in stone. In the 13th c., the army of Spoleto ousted the Arroni and incorporated the town into its Duchy. In 1799 it was sacked and set afire by the French army.
>   Today, the town is a center of the Valnerina recreational area and is known for its celebration of John the Baptist annually on 24 June. Arrone's charming narrow alleys and steep streets lead up to its medieval castle, Torre degli Olivi, and to its tiny 12th–14th-c. Church of San Giovanni Battista, which holds 15th-c. frescoes from the Umbrian school.

## THE WAY OF ST FRANCIS — VIA DI FRANCESCO

♣ **La Loggia Sul Nera** O Pr R K Cr W S 4/19, €55/person, €65/couple, Via Mezzacosta 14, info@loggiasulnera.com, www.loggiasulnera.com, tel 347 4970188. 10% discount at nearby restaurant. 1 apartment has room for a bicycle.

♣ **Casa Argenti B&B/Home Restaurant** Pr R Br Dr Cr S 1/1, €80/single, €120/couple, Via degli Olivi 1, elga.argenti@gmail.com, www.casaargenti.it, tel 328 6794509, 392 3872580. Dinner and wash service available. Open Apr to Jan.

♣ **La Rocchetta** O Pr R K Br Dr W 2/6, €-/60/100/135, Via della Rocchetta 21, info@larocchettainumbria.it, www.larocchettainumbria.it, tel 335 77717129, tel 335 7292242. Self-serve breakfast and dinner.

♣ **Casa Mattei** O Pr Do R K Br W S 10/14, €35/55/70/105, Voc. Isola 13a, agriturismocasamattei@gmail.com, www.casamattei.it, tel 338 9140559, tel 0744 420513. Baggage service, restaurant and grocery nearby.

the SP4 highway. Turn left here and in a few hundred meters come to the Church of Santa Maria Assunta in **Arrone** (**4.9km**).

Take the steps left of Santa Maria Assunta Church and head to the valley floor, where a walkway curves around the castle mount. Head under the SP17 highway bridge and follow signs that have you fork left among homes onto a road leading across the flat valley to the hill town of **Casteldilago** (**1.8km**), just ahead.

**Casteldilago** was once an island castle in the middle of a long-drained lake (hence its name), but there are few traces left of the castle. The ancient *borgo* (town) remains, though, and a pleasant adventure is to stroll the lanes to the top. Today an *albergo diffuso* (literally, a 'scattered hotel') occupies many of the buildings (www.castellolago.com).

Follow signs leading around the town and toward the SP209, but before arriving at the roadway, turn left to join a road along the Nera River's southern

*Cascata delle Marmore (Marmore Falls) is the largest human-made waterfall in Europe*

## STAGE 20 – MACENANO TO PIEDILUCO

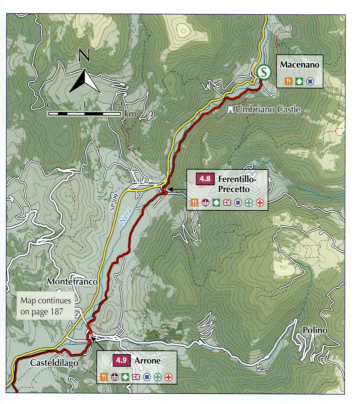

bank. At the next river bridge, turn left onto Strada Santa Maria del Caso, which snakes its way toward the forested hillside ahead. Once in the forest, watch carefully for a right fork that leads to the lower access to **Cascata delle Marmore**. (Going straight leads you to the upper falls route, which then requires a descent through the park to see the falls then another ascent to return to the top.)

On the recommended route, pass through a parking lot toward the ticket office (food and souvenir kiosks, restrooms). Pilgrims with a valid credential are granted free park entry tickets. Continue on the walkway and enter the park through turnstiles. Take Path 1, which leads along the waterfall on steps, giving you the best overlook just before the top (**6.4km**).

### 8.2KM MARMORE (ELEV 376M, POP 1602) 🍴 🛖 ⦿ ⦿ ℹ️ (146.9KM)

The breathtaking 165m **Cascata delle Marmore** is a creation of the ancient Romans who, in 271BC, chose to divert some of the waters of the Velino River over the natural cliffs at Marmore to drain the swamps around Rieti. Although this solved Rieti's problem, it led to difficulties at Terni, where the Nera River would now sometimes flood its banks, threatening the inhabitants. In the 1st c. BC, the Roman Senate debated the problem, with Aulus Pompeius representing Terni, and Cicero representing Rieti. But it was not until the 15th–16th c. that a succession of popes completed canals and other modifications that resolved the dangerous floods.

In the late 19th c., the water flow was harnessed for hydroelectricity, and today the falls are switched on and off at certain times of the day when the water flow is diverted to power-generating turbines. Scenic viewpoints at intervals on the mountainside ensure a dramatic and refreshing visit (www.cascatadellemarmore.info, free with Francesco credential; consult the website for timing of your visit since the waterfall operates on a variable schedule).

⛺ **Hotel Velino** O Pr R Br Dr Cr S Z 16/30, €-/50/70/90, Via Pilastri 6, info@hotelvelino.com, www.hotelvelino.com, tel 348 9628954. Riccardo is your host. Restaurant onsite.

*The town of Piediluco becomes visible through the trees*

## STAGE 20 – MACENANO TO PIEDILUCO

Exit the park by crossing a small footbridge and find the tourist information center (credential stamp) to the right. Turn left after the information center onto the **SS79**, alongside which you walk on a small path until forking to the right in a few hundred meters at an outdoor sports complex. Signs lead now onto a gentle walk along the dike on the Velino River canal, which feeds the waterfall you've just visited. The path is interrupted by the crossing of the **SP62** (**2.3km**), which heads south across the Velino, but then the path picks up again on the other side of the road, continuing until it merges with the **SS79** just after a lovely view across the lake to Piediluco. Carefully walk the next 400 meters on the roadway.

Fork left to climb up Via Fonte del Prato, which takes you first on a road and then a cross-country pathway to avoid the SS79. Watch very carefully for a narrow path that switches back on the right, and descend to the **SS79**. Cross it straight ahead onto Corso Raniero Salvati, which leads through town. Soon arrive at the Church of San Francesco in **Piediluco** (**3.2km**).

### 5.5KM PIEDILUCO (ELEV 375M, POP 1007) 🍴 ⊕ ⌂ ⓒ ⦿ ⊕ (141.5KM)

The first recorded mention of Piediluco is in 1028, when Castello di Luco was listed as a possession of the Arrone family. A small village sat at the foot of the castle – hence the name Piediluco (foot of the lake). The town's proximity to the Cascata delle Marmore put it on the list of cities to visit in the Grand Tours conducted for European nobility beginning in the 17th c. The modern town sits on the lakeshore, stretched into a long, thin line against the mountainous rock crowned by the ruined castle. Its historic jewel is the **Church of San Francesco**, which commemorates the passage of Francis through the territory in 1208.

Except for a few modern buildings, the picturesque lakeside village remains largely unchanged since the Middle Ages. Its annual Feste delle Acque celebrates boating sports, and the lake is home to the Italian national rowing team, whose sculls can be seen making practice runs during the summer months. Pyramidal Monte Caperno sits across the lake, and at its peak is a 2m-tall white statue of the Madonna made from weapons recycled from the Ethiopian War. The Madonna dell'Eco is named for the astounding 11-syllable echo possible from its location.

⌂ **Casa del Pellegrino, Parrocchia Santa Maria del Colle** O Pr Do R K S 9/34, €Donation (min €10 please), Corso Raniero Salvati 63, parrocchia-piediluco@tiscali.it, tel 338 8727918, tel 329 7475671. Bunk beds for pilgrims and church groups. On arrival, contact the parish office in the churchyard.

⌂ **Hotel Miralago** Pr R Br Dr Cr W S Z 32/100, €Seasonal rates (check online), Via Noceta 2, info@miralagohotel.net, www.miralagohotel.net, tel 0744 360022.

⌂ **Hotel del Lago** O Pr R Br Dr Cr Z 46/80, €See website for seasonal rates, Strada del Porto 71, info@hoteldellago.com, www.hoteldellago.com, tel 0744 368450, 347 3214352.

---

### FRANCIS AT LAGO PIEDILUCO

With his brothers, Francis crisscrossed Lago Piediluco, preaching to the locals. While he was on a boat at the shoreline, a local fisherman gave him a fish to eat. He immediately put it back in the water to free it. The fish remained alongside the boat, leaving only after Francis had preached a sermon and given his blessing. At Piediluco, Francis and his companions built a small mud-and-reed hut on the site of the current church and called it a *convegno*, from which use the word 'convent' was given to Franciscan gathering houses.

# STAGE 21
*Piediluco to Poggio Bustone*

| | |
|---|---|
| **Start** | Church of San Francesco, Piediluco |
| **Finish** | Piazza Battisti, Poggio Bustone |
| **Duration** | 6½hr |
| **Distance** | 20.9km |
| **Total ascent** | 879m |
| **Total descent** | 517m |
| **Difficulty** | Hard due to elevation changes |
| **Percentage paved** | 62% |
| **Lodgings** | Labro 4.9km, Poggio Bustone 20.9km |

Essentially one long, sustained climb, the stage's first ascent is to the tiny, ancient, depopulated hill town of Labro, forgotten in time and worthy of an exploration. This last urban moment is followed by the second steep climb of the stage, a climb in the forest to lofty, tranquil, and remote Faggio San Francesco – the Beech Tree of St Francis. A long downhill march is rewarded with an overnight in the medieval town of Poggio Bustone, with its wide vistas across the Rieti Valley far below and its close connection to St Francis, remembered in the Convento di San Giacomo and Sacro Speco 'Grotto of Revelation' cave above town.

Look east along the lake and see a hilltop town among the green mountains: this is Labro, the first goal of the day. Begin by continuing past the church as the street curves among shops and cafés, then passes the Hotel Miralago. After the hotel and parking lot, either follow the signs to turn right and walk the lakeside path or simply follow the road and turn right in a couple of hundred meters. The two routes rejoin to pass a **campground** and then come to the **SS79** roadway.

Turn right and at the second road in a scant 400 meters fork left as the signs direct, soon turning right (where you cross out of Umbria and into the region of Lazio). Climb the road up to the town of **Labro** (**4.9km**). Either enter the village gate for a quiet exploration of the serpentine alleys of this deserted but scenic hill settlement, or continue to the right, following the road directly upward to the café/bar.

## THE WAY OF ST FRANCIS — VIA DI FRANCESCO

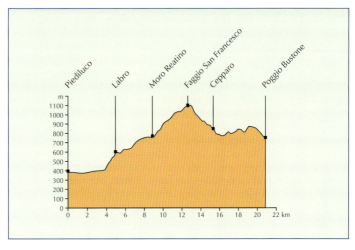

190

***Stage 21 – Piediluco to Poggio Bustone***

### 4.9KM LABRO (ELEV 628M, POP 368) 🏨 ⛪ (136.6KM)

The town's name derives from the Latin *aprum* (boar), and the town's coat of arms includes an image of a boar. In the year 956 the first Lord of Labro was installed. The town often engaged in battle with its neighbor, Piediluco.

Following World War II, the town was depopulated, and in the late 1960s a project began to restore its buildings, which include the castle, the Church of Santa Maria Maggiore, and many private homes, some of which have been gathered together into the four-star Albergo Diffuso Crispolti.

🏠 **Albergo Diffuso Crispolti** Pr R Br Cr S 7/20, €-/70/85/-, Via Cadorna 10 (for check-in), info@albergodiffusocrispolti.com, www.albergodiffusocrispolti.com, tel 335 5391560, tel 392 8395481.

Continue past the town and its **bar** until you reach the **Carabinieri office** (police). Instead of turning right or left on the SP5 roadway, go straight onto a path that climbs through woods to an asphalt road above. Continue on the road, coming again to the SP5. Turn right (water faucet), then fork left onto a road that takes you past a cemetery and soccer pitch to the SR521 road. When the road turns, go straight on Via delle Casette to meet the SR521 again at the hamlet of **Morro Reatino** (3.9km, café-restaurant).

Now cross the SP3 and go straight, with an arched steel building on your left, for the final, sometimes very steep, ascent. Follow signs leading uphill on either gravel (for moderate climbs) or concrete (for steep climbs). As you near the top, don't miss the left fork onto a pathway that affords a shortcut from the road by cutting off a long switchback. The path returns to the road below a tall, wooden cross. From here it is easiest to take the road, continuing uphill for a few hundred meters to the Church of San Francesco (3.9km). The chapel, although usually locked, has a couple of benches for a much-deserved rest after the challenging climb. The **Faggio San Francesco** is a few meters down the path and north of the church.

### THE BEECH TREE OF ST FRANCIS

Legends say that, while walking through these mountains, Francis was suddenly overwhelmed by a strong storm. Taking shelter under the branches of a beech tree (*faggio* in Italian), Francis noticed that the tree's branches gathered over him like an umbrella, protecting him from the elements. Francis blessed and thanked the tree, which tradition locates here, at what is confirmed to be one of the oldest living beech trees in the world. Its serpentine shape is unusual for the beech species and its trunk has a maximum circumference of 4 meters.

*The ancestor of the beech tree 'Faggio San Francesco' is said to have sheltered St Francis in a storm*

If you're not afraid of steep trails, a shortcut to Poggio Bustone begins at the chapel.

### Steep shortcut
Cross to the bottom of the cow pasture behind the chapel to a fire pit, where you'll see a CAI marker reading 'Poggio Bustone.' Follow this trail downhill on a steep bank to a gravel road below. Turn right on the gravel road and follow it to a marker for the **CAI 419 trailhead**, where you rejoin the longer route. Turn left on the trail and proceed as described below.

If not taking the shortcut, return on the road to the wooden cross, and go past it onto the same path from which you came. **Watch carefully for yellow/blue painted markings that lead you to fork off the path and downhill.** Meet the road again, which has since taken a lazy switchback to get to this spot, and cross again to shortcut another series of switchbacks in a downhill, cross-country path. Watch for steep and slippery banks when you return to the roadway. After the second shortcut, continue downhill on the asphalt road, which leads you to the mountain hamlet of **Cepparo** (**2.6km**, no services).

Continue beyond the hamlet and, when the road takes a tight, hairpin curve, go straight onto a **gravel road**. Climb again for just 600 meters and then turn right, following signs for both the Via di Francesco and **CAI 419** that read 'Poggio Bustone: 1hr.' Now find a pleasant and fairly level woodland path that

## Stage 21 – Piediluco to Poggio Bustone

stretches along the mountainside until ascending and becoming first a gravel road and then a road of asphalt.

The first houses of Poggio Bustone appear, views open to the Reatina (Rieti) Valley, and the road merges with Via della Casetta to descend into town. Cross Via Francescana and continue downhill on Via San Marco. Switch back at Via Volturno in the labyrinthine streets of this hill town and come to Piazza Battisti and its bar, pharmacy, and viewpoint in central **Poggio Bustone** (**5.6km**).

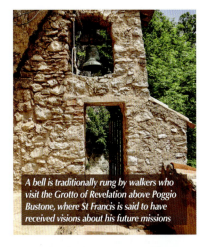

*A bell is traditionally rung by walkers who visit the Grotto of Revelation above Poggio Bustone, where St Francis is said to have received visions about his future missions*

### 16.0KM POGGIO BUSTONE (ELEV 756M, POP 1960) 🍴 ⊕ 🏠 © ⊙ ⊕
(120.6KM)

Perched high above the Rieti Valley, the well-preserved and picturesque medieval hillside town of Poggio Bustone is home to one of the Holy Valley's four main Franciscan sanctuaries. The dramatic setting among steep hills gives it extraordinary views to the valley below, and the narrow streets and simple stone homes and shops at its center evoke centuries long past.

The 12th-c. **Convent of San Giacomo** atop the town includes several small medieval chapels and cells. To reach the convent, go directly uphill from the Porta del Buongiorna. A stairway above the convent leads 1km uphill to the **Grotto of Revelation**, where it is customary to ring the bell on your arrival.

The town's most famous son is Lucio Battisti (1943–1998), one of Italy's most popular singers, whose career hit its peak in the 1970s and 1980s with songs like 'Il Mio Canto Libero,' 'Ancora Tu,' and 'Acqua Azzurra, Acqua Chiara.' A surprise delight of the town is its sumptuous restaurant/wine bar, L'Antico Arco, tucked away in a side alley and worth a splurge (Via Umberto I, 2, tel 339 8959469).

🏠 **San Francesco Suite** O Pr R Br S 5/12, €-/60/75/100, Via Vittorio Emanuele 18, tesseale@libero.it, tel 366 2741665. Located in historic center.

🏠 **Convento di San Giacomo** Do R K 1/30, €Donation €10+, Piazzale Missioni Francescane, convpbustone@libero.it, www.santuariovallesanta.com, tel 0746 688916 Fr Renzo. Request to be generous to support the mission. From 1 May to 15 Oct. Chapel is always open for reflection.

🏠 **B&B La Casetta** Via della Casetta, bblacasetta2022@libero.it, tel 349 4687364, Sergio is your host.

🏠 **Casa del Pellegrino Da Dina** O Pr R K S 2/5, €Donation, Via Roma 25, battisti.francesconw@gmail.com, tel 347 5133030. Francesco is your host.

🏠🏠 **Locanda Francescana** O Pr Do R Br Dr Cr W S Z 11/47, €25/60/70/105, Via Francescana 13 (hostel) and Via Roma 4 (restaurant), info@locandafrancescana.com, tel 0746 688688, tel 347 4150455 (Feliciano). Nearby new B&B.

🏠 **Casa Vacanze San Giacomo** O Pr R K Br Dr W S Z 5/10, €35 per person (including breakfast), Via San Giacomo 4, casavacanzesangiacomo@gmail.com, tel 339 5645493, tel 338 8391706. Annunziata is your host.

🏠 **Casetta Mariani** Pr R K S 3/6, €Donation, Via del Santuario, casettamariani@gmail.com, tel 349 4639384. Garden. Accepts animals. Open Apr to Oct. Valeria is your host.

## REVELATION AT POGGIO BUSTONE

In 1208, in a small Sacro Speco cave above Poggio Bustone now sometimes called the 'Grotto of Revelation,' Francis had two important spiritual experiences. In the first, he was overwhelmed by a sudden and complete sense of assurance that God had entirely forgiven all his sins. In the second, a dream suffused in light gave him an image of the future. 'I saw a great many men who wanted to share our way of life,' he told his brothers later. 'The roads were filled with Frenchmen, Spaniards, Germans, Englishmen, and many others, speaking various languages and hurrying toward us.'

The effect of the experiences was immediately evident in Francis' contagious joy. Coming out of the cave and down the mountain, he entered the town at the gate now aptly called the Porta del Buongiorno and greeted the residents of Poggio Bustone with a cheerful, 'Good day, good people.' The joyful greeting from the simple man is well remembered to this day and commemorated on a stone slab in the heart of the village.

*The buildings of Poggio Bustone cling to a hillside above the Holy Valley of Rieti*

*The Way of St Francis — Via di Francesco*

# STAGE 22
*Poggio Bustone to Rieti*

| | |
|---|---|
| **Start** | Piazza Battisti, Poggio Bustone |
| **Finish** | Duomo, Rieti |
| **Duration** | 5¼hr |
| **Distance** | 17.0km |
| **Total ascent** | 285m |
| **Total descent** | 626m |
| **Difficulty** | Moderate due to elevation changes |
| **Percentage paved** | 67% |
| **Lodgings** | Cantalice 5.7km, San Felice all'Acqua 9.2km, Rieti 17.0km |

The stage includes a lovely walk through forests, fields, and farms on the hillsides above the 'Holy Valley of Rieti' to the charming hill town of Cantalice, followed by a visit to the important Franciscan site at Santuario della Foresta. While the last two kilometers are suburban, Rieti's city center offers shopping, restaurants, a rich history, and a beautiful cathedral. A rest day in Rieti allows quick and easy travel to the Franciscan sanctuaries at Greccio and Fonte Colombo.

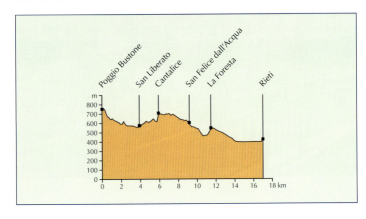

## STAGE 22 – POGGIO BUSTONE TO RIETI

Head uphill to Poggio Bustone's Church of Giovanni Battista and its Municipio. At the Porta Buongiorno, with the archway to your back, turn right to take the marked sidewalk leading downhill, first on steps and then on gray paving stones. In 40 meters go right on a concrete drive, which then turns left, heading downhill. Follow signs that curve toward the bottom of the valley, where you cross a stream before coming to the **trailhead** of a gravel path, bordered with wooden X-frame fencing. The X-frame fencing will be a regular feature of the paths here in the Rieti Valley, often called the 'Holy Valley' because of its many Franciscan sanctuaries.

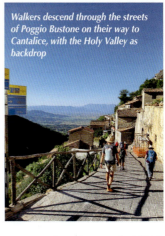

*Walkers descend through the streets of Poggio Bustone on their way to Cantalice, with the Holy Valley as backdrop*

The path joins an asphalt road set in pastures and continues to the hillside hamlet of **San Liberato** (**3.9km**, no services). The first ascent of the day now begins on a sometimes-narrow, wooded path that traverses the mountainside. Continue as the path joins a road and comes to an overlook above the next town. Descend to the main road, Via Dante Alighieri, and turn left to find the bars and shops of photogenic **Cantalice** (**1.8km**).

---

**5.7KM CANTALICE** (ELEV 660M, POP 2428) (114.9KM)

The town's name may derive from the Latin *catata ilex* (referring to holm oak). According to legends, an oak tree emerged from a cracked stone inside the sacristy of the town's Church of Santa Maria delle Grazie. The oak was considered miraculous and the cracked stone became an object venerated for its promotion of fertility. It was later removed in 1200 by order of Pope Innocent III, who considered its veneration too pagan. The stone can today be seen near the town's Scentella fountain.

Cantalice is surmounted by a fortress, which in prior centuries guarded the border between Rieti and Spoleto. The town's most famous son was Felice Porri (1515–1587), a Capuchin friar who begged food in Rome so he could feed hungry people. He was a close friend of San Filippo Neri and Carlo Borromeo, and was canonized San Felice in 1712. The town has a volunteer Pilgrim Office to serve people on the Via di Francesco.

**Ostello San Felice all'Acqua** is on the route 3.5km after town: see below for details.

# THE WAY OF ST FRANCIS — VIA DI FRANCESCO

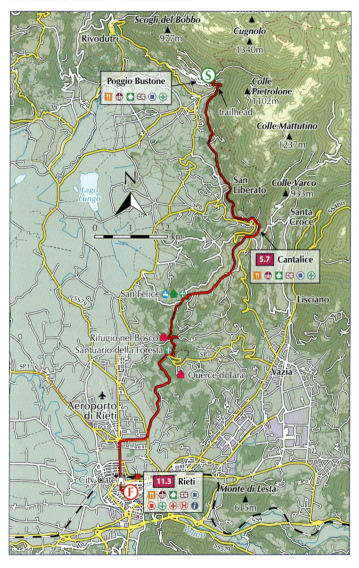

## STAGE 22 – POGGIO BUSTONE TO RIETI

Take the stairway to the right of the café/bar and wind your way upward through Cantalice to the piazza and fountain in front of the large, yellow, 19th-c. Church of San Felice. Turn right at the fountain and follow the walkway, at the foot of the fortress above; the walkway soon becomes a road going along the ridge out of town, passing homes and a bakery. Go right at the end of the road toward a bar; pass the bar and go left at the next fork, the Via San Gregorio. Rieti is visible in the distance in the valley below.

The road now follows a long ridgeline downhill. Pass the Saletta dei Ricordi Museum on your left. This small museum remembers the life of actress Marcella Mariani and other victims of the Monte Terminillo air disaster in 1955. The road finally ends at the chapel of **Santuario di San Felice all'Acqua** (**3.5km**, water, restrooms. ⛺ **Ostello San Felice All'Acqua** O Do R K S 3/8, €Donation, Via G Pascoli 46-47, tel 338 7782930, 347 0869032. Pantry with food items. Linens provided. Enrico is your host).

> Legends associated with **Santuario di San Felice all'Acqua** tell the story of Felice Porri resting here with his companions, parched from their work of caring for crops and livestock. After praying for water, Felice struck the ground with his staff and a spring emerged from the ground, ever since that time providing fresh water to the neighboring community.

Follow signs that lead onto a road to the left, going downhill on asphalt. Now the road winds its way downward between farm buildings. Pass the **Rifugio nel Bosco B&B** (www.andandoporelmundo.com/italia/rieti/rifugio-nel-bosco) and turn left on the gravel road, coming finally to the valley floor after the long descent from Cantalice. Fork right here and follow signs up a road; before the gate of an estate, you turn right on a rutted path with the familiar X-framed railing. In 400 meters you come to **Santuario della Foresta** (**2.3km**), the second of the Franciscan sanctuaries you will pass in the Holy Valley (⛺ **Le Querce di Tara** O Do R K Br Dr W S 2/16, €Donation, Via Foresta 37 (Rieti), mauro.rinaldi@damaitaliasrl.it, tel 348 4273023).

### THE MIRACLE OF THE WINE

Late in his life, an illness in his eyes caused Francis to gradually lose his sight. Cardinal Ugolino of Rieti begged him to come to his town to undergo treatment from a prominent doctor nearby; but large crowds had begun to follow Francis. Needing rest and a respite from the crowds, he chose to remain at the nearby Church of San Fabiano.

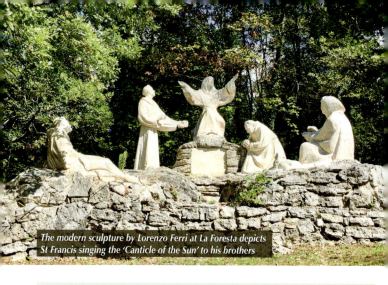
*The modern sculpture by Lorenzo Ferri at La Foresta depicts St Francis singing the 'Canticle of the Sun' to his brothers*

He stayed here for more than 50 days, while the crowds assembled in the surrounding vineyards, consuming nearly the entire year's crop of grapes. The local farmers, seeing that their livelihood was destroyed, entreated Francis to do something. According to legend, he had them bring their remaining grapes to the winepress at the church and, to their astonishment, after pressing the grapes, the winepress yielded double the juice it had in the previous year's crop. This became known as 'the miracle of the wine,' and San Fabiano Church ultimately became the Franciscan convent of La Foresta ('the guesthouse').

Leave the church behind you and go straight ahead on the asphalt driveway that sweeps in a circle to the right, around gardens and vineyards with Stations of the Cross on tiles at intervals. At the gate, go straight onto Via Foresta, a two-lane asphalt road leading downhill. Follow this road until you come to an intersection with the main arterial, Via Angelo Ricci.

Cross the road after the traffic circle and take an immediate right onto Viale Giulio de Juliis, a wide boulevard with apartment blocks on both sides. Cross to the left and at the next traffic circle turn left onto Viale Emilio Maraini. Follow this road straight through the city gate and into the old city. It curves as it goes uphill, becoming Via Cintia, which leads to the Duomo of **Rieti** (**5.5km**) in the heart of the city.

## STAGE 22 – POGGIO BUSTONE TO RIETI

## 11.3KM RIETI (ELEV 405M, POP 45,278) 🍴 ⊕ 🏠 € ● ● ⊕ ⊕ Ⓗ ❶ (103.6KM)

The ancient town of Rieti is capital of the Sabine region and traces its roots to nearly the year 1000 BC. In its first territorial expansion, Rome conquered Rieti and its surrounding Sabine region and, according to legend, abducted its women to serve as concubines. *The Rape of the Sabines* by Giambologna, commissioned by Cosimo I de Medici, is one of the most famous sculptures of the Renaissance. From this point onward Rieti was part of Roman hegemony in Central Italy. In the 3rd c. BC, the Roman consul Manius Curius Dentatus oversaw the draining of Lacus Velinus, the lake that had filled the valley below town. Rieti became an important stopping point on the Salt Road (Via Salaria) that crossed the Italian peninsula.

In the 12th c. AD, Saracens sacked Rieti, and in the 20th c. the town was partially destroyed by Allied bombardment. However, much of the 13th-c. medieval wall still stands, particularly on the north side of the city, and continues to shelter its quaint streets.

Rieti's 13th–16th-c. **Duomo** and its tower mark the center of town, and the narrow pedestrian streets on the downward slope to the Velino River hold busy shops. An unusual archeological feature is **Underground Rieti**, where portions of the ancient Roman Salt Road, the Via Salaria, can be seen. On the riverfront stands the historic **Chiesa di San Francesco** (13th c.) with its frescoes from the school of Giotto depicting the life of St Francis. Today, Rieti is sometimes called 'the navel of Italy' due to its geographic location.

The serene **Santuario Fonte Colombo** sits above Rieti among the lush oak forests of Monte Rainiero, and can be reached from Piazza Cavour on Line 333 of the ASM Rieti bus service in just 15min (www.asmrieti.it). The **Santuario Francescano del Presepe di Greccio** is a 40min bus ride via San Marco from Rieti's Viale Morroni on the Cotral bus service (www.cotralspa.it). The train from Rieti also serves Greccio from about 4km below the sanctuary (www.trenitalia.com).

🔺 **B&B La Terrazza FioRita** O Pr Do R Br Dr Cr W S Z B&B and apartment, €30 per person, Via Pelliccheria 5, rietidascoprire@rietidascoprire.it, tel 347 7279591, tel 350 5996168. Price includes breakfast and kitchen use. Ask Rita about Rieti subterranean tours. Rita has three separate properties in Rieti.

🔺 **L'Angelo Pellegrino** O Pr R K Cr W S 3/7, €-/50/60/-, Vicolo Barilotto 22, langelopellegrino@gmail.com, www.langelopellegrino.it, tel 351 5452758.

🔺 **B&B La Camelia** O Pr R K Br W S 1/1, €-/40/60/-, Via Santa Anna 21, giulianaconsumati@yahoo.it, https://beb.it/lacameliarieti/it/, tel 3498 467496. Linens available. Breakfast included. 1 apartment with washing machine. Ask for pilgrim price.

# THE WAY OF ST FRANCIS — VIA DI FRANCESCO

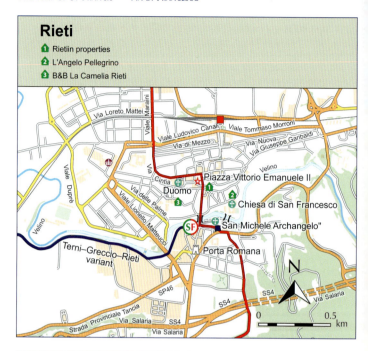

## FRANCIS AT THE HOLY VALLEY OF RIETI

At Fonte Colombo, Francis completed his rule for communal life in 1222–1223, remaining there six weeks while he dictated its contents to his followers. Here also in 1224 doctors cauterized Francis' eyes in an attempt to cure his illness. Although his disciples could not bear to watch the branding of his eyes, Francis insisted he could not feel any pain at all.

About 15km from Rieti, the steep cliffs at Greccio offered grottoes favored by Francis for solitude and meditation. Here, on Christmas Eve of 1223, Francis brought together farm animals and villagers to recreate the scene of Christ's birth at Bethlehem. The tradition of Christmas manger or crèche scenes spread from Greccio throughout the world.

# SECTION 3A: VARIANT ROUTES TO RIETI

*The trail above Greccio is one of a ring of trails around the Holy Valley of Rieti (Variant 3.1)*

## VARIANT 3.1
*Arrone to Terni, Greccio, and Rieti*

| | |
|---|---|
| **Start** | Arrone |
| **Finish** | Rieti |
| **Duration** | 19hr (3 days) |
| **Distance** | 61.1km |
| **Total ascent** | 1754m |
| **Total descent** | 1600m |
| **Difficulty** | Hard due to elevation changes |
| **Percentage paved** | 60% |
| **Lodgings** | Marmore 7.0km, Terni 15.6km, Stroncone 25.5km, Contigliano 45.2km, Fonte Colombo 55.9km, Rieti 61.1km |

The Franciscan sanctuaries stand on the sides of a ring of mountains that surround the Rieti Valley, whose valley floor was once covered by a large lake. With the top of the ring at Marmore and the bottom of the ring at Rieti, there are two sanctuaries on each side, forcing a choice as to whether to walk the east side of the valley and see the sanctuaries at Poggio Bustone and La Foresta, or the west side of the valley to visit the sanctuaries at Greccio and Fonte Colombo. The main (east) route assumes the former, covering the distance from Marmore in 43.3km. The west variant described here takes an additional 10.8km to reach Rieti through Greccio.

The city of Terni is large and interesting, while the villages of Stroncone, Greccio, and Contigliano are picturesque. A walk up the pass from Stroncone through I Prati is remote, secluded, and very beautiful.

### Stage 1: Marmore to Stroncone (25.5KM)

From Marmore, cross the highway and, just before the auto tunnel, take a stairway directly up the mountainside, making a 200m climb to the tiny village of **San Liberatore** (9.4km). Descend first through olive groves and then through industrial estates to urban **Terni** (6.2km), a provincial capital of Umbria. (🏠 **Hotel de Paris** O Pr R Br Cf W S Z 40/80, €-/71/85/95, Viale della Stazione 52, info@hoteldeparis.it, www.hoteldeparis.it, tel 0744 58047. 🏠 **Il Pozzo** O Pr R Br Dr Cf S Z 8/22,

## Variant 3.1 – Arrone to Terni, Greccio, and Rieti

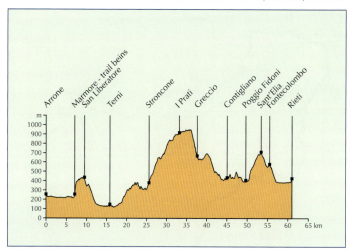

€-/55/75/120, Strada di Collescipoli 19, countryhouseilpozzo@gmail.com, www.ilpozzoterni.com, tel 340 4684417.)

Continue from Terni up roads and trails to **Stroncone**, a hilltop city with a quiet, medieval center. (🏠 **La Sosta B&B** O Pr R Br Cr 2/5, €-/-/70/100, Via L. Lanzi 5, paolobrunetti1965@libero.it, tel 327 8767147. Outside bike storage. Paolo is your host.)

### Stage 2: Stroncone to Contigliano (19.7km)

The long uphill followed by the steep downhill to **Greccio** makes this a challenging stage. (🏠 **Il Cantico B&B** O Pr R Br Cr S 2/4, €-/50/80/120, Via dei Frati 102, ilcantico2007@libero.it, tel 328 9642274. From Apr 1 to Jan 6.)

Continue on to **Contigliano** over roads and trails. (🏠 **La Bottega del Fabbro** O Pr R K Cr S 2/5, €40–60/person, Via Cairoli 20, labottegadelfabbroab@gmail.com, www.bottegadelfabbrocontigliano.com, tel 328 0718566, 328 3057365. Maurizio is your host. 🏠 **Ostello Villa Franceschini** O Do R Br Dr Cr S Z 11/62, €20/person including breakfast, €30/person including half-board, €40/person including full board, Via Ettore 7, ostellovillafranceschini@gmail.com, www.ostellovillafranceschini.com, tel 0746 1766583.)

Information and a pilgrim rest area can be found at Punto Sosta Le Farfalle, Contigliano (Via Madonna 2, missgiuliast@libero.it, tel 347 4035827).

## THE WAY OF ST FRANCIS — VIA DI FRANCESCO

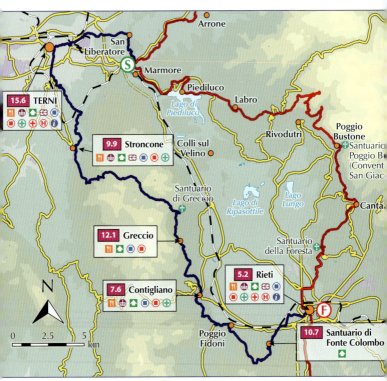

### Stage 3: Contigliano to Rieti (15.9KM)

Roads and trails lead you from the hilltop town of Contigliano to the sanctuary at **Fonte Colombo**. (🏠 **Santuario Fonte Colombo** Via Fontecolombo 40, santuariofontecolombo@gmail.com, tel 347 2938643. Religious accommodation. Aldo is your host. Tel: 339 3270660 Padre Francesco è il il Nuovo host. The sanctuary is undergoing a renovation and will open in 2026 with private rooms. In the meantime, only sleeping bags and tents can be accommodated.) A path leads directly down from the sanctuary to the SP46 at the valley floor. From here it is mostly on busy roads to central **Rieti**. See Stage 22 for accommodation options in Rieti.

# SECTION 4: RIETI TO ROME

*Olive groves cover the nearby hills on the descent from Colle Peloso (Stage 24)*

## THE WAY OF ST FRANCIS — VIA DI FRANCESCO

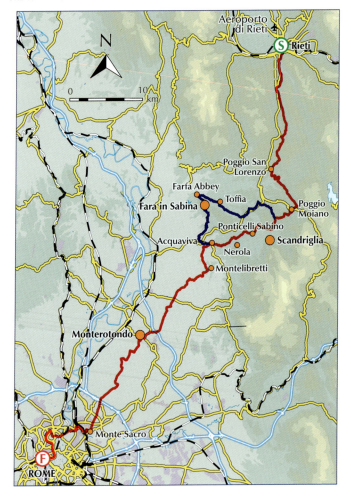

The route crosses from the Rieti plain over low ridges through the region of Sabina, known worldwide for the premium quality of its olive oil. The area is dotted with small, proud towns, each with its own history traced back to the Romans and beyond. After Ponticelli Sabino, the mountains gradually give way to

## SECTION 4 — RIETI TO ROME

*A plaque on the trail near Nerola reads 'The only journey is the internal one.' – Rainer Maria Rilke.*

the vast and fertile Tiber River plain. Before arriving in urban Rome, the itinerary passes through the protected wilderness areas of Riserva Macchia di Gattaceca and Riserva Naturale della Marcigliana, both quiet and protected from automobile traffic. The climax of the walk comes with an entry along the colonnaded Piazza San Pietro to one of the most spectacular and beloved buildings in the world – Saint Peter's Basilica.

*The Way of St Francis — Via di Francesco*

# STAGE 23
*Rieti to Poggio San Lorenzo*

| | |
|---|---|
| **Start** | Duomo, Rieti |
| **Finish** | Piazza Marconi, Poggio San Lorenzo |
| **Duration** | 6hr |
| **Distance** | 20.5km |
| **Total ascent** | 359m |
| **Total descent** | 266m |
| **Difficulty** | Moderate due to elevation changes |
| **Percentage paved** | 58% |
| **Lodgings** | Torricella in Sabina 18.2km, Poggio San Lorenzo 20.5km |

A mostly flat and mellow stage that walks along creeks and fields into forests, ending with some steep but low climbs just before tiny Poggio San Lorenzo. The town is a gem of rural village life in Sabina, and worthy of a relaxed beverage in its Piazza Marconi as children play and workers arrive for a refreshment before heading home for the day.

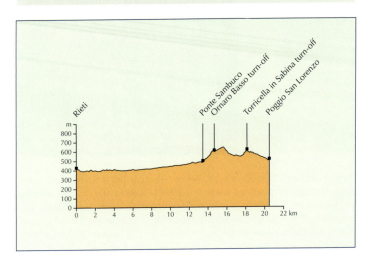

## STAGE 23 – RIETI TO POGGIO SAN LORENZO

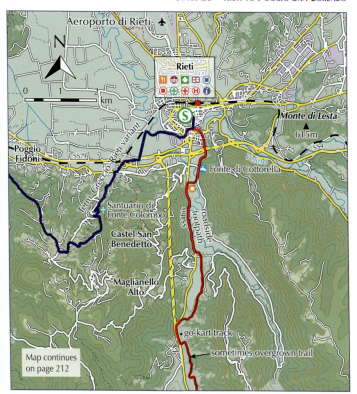

From Rieti's main square, Piazza Vittorio Emanuele II, walk downhill along the shops of Via Roma. Cross the Velino River, where you may see the submerged piers of the original Roman bridge on the left side. Turn left at the Monument to the Lira. Straight ahead within a block are a grocery store, fruit store, cash machine, and café/bar. Then pass the large **Church of San Michele Arcangelo** on the left. Turn right before the Monumento alle Vittime del Bombardamento war memorial and pass through the quaint neighborhood of Borgo Sant'Antonio.

Follow this road across Via Giacomo Matteotti as it becomes Via Fonte Cottorella. Pass under the highway bridge and continue to the Cottorella water-bottling plant. Just across the road is the '100 Kilometers to Rome' waymark sign. Continue left 200 meters and fork right onto a trail to the **SS4bis** Via Salaria

*The Way of St Francis — Via di Francesco*

Vecchia highway ahead. Turn left at the highway (gas station with cafe/bar) and walk on the pleasant and safe path along the shoulder of the tree-lined highway until the waymarks point you to the left, where you turn to join a path that parallels the highway. Return to the path alongside the highway just before a **go-kart track** and parking lot. Turn left and now pick up another sometimes-overgrown path leading alongside a drainage canal, which ends at the quiet, asphalt **SP34**.

*Pilgrims climb on a gravel road after Ponte Sambuco*

Turn left and follow this road gradually uphill. Follow signs that have you fork right onto the **Via della Noce** and continue on this gravel road under trees until signs point you right at a meadow. Come to a gravel road and rest area at **Ponte Sambuco** (**13.5km**, picnic tables). This well-preserved 2nd-c. Roman bridge of large, white stones served the Via Salaria in ancient times. Cross the bridge and head uphill on gravel for the biggest climb of the day, which leads to the asphalt

*A member of the Agamennone family describes the process of making oil at the family's 2000-year-old Capo Farfa olive mill in Poggio San Lorenzo*

Via Salaria Vecchia at the turn-off to **Ornaro Basso** (**1.2km**, turn right to find the town and its restaurant in 1km).

Turn left at the roadway and climb on this quiet road to the day's summit at the settlement of **Colonnetta** (no services), where you turn right at the Roman mile marker on Via Quinzia. Go downhill at first on the asphalt road, then left to a gravel road, and fork right, near the bottom of the valley, to a dirt path.

Watch carefully for waymarks along the trail in this dark and swampy forest and find a gravel path leading uphill. Come then to a gravel road and continue uphill to the asphalt roadway to reach a left turn to **Torricella in Sabina** (**3.5km**, see Poggio San Lorenzo below for details of lodging at Casa per Ferie Sacro Cuore, 400 metres off the route). If not heading for Torricella, go straight on this asphalt road (Via Quinzia), passing the entrance road to Agriturismo Santa Giusta. Continue into town and arrive at Piazza Marconi of **Poggio San Lorenzo** (**2.3km**).

**20.5KM POGGIO SAN LORENZO** (ELEV 492M, POP 517) 🍴 ⊕ 🏠 ⊙ **(83.1KM)**
The ancient Roman walls of tiny but captivating Poggio San Lorenzo buttress the town's flank and are still visible below the piazza, showing intricate Roman brickwork over 2000 years old. In Roman times, the town was known for its thermal baths. It was a stop on the ancient Via Salaria, and the Capo Farfa olive oil mill in town still produces oil there, as it has for nearly 2000 years. Near town are an ancient oak tree, believed to be the oldest in Europe, and the 4th-c. Church of the Madonna of the Penitents, whose caves sheltered residents during World War II bombings.

🔺 **Casa Per Ferie Sacro Cuore** O Do R Br Dr S 1/3, €Donation, Loc. Faioni 1, ancellescuore@libero.it, tel 0765 735017. Religious retreat house, primarily for groups. Half-board and linens included.

🔺 **Casa del Pellegrino** O Do R K Br Dr Cr W 2/16, €15 per person, Piazza Guglielmo Marconi, info@lacasadelpellegrino.it, tel 392 1445940. Breakfast included, linens.

🔺 **Agriturismo Santa Giusta** Pr R Br Dr Cr S Z 5/17, €-/80/85/110, Via Santa Giusti, Loc. Prato, agriturismo.santagiusta@gmail.com, tel 339 4984008, tel 0765 884166. Open Mar–Oct. Swimming pool in summer. Your host is Stefano.

## FRANCIS AND THE SULTAN

Francis tried several times to travel to the Holy Land. With the beginning of the Fifth Crusade (1217–1221), he especially hoped he could visit with Muslim leaders and either convert them to Christianity or at least bring about an end to the conflict. If neither came true, he hoped instead for martyrdom.

Arriving in the Middle East in 1219, Francis approached the battle lines, crossed into Muslim territory, and was taken prisoner. He asked to meet the Muslim leader and was brought into the presence of Sultan al-Malik al-Kamil. Legends say that Francis was asked to walk across a fire to show his faith, but there is no evidence this occurred. Some form of relationship was built, though, and it is known that the two developed great mutual respect. When Francis was about to depart, the Sultan wanted to give Francis lavish gifts, which the saint refused. Francis eventually accepted an ivory horn, which is on display in Assisi. Francis established a Franciscan presence in the Holy Land, and Franciscans ultimately came to be custodians of some of the region's most holy Christian sites.

*THE WAY OF ST FRANCIS — VIA DI FRANCESCO*

# STAGE 24
*Poggio San Lorenzo to Ponticelli Sabino*

| | |
|---|---|
| **Start** | Piazza Marconi, Poggio San Lorenzo |
| **Finish** | Piazza del Sole, Ponticelli Sabino |
| **Duration** | 6¼hr |
| **Distance** | 19.9km |
| **Total ascent** | 568m |
| **Total descent** | 732m |
| **Difficulty** | Moderately hard due to elevation changes |
| **Percentage paved** | 26% |
| **Lodgings** | Monteleone turn-off 5.6km, Poggio Moiano 10.4km, Ponticelli Sabino 19.9km |

Some steep climbs make this stage seem longer than it is, while spectacular mountain scenery and very pleasant walks through orchards, fields, and farms take your mind off the exertion. The goal is tiny, remote Ponticelli, served by only a sparse set of accommodations. Historic sites and small villages like Monteleone and Poggio Moiano – a logical lunch stop – are noteworthy diversions along the way. Olive groves are a constant companion, and don't be surprised by a resident flock of sheep on the route before Ponticelli. At Poggio Moiano, in 10.4km, you have the option of taking the variant route to the Abbey of Farfa (see Section 4A), adding about 13km to the total distance to Monterotondo.

## STAGE 24 – POGGIO SAN LORENZO TO PONTICELLI SABINO

From Piazza Marconi, walk downhill on the Via Quinzia leading out of town. At the children's play area, turn left, going downhill. At the following hairpin turn, you have the option of walking left just 50 meters to inspect the ancient brickwork of the Roman walls of San Lorenzo. Continue down the road on switchbacks leading to the valley floor, then head up the opposite side on a very steep climb where now you can look back on Poggio San Lorenzo high above. After you reach a summit, go back downhill again, this time emptying out onto the roadway of the **Via Salaria Vecchia** highway.

The signage points you to a pathway across the road, and you follow it heading downhill to **ford the stream** (Fosso delle Mole) on stones. Now begin your second big climb of the day, up nearly 200m to the SP35 roadway (**5.6km**). A right turn here leads in 750 meters to the town of **Monteleone Sabino** (café, restaurant, ● **B&B Santa Vittoria** O Pt R K Br Cf W S 6/14, €-/60/75/80/90 including breakfast, Via Trebula Mutuesca, 181, bbsantavittoria@gmail.com, www.bbsantavittoria.it, tel 347 5988875. Ask for pilgrim price). If not heading for Monteleone Sabino, turn left, pass a cemetery, and come to the entry of the **Trebula Mutuesca Archeological Park**.

> Scattered dwellings around a sanctuary to the Sabine goddess Feronia were aggregated into the Roman town of **Trebula Mutuesca** here in the 1st c. BC. Mentioned by Pliny and others, the town once included a forum, public offices, baths, and an amphitheater. The site was long deserted, but archeologists began excavations here in 2000 and portions of many of the buildings are now visible. Finds from the digs are kept at the Museo Archeologico Trebula Mutuesca in Monteleone (Via Lucio Mummio 11, Monteleone Sabino, www.museomonteleonesabino.it).

Follow the wide path through the park, then the trail at its end until coming to the road at the opposite side. Cross the road and come in 50 meters to the **Santuario di Santa Vittoria**.

> In the 5th-c. **Legend of Saint Victoria**, the Christian faith of a young girl of Trebula Mutuesca freed the region of a powerful dragon that had been terrorizing the population. Local pagan leaders martyred the girl, as she was unwilling to convert to their religion. Her remains were housed in the church, and local residents believe the waters of the spring here to be blessed, due to its proximity to the saint's tomb.
>
> The 12th-c. Santuario di Santa Vittoria was built on its 4th-c. predecessor, and many architectural details are preserved in its white stone facade, along with other artifacts from the Roman town which are kept on the lawn.

## THE WAY OF ST FRANCIS — VIA DI FRANCESCO

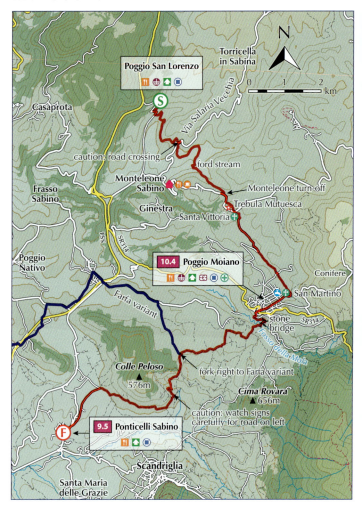

Continue down the road, passing memorials to partisans killed by Germans during World War II. Cross a small stream and afterward fork left, following signs, onto another narrower road that transits an area of vineyards. Go straight onto a

218

## STAGE 24 – POGGIO SAN LORENZO TO PONTICELLI SABINO

path when the road turns right and follow this road as it climbs up past the 10th-c. **Church of San Martino** (water, ⌂ **Ostello San Martino** – see Poggio Moiano below for lodging information) to the upper neighborhood of Poggio Moiano. Continue straight on through Piazza Papa Giovanni XXIII onto Via San Martino as it descends to the city center and comes to the town hall of **Poggio Moiano** (**4.8km**).

> **10.4KM POGGIO MOIANO** (ELEV 520M, POP 2797) 🍴 ⊕ ⌂ ⓔ ⓘ ⊕ (72.7KM)
> Relatively modern by Sabine standards, the town of Poggio Moiano first appears in records in 1083, but it is believed to have been a center for lumber products for a few centuries before. It was held variously by the Abbey of Farfa, then the Savelli, Orsini, and Borghese families of Rome.
>
> ⌂ **Ostello San Martino** Via San Martino, ostellosanmartino1@gmail.com tel 340 0807262. Norma is your host.

Turn left at the main piazza, pass to the left of the church, and head downhill on pink paving stones to the stream at the valley floor. Cross an ancient **stone arched bridge** and begin an extremely steep climb on concrete, gaining 100m in the next half kilometer. Finally, at the summit, the route becomes a pleasant, two-lane gravel road under trees. Continue in this wooded area among sheepfolds, until the route turns left to climb Colle Peloso (**3.8km**). You have now come to an important junction with the variant route to the Abbey at Farfa: a right turn takes you toward Farfa (see Section 4A), while a left turn takes you to Ponticelli.

Turn left and climb on gravel to the top of the ridge at 576m **Colle Peloso**. Wide vistas now open up among olive orchards, with mountains ahead. The road goes downhill on a series of switchbacks and in 1.8km comes to an intersection with barns for a sheep farm

*A gravel road among olive groves leads toward Ponticelli Sabino*

## THE WAY OF ST FRANCIS — VIA DI FRANCESCO

on the left. Take the rightmost turn onto the smaller, unmarked road, which is easily missed. Follow signs uphill now, with sweeping views of Scandriglia and the surrounding mountains to the left. Follow signs which take you first to a gravel road (go right) and then to an asphalt road (go left). Pass a cemetery on the right and walk downhill to the main piazza of **Ponticelli Sabino** (5.7km), just below its historic church and castle at the base of town.

### 9.5KM PONTICELLI SABINO (ELEV 300M, POP 515) (63.2KM)

Ponticelli may be more memorable for what is near it than for the tiny village itself. Across the valley is majestic Castello Orsini of the late Middle Ages, as well as the picturesque mountain town of Scandriglia. Ponticelli's Santa Maria delle Colle church has 6th c. roots. Its current construction features a simple Romanesque façade and interior frescoes of the 14–15th c.

♦ **Casale Il Viandante** Pr R K W S 4/10, €35/60/80/120, Via XX Settembre 13, cristina.stempel@gmail.com, tel 349 0914666. Open Mar–Oct. Breakfast at café is €5, dinner available at trattoria. Cristina is your host.

♦ **Casa di Riccardo** O Do R K Br Dr Cr W S 2/7, €Donation, Via Rieti 43, sabinaviva2015@gmail.com, tel 351 7803475, tel 076 589249. Above Bar Mariani, local food, mainly vegetarian. Riccardo and Patrizia of the Sabina Association are your hosts.

♦ **Apartment 1913** Pr R K Br Cr S Z 2/5, €-/60/70/80, Piazza Santa Maria al Colle 21, ilaria0107@gmail.com, tel 331 8538445. Open Apr–Oct. Breakfast included for pilgrims. Ilaria is your host. (Also site in Montelibretti.)

### FRANCIS AND CLARE

Younger than him by a dozen or so years, Clare of Assisi was drawn to the teachings of Francis. She met him several times, but on the night of Palm Sunday she left her parents' home and found her way to Francis and his companions. Francis and Clare established a second Franciscan Order, the Poor Clares, devoted to poverty in a cloistered life. Clare's order was given the Church of San Damiano in Assisi, and she lived a long life there, ultimately matching Francis in the esteem of others. Francis shared versions of his order with her, and of his 'Canticle of the Sun,' wanting her advice and approval.

When Francis died, his body was first taken to San Damiano so it could be viewed there by Clare. It then was taken to its first resting place at San Giorgio, where both Francis and Clare had been baptized as infants.

*Pilgrims descend a steep trail on the way to Ponticelli Sabino*

## STAGE 25
*Ponticelli Sabino to Monterotondo*

| | |
|---|---|
| **Start** | Piazza del Sole, Ponticelli Sabino |
| **Finish** | Duomo, Monterotondo |
| **Duration** | 8½hr |
| **Distance** | 29.4km |
| **Total ascent** | 536m |
| **Total descent** | 716m |
| **Difficulty** | Hard due to distance and elevation changes |
| **Percentage paved** | 70% |
| **Lodgings** | Acquaviva 7.7km, Montelibretti 12.8km, Monterotondo 29.4km |

Today you begin the transition from the Sabine mountains down into the widening Tiber Valley plain. This long and undulating stage on gravel and asphalt roads stretches through orchards and farmland, generally following the trajectory of the Roman Via Salaria and Via Nomentana while crossing the towns of Acquaviva and Montelibretti and the Macchia di Gattaceca Nature Reserve. The reward is central Monterotondo, a commuter town of Rome, with its characteristic pedestrian mall and old city. The town of Montelibretti makes an excellent overnight if you decide to divide the stage in two.

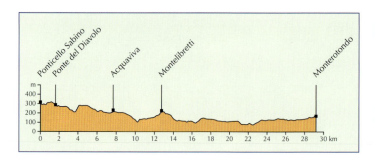

In the main piazza of Ponticelli, with the bar to your right, go straight ahead, walking downhill with the tall stone wall on your left. At the first fork, go steeply downhill to the right, aiming at the main road out of town. Follow signs to cross the road and continue onto Via San Martino, heading uphill. Soon arrive at the Via Salaria Vecchia roadway, which you cross, going downhill. Don't miss on the right side in 400 meters an interesting and ancient construction, the Roman bridge known as the **Ponte del Diavolo** (**1.6km**, rest area).

> While called a 'bridge,' the 3rd-c. BC **Ponte del Diavolo** is actually a retaining wall built to support the Via Salaria Vecchia while channeling a small stream below the roadway. The wall measures about 13 meters high and 20 meters long, and is made of a stack of substantial travertine blocks.

Continue along the road and come to the asphalt SP40 roadway in the village of **Poggio Corese** (no services), where you turn right and walk along the quiet

## THE WAY OF ST FRANCIS — VIA DI FRANCESCO

roadway for about 200 meters. Branch left here onto a path that takes you downhill before sending you back uphill on the Via Capo Croce to the **SP28a** roadway.

> A left turn here would take you in about 1km uphill to Nerola and its **Castello Orsini**, the monumental 15th-c. castle that you have seen since just before Ponticelli. Today, it is a posh wedding venue and luxury hotel (www.castellorsini.it).

Cross the road and continue on a series of paved and gravel roads, generally in a downhill direction, to meet the **SP636**. Turn right and come again to the SP28a, this time in the roadside village of **Acquaviva** (**6.1km**).

---

**7.7KM ACQUAVIVA (ELEV 218M, POP 756)** 🍴 ⛪ 🏠 ⓘ ✚ (55.5KM)
Though few signs exist today of its history, the village is thought to have been the seat of a bishop since antiquity.

🔻 **Nel Cuore della Sabina B&B** O Pr R K Br Dr W S 1/2, €40 per person, Via Probato Abate 22, provenzianicarla@gmail.com, tel 339 6185251, 327 0311729 Carla. Kitchen available for €10.

---

The Farfa route rejoins the main route just west of town, so be careful not to confuse markings to Farfa on the north side of the SP28a with the main route to Montelibretti on the south side of the road. A series of roads and paths through farmland now take you downhill below Montelibretti, and then back uphill, with buildings of the old town on the ridge to the left. Once you arrive at the valley

*Near Montelibretti the countryside begins to flatten out into the Tiber plateau*

## STAGE 25 – PONTICELLI SABINO TO MONTEROTONDO

floor, you begin one of the steep climbs of the stage, heading up the hill on asphalt to a ridgetop arm of suburban **Montelibretti** at the SP26a (**5.1km**, café, bakery, groceries. Turn left to find the center of town in about 700 meters).

**5.1KM MONTELIBRETTI (ELEV 232M, POP 5103)** (50.4KM)
A *comune* (community) in the Metropolitan City of Rome, Montelibretti was founded in Roman times. Over the centuries its castle was held by notable Roman families, including the Orsini, Barberini, and Sciarra.

🏠 **B&B I Due Gelsi** O Pr R K Br Cr S 4/9, €-/50/60/80, Via Garibaldi 23, bbi-duegelsi@gmail.com, tel 3476 412908, tel 346 1881485. Please notify host of arrival time.

🏠 **Apartments 1913** O Pr R K Br Cr W S Z 3/7, €-/45/68/85, Via Valle Dei Prati 60, ilaria0107@gmail.com, tel 3318 538445. Ilaria is your host.

🏠 **Il Tronchetto** Pr R K Br Cr W S 2/5, €-/40/70/100, Via Roma 160, tancredino-vella@gmail.com, tel 334 9599935, tel 0774 609830. Breakfast included.

🏠 **Il Rifugio di Noi** O Pr R K Br Dr Cr W S 2/7, €Donation, SP Pascolare 175, ilrifugiodinoi@gmail.com, tel 349 4245734. Tent camping available. Simona is your host.

Cross the road and veer right onto Via Vignacce, between the bar and bakery. Follow this asphalt road as it leads down and out of Montelibretti in a long descent. The towns of Palombara Sabina and Guidonia are visible on the distant hills to the left. Gravel roads then lead you among farms to the bottom

*Tickets on the wall at Marco's Bar in Montelibretti are receipts for bar patrons who are sponsoring a drink for thirsty pilgrims*

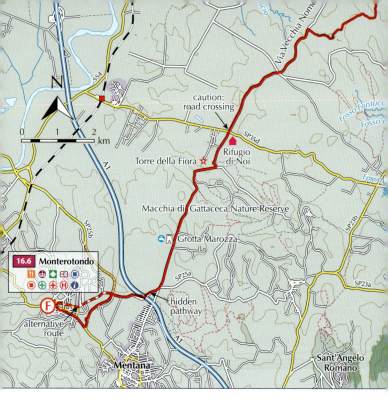

of the valley at the asphalt **Via Vecchia Nomentana**. Turn left here and begin a climb uphill on the roadway. The roadway flattens out as you cross a series of rural farm commodities warehouses and industrial estates. Merge with the Via dell'Osteria di Moricone and continue as you cross the **SP35d**. (A left turn on the SP35d leads you in a few hundred meters to ⛺ Il Rifugio di Noi – see Montelibretti above.)

The road now becomes the Via Santa Maria delle Camere, leading downhill into the Macchia di Gattaceca Nature Reserve. Turn right to proceed into the midst of the reserve, with the **Torre della Fiora** on your right.

The 996-hectare protected area of the **Macchia di Gattaceca Nature Reserve** safeguards agricultural and forest land between the Tiber River and the Cornicolani Mountains.

## STAGE 25 – PONTICELLI SABINO TO MONTEROTONDO

From the 13th c., the **Torre della Fiora** was part of the fortified village of Podium de Flora. This tall brick ruin is the most prominent of the remaining structures of the long-abandoned village.

The quiet of the countryside continues as the road rises to meet the Località di Ficorella and comes to the pink farmhouse and pastures of the Grottamarozza farm (water), just below the **Castello di Grotta Marozza**, which you pass on your right.

The settlement at **Grotta Marozza**, which flourished from Roman times until the Middle Ages, was likely abandoned in the 14th c. due to the effects of the Black Death. In the early 19th c. it became a private estate, and in 1924 it passed to Antonio Fratini, whose family still oversees the agricultural property.

The route continues straight ahead, now on asphalt under umbrella pines, although the quiet of the countryside is about to be disturbed by your first experience of the Roman suburbs. Monterotondo becomes visible on the hill straight ahead, but there are busy roads in between, including the A1 Autostrada del Sole freeway.

Come to the **SP25a**, a busy road, and follow it right. Carefully continue alongside the road for just 300 meters. Importantly, do not attempt to continue on the roadside of the SP25a; instead, enter the restaurant parking lot and find a **hidden pathway** that takes off above the roadway, before descending to the underpass sidewalk to cross below the A1. Continue on the pathway above the SP25a on the other side of the Autostrada. From here, connect through a gate to a pathway safely tucked on the north side of the road, away from traffic. Now follow the metal-grate sidewalk along the highway to the stoplight at the **SP25b**.

Here, you have a choice of two options for reaching the historic center of Monterotondo. On the official route, turn left onto a green **bike trail**, then right on the Via Nomentana to reach the center of town. Alternatively, to save a few hundred meters in distance, cross the SP25b and head uphill on the sidewalk of the SP25a to the town center.

The two routes converge at the west end of Monterotondo's Passeggiata pedestrian mall. Continue uphill to the Fontana del Cigno (Swan Fountain) and turn right, passing in front of the town hall at Palazzo Orsini. Walk round right from the back to the front of the Duomo of Santa Maria Maddalena in **Monterotondo (16.6km)**.

*The Way of St Francis — Via di Francesco*

**16.6KM MONTEROTONDO** (ELEV 165M, POP 41,027) 🍴 🏨 🛖 Ⓒ ⦿ ⦿ ⊕ ✚ ⓗ ⓘ (33.8KM)

Although the site of the ancient city of Eretum is just to the north, the city of Monterotondo itself is not mentioned in historical documents until the 11th c. In its early centuries, the town and its fortress were properties of the Capocci and then Orisini families. In the 17th c., the Barberini family acquired the town, and the grand **Palazzo Orsini-Barberini** still dominates its center, now serving as the town hall. The 17th-c. **Basilica of Santa Maria Maddalena** faces the central street of the old city, and on its ceiling are frescoes by Domenico Piestrini.

Now a commuter town of Rome, Monterotondo bustles with people of all ages in the *passeggiata* – the Italian evening stroll – either on a lower course that leads from Palazzo Orsini-Barberini downhill along the north side of Via Bruno Buozzi, or on an upper course among the restaurants, pizzerias, and *gelato* shops of the old city on Via Cavour, between the basilica and Piazza dei Leoni.

🔺 **La Cupella B&B** Via Vincenzo Bellini 36, info@lacupella.it, tel 338 4224137.

🔺 **B&B SáDi** O Pr R K Br Cr 1/4, €-/60/65/90/115, Via Nazario Sauro 17, info@bbsadi.it, www.bbsadi.it, tel 351 8578371. €5 pilgrim discount. Bruno is your host.

🔺 **L'Alighieri B&B** Pr R Br Cr 3/8, €-/70/75/100, Via Dante Alighieri 27, hello@lalighieri.it, www.lalighieri.it, tel 333 4146459. Closed Aug. Pamela is your host.

🔺 **Casa di Sasha** O Pr R Br S 3/6, €30/person including breakfast, Via Massimo Pelosi 15, ritabizzarri@libero.it, tel 328 3760262. Rita is your host.

## YOUNG FRANCIS AND THE BEGGARS

Before Francis began his ministry, he had an unusual attachment to people who were poor. It is said that, while he was selling his father's cloth at the marketplace, a person in need asked him for alms. Francis immediately gave the poor person everything he had received from his sales. A sincere, devout, and economically poor man lived in Assisi, and he is said to have taken off his cloak each time he saw Francis and laid it on the ground for Francis to walk on, as a sign of respect for the future saint.

# STAGE 26
*Monterotondo to Monte Sacro*

| | |
|---|---|
| **Start** | Duomo, Monterotondo |
| **Finish** | Piazza Sempione, Monte Sacro, Rome |
| **Duration** | 5½hr |
| **Distance** | 18.9km |
| **Total ascent** | 286m |
| **Total descent** | 401m |
| **Difficulty** | Moderate due to elevation changes |
| **Percentage paved** | 89% |
| **Lodgings** | Monte Sacro 18.9km |

The first half of the stage is a refreshing walk through farmlands, while the second half becomes a suburban slog into the busy and somewhat bleak suburbs of Rome. On the other hand, the bars, restaurants, and *gelato* shops offer many options for a refreshing respite. Signage now becomes stickers on posts; while the directions are quite simple, the stickers will confirm you are heading the right way.

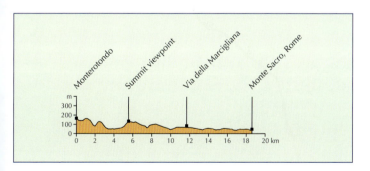

Retrace your route from yesterday, heading to the back of the Duomo, past the Swan Fountain, and down the Passeggiata. At the Fausto Cecconi Arch, turn right and walk uphill on Via Fausto Cecconi. Note the grocery store below and to the right in 100 meters. Continue up the hill and, just after the Convento Frati Cappuccini on the left, take the right fork that continues uphill. In 200 meters

229

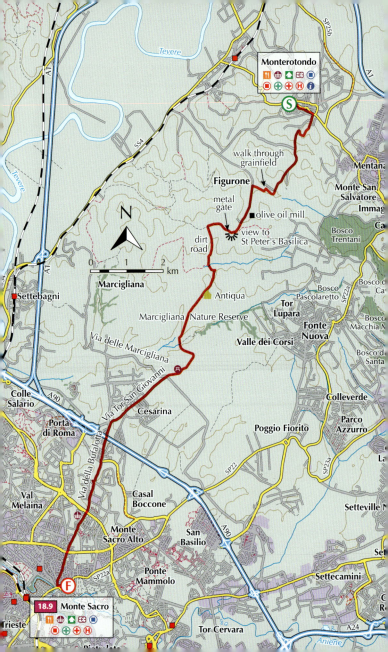

## STAGE 26 – MONTEROTONDO TO MONTE SACRO

arrive at a summit, where you can look ahead to the rolling hills you will travel today and tomorrow to Rome.

Walk downhill and in another 100 meters turn right onto Dei Frati Minori. Follow signs continuing downhill on Via Sant'Angelo, where you descend first into a narrow valley with homes along the hillsides. The road ascends steeply before making a hard right turn among farms and wide **grainfields** at the valley floor. Instead of turning right onto the street, turn left to pick up a path among the fields, which will take you around to the right, circling behind a row of homes.

Come to a street in the village of **Figurone** (no services). Turn left when the street ends and begin a walk uphill on the Via di Valle Ricca asphalt road. Pass an **olive oil mill** and arrive at the summit (**5.9km**), where the road ends. On a clear day from here you can see the dome of St Peter's Basilica in the far distance. Turn right and come to a closed **metal gate** at a neighborhood of large homes on acreage. Pass around the gate and continue on the gravel road. In about 1 km, turn left onto an often-unmarked dirt road that leads downhill into the **Marcigliana Nature Reserve**.

The **Marcigliana Nature Reserve** covers more than 4000 hectares, preserving agricultural lands and archeological sites between the Via Salaria and Via Nomentana on the left bank of the Tiber. Roman villas and scattered medieval villages dotted the countryside in this vast, rolling terrain. Most notable of the remains are two 16th–17th-c. towers, Torre San Giovanni and Torre della Marcigliana.

*Pilgrims walk among fields in the Marcigliana Nature Reserve after Monterotondo*

*The Way of St Francis — Via di Francesco*

Continue on this road among woods, fields, and the occasional lodging. Pass a **picnic area** and then finally come to a stop sign where the road ends at **Via della Marcigliana** (**6.0km**). Farmlands, vineyards, and olive groves are now all behind you as you enter **Cesarina**, the first of Rome's ring of suburbs.

Go straight ahead, following the sidewalk on **Via Tor San Giovanni** past strip malls with the occasional café. Veer to the left as the road joins the busy **Via della Bufalotta**, which merges from the right and becomes your primary route into Monte Sacro. Follow this road under the **A90 freeway** overpass and remain on it in a generally downhill trajectory while enjoying the plethora of shops and cafés available from its sidewalks. Cross the Viale Jonio, where the road becomes the Viale Adriatico, continuing downhill to its end at a maze of streets before the bridge across the Aniene River. The stage ends with a left turn here and a one-block walk into Piazza Sempione and the Chiesa dei Santi Angeli Custodi in **Monte Sacro** (**6.9km**).

---

**18.9KM MONTE SACRO** (ELEV 40M, POP 58,685)
(15.0KM)

Monte Sacro is the 16th *quartiere* (quarter) of Rome, sitting on the far north-northeast edge of the metropolis. The name derives from the ancient sacrifices and auguries made at this low ridge above the Aniene River. The Ponte Nomentano across the Aniene was one of the strategic entries into Rome. The area reached notoriety in the Plebeian Revolt of 494BC, when the lower classes took up residence at Monte Sacro in rebellion against the Patricians. During the Middle Ages the area was largely depopulated, but with urbanization it was incorporated into metropolitan Rome, at first under the name Garden City and then, in 1951, under its new-old name, Monte Sacro.

The 20th-c. **Chiesa dei Santi Angeli Custodi** replaces an earlier building demolished in the late 1920s. Frescoes painted by Aaron del Vecchio in 1962 richly adorn the vault.

♠ **Casa Dino** O Pr R K Br Dr W 1/2, €Donation, Via Val Chisone 35, gherardodinoruggiero@gmail.com, tel 338 7965614. Room in private home. Linens provided. Gherardo is your host.

♠ **Holiday Home Roma Casa Vacanze** O Pr R K Br 2/5, €Donation, Via di Montesacro 20, dora.antonini@gmail.com, tel 347 3662814. Dora is your host.

♠ **Galatea's House** Via dei Monti Lepini 2, barbarasimari@gmail.com, tel 333 1520473, Hospitality in private home.

*Stage 26 – Monterotondo to Monte Sacro*

### THE CANONIZATION OF FRANCIS

After the death of Francis, Pope Gregory IX was already convinced of Francis' case for canonization as a saint. Still, he had documents drawn up that attested to miracles and he sent the documents to other prelates, asking for concurrence. It was unanimously agreed that Francis deserved the title of 'saint,' and his canonization ceremony was held on 16 July 1228, a mere 21 months after his death. Two years later, his body was transferred to the crypt of a new basilica designed by Brother Elias of Cortona and built in his honor.

*Monte Sacro's Chiesa dei Santi Angeli Custodi (Holy Guardian Angels)*

# THE WAY OF ST FRANCIS — VIA DI FRANCESCO

## STAGE 27
*Monte Sacro to Vatican City, Rome*

| | |
|---|---|
| **Start** | Piazza Sempione, Monte Sacro, Rome |
| **Finish** | Piazza San Pietro, Vatican City, Rome |
| **Duration** | 4hr (3.5hr via park route) |
| **Distance** | 15.0km (12.3km via park route) |
| **Total ascent** | 59m (161m via park route) |
| **Total descent** | 66m (169m via park route) |
| **Difficulty** | Easy (easy via park route) |
| **Percentage paved** | 92% (71% via park route) |
| **Lodgings** | Rome 15.0km |

Today's walk is full of excitement as you transit Rome, unarguably one of the great cities of the world, on your way to the capital of Christendom at Vatican City. The official route avoids much of the noise and traffic of urban Rome by guiding you alongside parks and then across the Tiber (Tevere) at Ponte Milvio, along the channeled Tiber River on the Lungotevere bike/pedestrian route. An alternative way goes directly through Rome's largest parks to enjoy a few urban, pilgrim-oriented highlights like Piazza del Popolo and Via dei Coronari. For both routes, St Peter's Basilica at the Vatican is the emotional climax of the entire walk. Food and other services are available within a few blocks all along the way.

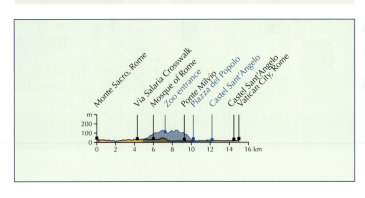

## STAGE 27 – MONTE SACRO TO VATICAN CITY, ROME

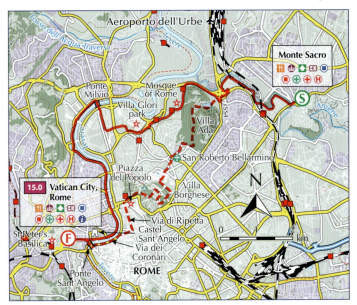

With your back to Santi Angeli Custodi Church, walk straight ahead along the Corso Sempione and cross the Viale Tirreno. Cross the **Aniene River** on the Ponte Tazio and immediately turn right onto the bike path. This will lead you all the way to a cloverleaf complex of roads where the Via Salaria (now a major arterial) crosses the Circonvallazione Salaria *autostrada* (freeway). Carefully follow signs that lead you alongside the first automobile access roadway, then right, under the Circonvallazione roadway. Follow alongside a second set of access roadways and turn left at the **SS4** (Via Salaria). Walk two blocks and then cross the arterial at the stoplight on the Via Salaria (**4.1km**), where you have an important choice.

### Official route

Turn right and follow the roadside bike path as it winds around the Monte Antenne park, passing the **Mosque of Rome** on your right. Pass the aqua fitness center on your left and continue alongside the **Villa Glori** park. The park and neighborhood have several restaurants and bars. Come to the Viale Pilsudski, which you follow as it veers right alongside the park and its equestrian center. Take the first right onto Via Giulio Gaudini and then the first left onto Viale Pietro de Coubertin, where you enter the Parco della Musica with its auditoriums on the left.

235

*The Way of St Francis — Via di Francesco*

Join the bike path again as it goes under the highway overpass on the south side of the domed Palazzetto dello Sport. Turn right onto Via Tiziano, adjacent to a children's park and its giant red geometric sculpture. Cross the **Ponte Milvio** bridge and head down to the Lungotevere bike trail along the Tiber River. Continue all the way to **Castel Sant'Angelo** (**10.2km**), where you meet the alternative route.

### Park route via Villa Ada and Villa Borghese

At the Via Salaria, instead of taking the bike path to the right, head down a sloping access lane, through a parking lot, and come to the entrance to the **Villa Ada** park. Upon entering the park, go left of Lago Villa Ada and, after a field, pick up a wide trail that heads directly south through woods in the park. The trail through the park is busy and safe with many pedestrians and cyclists.

*Ponte Milvio, scene of one of the pivotal battles of the late Roman Empire, is a traditional pilgrimage entry point to Rome*

The southern terminus of all the north–south trails is the park boundary along Via Panama. Once you reach it, turn right, and two blocks later come to the **Church of San Roberto Bellarmino**. Immediately across from the church, take Viale Gioacchino Rossini south, in just two long blocks coming to the **zoo** (Bioparco di Roma) at the north end of **Villa Borghese** park (**7.3km**, restaurants and food kiosks). There is much to explore here, and the atmosphere on a sunny afternoon is relaxed and vibrant.

In the 17th c., **Cardinal Scipione Borghese** began to transform his vineyard into extensive gardens. Today, the 80-hectare property is the most lively and beautiful of Rome's extensive park system. Inside the park are many gardens, a replica of Shakespeare's Globe theater, and two important museums: the Galleria Borghese in Villa Borghese, which contains works by Bernini, Caravaggio, Raphael, Titian, and Rubens; and the National Gallery of Modern Art, with important works by Italian and other European artists.

## STAGE 27 – MONTE SACRO TO VATICAN CITY, ROME

Continue in a generally southwest direction to the park's boundary at Viale Guardia, where you descend on a sidewalk to come to the Porta Flaminia gate, commonly used by pilgrims to enter Rome. Turn left, pass Santa Maria del Popolo, and enter **Piazza del Popolo**.

> Redesigned in the 19th c., the large urban square of **Piazza del Popolo** features the ancient 24m-tall obelisk of Rameses II, brought to Rome in 10BC by order of Augustus. Between the twin churches opposite the Porta Flaminia is the Via del Corso, the main commercial street of Rome. Behind is the Church of Santa Maria del Popolo, an ancient church and chapel of a former Augustinian monastery, which today is perhaps most famous for housing two precious Caravaggio canvases, the *Conversion of Saint Paul* and the *Crucifixion of Saint Peter*.

Proceed through the square, forking right onto **Via di Ripetta**. Pass between the Museo dell'Ara Pacis (https://ara-pacis-museum.com), which houses an ancient Roman altar, and the **Mausoleum of Augustus**.

> Built in 28BC by Emperor Augustus to celebrate his conquests, the **Mausoleum** fell into decay for centuries. After extensive renovations, it opened to visitors in 2021 (www.mausoleodiaugusto.it/en).

Continue on Via Ripetta until you turn right on Via di San Agostino. Pass the northern entrance to **Piazza Navona**, noting the archeological exhibit to the right that shows part of its buried structure.

> **Piazza Navona**, one of the best-loved public squares in Rome, was originally the site of the 1st-c. AD Stadium of Domitian and still retains the oblong form of its racecourse. Today, the square houses the famous Fountain of the Four Rivers by Bernini.

Continue along San Agostino as it now becomes Via dei Coronari, which includes mostly 15th–16th-c. buildings and preserves the character of Rome during the period of the Renaissance. The name Via dei Coronari derives from the selling here of *corone* (rosary beads) and other Christian miniatures and holy objects. After a relaxing stroll along this shaded and pleasant Roman street, turn right at its end to come in one block to **Ponte Sant'Angelo**.

> Built by the Emperor Hadrian in AD134 to serve his Mausoleum, the five-arched **Ponte Sant'Angelo** retains three of its original, ancient Roman arches. Today, the bridge is adorned with replicas of statues commissioned to Bernini, depicting ten angels holding the instruments of the Passion of Christ.

## THE WAY OF ST FRANCIS — VIA DI FRANCESCO

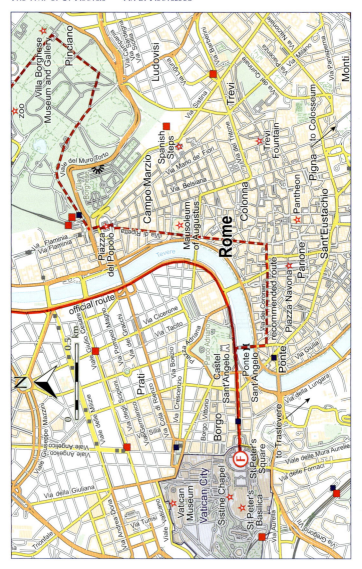

## STAGE 27 – MONTE SACRO TO VATICAN CITY, ROME

Cross the bridge and continue straight ahead to join the official route at **Castel Sant'Angelo**.

Once Hadrian's Mausoleum, the **Castel Sant'Angelo** became a fortress of the popes in the 5th c., and later a prison. Today, it houses the National Museum of Castel Sant'Angelo, with displays about its history (http://castelsantangelo.beniculturali.it).

Both routes now proceed west to come to the **Vatican City** and **St Peter's Square** (**0.6km**).

### 15.0KM VATICAN CITY, ROME (ELEV 21M, POP 2,746,382) (0.0KM)

St Peter's Basilica, completed in the 17th c., is the crown jewel of Vatican City, the capital of the Roman Catholic Church, a tiny and independent country in its own right, and one of the most celebrated pilgrimage destinations in the world. The Vatican's 44 hectares hold the Vatican Museum and Library, which include unsurpassed collections of art and literature accumulated over the last 2000 years. The Vatican, of course, is home to the Pope, and from here he leads a church of some 1.3 billion adherents.

A tour of the Vatican begins within the 17th-c. colonnade around St Peter's Square, designed by the sculptor Bernini. At the center is an ancient Egyptian obelisk (circa 2400BC) known as 'The Witness,' which originally stood at the Circus of Nero and is believed to have witnessed the crucifixion of St Peter. The vast square surrounds the obelisk and fountains, and atop the colonnade that rings the square are 140 statues of saints and martyrs. You will find the statue of St Clare of Assisi as the tenth from the right on the square's north (right) side, with Francis of Assisi the nineteenth.

Opening to the piazza are the doors of St Peter's Basilica, a marvel of architecture and one of the largest churches in the world. Rebuilt on the site of the 4th-c. church built for Constantine, which itself was built over the traditional site of St Peter's tomb, the building of the 'new' St Peter's spanned 120 years, beginning in 1506. Most famous of its architects was Michelangelo, who designed the massive dome that can be seen from throughout Rome. His *Pietà* sculpture is on the right aisle of the nave.

Pilgrims for centuries rubbed the foot of the bronze statue of St Peter by Cambio, also in the nave, but this practice was recently ended since over the centuries the bronze had nearly been rubbed off. For €7 it is possible to walk through the inside of the dome, 551 steps above to the cupola to enjoy its unparalleled view of Rome and its environs. Note that strict adherence to modesty is required in the Vatican,

The monumental scale and intricate decoration of St Peter's Basilica can be seen from this side entry to the Vatican

## STAGE 27 – MONTE SACRO TO VATICAN CITY, ROME

and shoulders and knees must be covered. It is wise to purchase the €16 tickets for the famed Vatican Museum and Sistine Chapel in advance at www.museivaticani.va.

A *testimonium* completion certificate is given to those with a completed credential documenting at least 100km of walking to Rome (although members of staff are not diligent in confirming the distance). You can skip the line by going directly to the metal detector under the colonnade at St Peter's Square and showing your credential. After the security check, go toward the front doors of the basilica, but turn right before the steps to the coat check area and look for the security guards or a reception volunteer in a yellow vest. Introduce yourself as a pilgrim and show your credential; they will welcome you, congratulate you for your walk, give you a short, written questionnaire, then will fill out a *testimonium* certificate for you as a keepsake of your achievement. It's common then to take a photo of yourself with your *testimonium* inside the basilica. You've earned this moment of joy, and it's quite an achievement to have walked to Rome.

🔺 **Spedale della Divina Provvidenza di San Giacomo e Benedetto Labre** O Do Br Dr S 2/24, €Donation, Via dei Genovesi 11-B, segreteria@pellegriniaroma.it, www.pellegriniaroma.com, tel 353 4286139. 2 night max. Rome's main walking pilgrimage hostel.

🔺 **Casa per Ferie Santa Maria alle Fornaci** O Pr R Br Cr S Z 54/108, €-/80/110/180, Piazza Santa Maria alle Fornaci 27, info@santamariafornaci.com, www.santamariaallefornaci.it, tel: 0696 044811, 0696 044812. Religious accommodation with hotel rooms.

Bike pedestrian lanes make up much of the route from Monte Sacro to the Vatican.

## THE WAY OF ST FRANCIS — VIA DI FRANCESCO

### FRANCIS IS CALLED TO ROME

The religious authorities in Rome took notice of Francis and his growing band of followers, and, in his biggest test, Francis was summoned in 1210 by Pope Innocent III to explain his unauthorized gospel ministry. When he appeared in Rome with his scruffy band of followers at St John Lateran, the Pope's cathedral, the Pope is said to have uttered in disgust at their appearance, 'Why don't you go roll with the pigs? You look like you belong to them!' The band left to spend the night with the pigs, and came back the next day, smeared in mud from the pigsty.

Aptly remembered as one of the wisest of all popes, Innocent then carefully pondered the ragged man in the tattered brown robe before him. Afterward, in a dream, the Pope saw Francis holding up the pillars of his church, which was tottering in an earthquake. The next morning he gave his blessing and Francis began a preaching mission that would send him across the Western world. Historians attest that Innocent III's approval of Francis reset the priorities of the Church and reminded it to attend to nature, to deep prayer, and to the needs of the poor.

*St Francis and his followers are depicted in this statue across from the Church of St John Lateran where they met Pope Innocent III in 1209*

# SECTION 4A: VARIANT ROUTE TO MONTEROTONDO

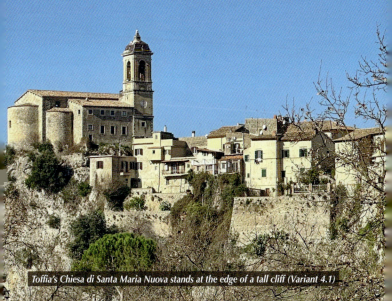

*Toffia's Chiesa di Santa Maria Nuova stands at the edge of a tall cliff (Variant 4.1)*

THE WAY OF ST FRANCIS — VIA DI FRANCESCO

## VARIANT 4.1
Poggio San Lorenzo to Monterotondo via Farfa Abbey

| | |
|---|---|
| **Start** | Piazza Marconi, Poggio San Lorenzo |
| **Finish** | Duomo, Monterotondo |
| **Duration** | 18½hr (2–3 days) |
| **Distance** | 62.2km |
| **Total ascent** | 1436m |
| **Total descent** | 1785m |
| **Difficulty** | Moderately hard due to elevation changes |
| **Percentage paved** | 59% |
| **Lodgings** | Osteria Nuova 17.8km, Toffia 26.1km, Farfa Abbey 29.6km, Fara in Sabina 31.5km, Monterotondo 62.2km |

While this option adds 13km to the distance from Poggio San Lorenzo to Monterotondo on the main route, it offers some interesting sites, particularly the villages of Toffia and Fara in Sabina as well as the historic Farfa Abbey, tucked away for centuries on an olive-clad mountainside. The route undulates in 100m bumps, except for the 300m climb after Toffia to Fara in Sabina.

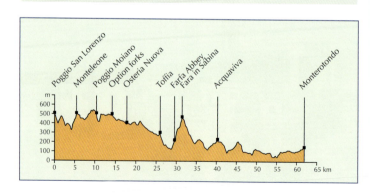

244

## Variant 4.1 – Poggio San Lorenzo to Monterotondo via Farfa Abbey

This option splits from the main route at the start of the climb up Colle Peloso, 3.8km after Poggio Moiano, and then heads over farm and secondary roads to Osteria Nuova, Collano, and Toffia. It then climbs to Fara in Sabina, a walled city high above the surrounding hills and valleys, from which it descends to the main route, merging with it at Acquaviva. While there are intermediate options, the primary staging plan for this interesting variant to historic Farfa Abbey is:

### Stage 1: Poggio San Lorenzo to Farfa Abbey (29.6KM)
Intermediate stays are possible in **Toffia**: ▲ La Casetta di Col di Melo O Pr R K Br Dr Gr W S Z 4/8, €Donation, Loc. Col di Melo, nadah.spreafico@gmail.com, tel 334 3388900, tel 076 326285. Nadah is your host. ▲ Monti degli Elci B&B O Pr R K Br Dr W S Z 4/8, €-/50/70/90, Via Farense 33, claudiazonetti@gmail.com, tel 347 4747012. Dinner and bag transport available by reservation. Claudia is your host.

Overnights at **Farfa**: ▲ Abbazia di Farfa O Pr R Br Dr S 20/40, €40/person including breakfast or €50/person includes half-board, Via del Monastero 1, men: farenprior@libero.it, groups: suorefarfa@brigidine.org, www.abbaziadifarfa.it, tel 0765 277087, 0765 277065.

### Stage 2: Farfa Abbey to Monterotondo (32.6KM)
Intermediate accommodation is available in **Fara in Sabina** at the historic Clarisse Monastery: ▲ Monastero delle Clarisse Eremite Via Santa Maria in Castello 4, clarisse.farasabina@libero.it, danielinapos@yahoo.it, tel 329 6061580. Religious accommodation.

The route rejoins the main route just west of **Acquaviva**: see Stage 25 for map and route description from Acquaviva to Monterotondo.

# APPENDIX A
## *Stage planning table*

| Book stage | Location | Distance from start | Distance from previous | Stage distance | Your itinerary |
|---|---|---|---|---|---|
| 1 | **Florence** | **0.0** | | | |
| 2 | **Pontassieve** | **18.4** | **18.4** | **18.4** | |
| | Diacceto | 24.3 | 5.9 | | |
| | Ferrano | 27.9 | 3.6 | | |
| 3 | **Consuma** | **35.2** | **7.3** | **16.8** | |
| | Gualdo | 38.0 | 2.8 | | |
| | Villa (turn-off) | 42.3 | 4.2 | | |
| | SP75 Castel Castagnaio | 43.6 | 1.4 | | |
| 4 | **Stia** | **49.7** | **6.1** | **14.6** | |
| | Lonnano | 54.4 | 4.7 | | |
| | Casalino turn-off | 56.5 | 2.1 | | |
| | Fork to Valagnesi | 57.5 | 1.0 | | |
| | Rifugio Asqua | 60.8 | 3.3 | | |
| | Camaldoli | 66.0 | 5.2 | | |
| | Rifugio Cotozzo | 67.8 | 1.8 | | |
| | Rifugio Casanova | 72.8 | 5.0 | | |
| 5 | **Badia Prataglia** | **73.6** | **0.8** | **23.8** | |
| | Santicchio (turn-off) | 81.3 | 7.7 | | |
| | Biforco (turn-off) | 83.8 | 2.5 | | |
| 6 | **Santuario della Verna** | **89.5** | **5.7** | **15.9** | |
| 7 | **Pieve Santo Stefano** | **104.1** | **14.6** | **14.6** | |
| | Cerbaiolo | 109.7 | 5.7 | | |
| | Passo Viamaggio | 113.5 | 3.7 | | |
| | Pian della Capanna | 120.2 | 6.7 | | |
| | Il Palazzo B&B | 125.7 | 5.5 | | |
| 8 | **Montagna** | **126.7** | **1.1** | **22.6** | |
| | Montecasale | 132.1 | 5.4 | | |
| | San Martino d'Afra | 133.7 | 1.6 | | |
| 9 | **Sansepolcro** | **137.9** | **4.2** | **11.2** | |

## APPENDIX A – STAGE PLANNING TABLE

| Book stage | Location | Distance from start | Distance from previous | Stage distance | Your itinerary |
|---|---|---|---|---|---|
|  | Zoccolanti | 149.2 | 11.3 |  |  |
| 10 | **Citerna** | **150.1** | **0.9** | **12.2** |  |
|  | Agriturismo Le Burgne | 155.1 | 4.9 |  |  |
|  | Lerchi | 160.7 | 5.6 |  |  |
| 11 | **Città di Castello** | **169.2** | **8.6** | **19.1** |  |
|  | Candeggio | 182.8 | 13.5 |  |  |
|  | Pieve de' Saddi | 188.5 | 5.7 |  |  |
| 12 | **Pietralunga** | **197.9** | **9.5** | **28.7** |  |
|  | Borgo San Benedetto turn-off | 201.0 | 3.1 |  |  |
|  | Loreto | 213.7 | 12.7 |  |  |
| 13 | **Gubbio** | **224.1** | **10.4** | **26.2** |  |
|  | Ponte di Riocchio | 232.9 | 8.8 |  |  |
|  | Brocca di Valdichiascio | 235.1 | 2.1 |  |  |
|  | Casalotto Francescano | 235.6 | 0.5 |  |  |
|  | Il Beccafico | 236.9 | 1.3 |  |  |
| 14 | **Valdichiascio** | **240.1** | **3.2** | **15.9** |  |
|  | Tenuta di Biscina | 245.2 | 5.2 |  |  |
|  | Agriturismo Borgo Sambuco | 252.5 | 7.3 |  |  |
| 15 | **Valfabbrica** | **260.9** | **8.3** | **20.8** |  |
|  | Agriturismo Il Pioppo | 262.7 | 1.8 |  |  |
| 16 | **Assisi** | **274.1** | **11.4** | **13.2** |  |
| 17 | **Spello** | **286.8** | **12.9** | **12.9** |  |
|  | Foligno | 293.3 | 6.4 |  |  |
| 18 | **Trevi** | **305.9** | **12.6** | **19.0** |  |
|  | Poreta | 317.7 | 11.7 |  |  |
|  | Bazzano Superiore | 325.2 | 7.5 |  |  |
| 19 | **Spoleto** | **333.0** | **7.8** | **27.1** |  |
|  | Monteluco | 335.5 | 2.5 |  |  |
|  | Ceselli | 347.6 | 12.2 |  |  |
| 20 | **Macenano (turn-off)** | **352.7** | **5.1** | **19.7** |  |
|  | Arrone | 362.4 | 9.7 |  |  |
|  | Casteldilago (turn-off) | 364.3 | 1.8 |  |  |

## THE WAY OF ST FRANCIS — VIA DI FRANCESCO

| Book stage | Location | Distance from start | Distance from previous | Stage distance | Your itinerary |
|---|---|---|---|---|---|
|  | Marmore | 370.6 | 6.4 |  |  |
| 21 | **Piediluco** | **376.1** | **5.5** | **23.4** |  |
|  | Labro | 381.0 | 4.9 |  |  |
| 22 | **Poggio Bustone** | **397.0** | **16.0** | **20.9** |  |
|  | San Felice all'Acqua | 406.2 | 9.2 |  |  |
|  | La Foresta | 408.5 | 2.3 |  |  |
| 23 | **Rieti** | **414.0** | **5.5** | **17.0** |  |
|  | Ornaro Basso (turn-off) | 428.7 | 14.7 |  |  |
|  | Torricella in Sabina (turn-off) | 432.1 | 3.5 |  |  |
| 24 | **Poggio San Lorenzo** | **434.4** | **2.3** | **20.5** |  |
|  | Poggio Moiano | 444.8 | 10.4 |  |  |
| 25 | **Ponticelli Sabino** | **454.4** | **9.5** | **19.9** |  |
|  | Montelibretti | 467.2 | 12.8 |  |  |
| 26 | **Monterotondo** | **483.8** | **16.6** | **29.4** |  |
| 27 | **Monte Sacro, Rome** | **502.6** | **18.9** | **18.9** |  |
|  | **Vatican City, Rome** | **517.6** | **15.0** | **15.0** |  |

# APPENDIX B
*Useful contacts*

**Websites with lodging information**
Gronze.com
www.gronze.com/camino-san-francesco
(from Rome north to Assisi and from La Verna south to Assisi)

Network Association of the Via di Francesco in Lazio (lodging info from Poggio Bustone to Rome)
www.viadifrancescolazio.it

I Cammini di Francesco in Casentino (lodging info from Florence to Santuario della Verna)
www.viadifrancescofirenzelaverna.it

Caminoist (website of the author with updated lodging information)
https://caminoist.org/stfranciswaylodginglist

**Tourist information offices**
Additional information on lodging and sites of interest can be requested at tourist information offices along the way. As Italian government agencies, these offices can provide information about commercial hotels and campgrounds, but not unlicensed parochial or private hostels.

**Florence**
There are five provincial tourist information offices, including at Amerigo Vespucci airport (tel 055 315874, infoaeroporto@firenzeturismo.it) and across from Santa Maria Novella train station (Piazza Stazione 4, tel 055 212245, turismo3@comune.fi.it)

**Stia**
Municipal tourist office in nearby Pratovecchio (Piazza Maccioni 1, tel 0575 504877, anagrafe.pratovecchio@casentino.toscana.it)

**Camaldoli village**
Tourist information office of the Casentino National Forest (tel 0575 556130, cv.camaldoli@parcoforestecasentinesi.it) with park ranger staff members, an ornithological museum, books, and National Forest maps

**Badia Prataglia**
Tourism information office for the National Forest (Via Nazionale 14a, tel 0575 559477, cv.badiaprataglia@parcoforestecasentinesi.it)

**Sansepolcro**
Tourism office of the province of Arezzo, Valtiberina region (Via Matteotti 8, tel 0575 740536, info@valtiberinaintoscana.it)

**Città di Castello**
An office of the Umbria tourism department (Piazza Matteotti – Logge Bufalini, tel 0758 554922, info@iat.citta-di-castello.pg.it)

**Pietralunga**
A small municipal information office (Piazza Fiorucci 1, tel 0759 460721, commune@pietralunga.it)

### Gubbio
A municipal tourism office combined with the Umbria tourist office (Via della Repubblica 15, tel 0759 220693, info@iat.gubbio.pg.it)

### Assisi
Tourist information office of the region of Umbria (Piazza del Comune, tel 0758 138680, info@iat.assisi.pg.it)

### Spello
Municipal tourist information office (Piazza Matteotti 3, tel 0742 301009, info@prospello.it)

### Foligno
Tourism information office of the region of Umbria, on the main pedestrian street (Corso Cavour 126, tel 0742 354459, info@iat.foligno.pg.it)

### Trevi
Volunteer-run tourist information office, off Piazza Mazzini (Villa Fabri, tel 0742 332269, infoturismo@comune.trevi.pg.it)

### Spoleto
Municipal tourist information center. Provisional office at Largo Ferrer 6, open daily (tel 0743 218620, info@iat.spoleto.pg.it)

### Rieti
Municipal tourist information office in the city hall (Piazza Vittorio Emanuele II, tel 0746 488537, turismo@comune.rieti.it) and a tourist information office nearby for the region of Lazio (rieti@visitlazio.com)

### Monterotondo
Tourist information near the city hall (Piazza Libertà 30, tel 069 066683, prolocomonterotondo@libero.it) as well as a small, staffed kiosk on the Passeggiata (Viale Buozzi, tel 069 0622552)

### Rome
Rome has many large and small tourist offices. The main office is near the Repubblica metro station (Via Parigi 5, tel 060 60608, turismo@comune.roma.it). Smaller offices are near transportation centers like Fiumicino airport (Terminal 3) and Termini train station (Track 24, Via Giovanni Giolitti 34). In the historic center there are offices on Via Marco Minghetti (near the Piazza Venezia), near Piazza Navona (on Piazza delle Cinque Lune), near Castel Sant'Angelo (Piazza Pia) and near Santa Maria Maggiore (Via dell'Olmata).

## Public transport websites

### Bus
Tuscany
www.etruriamobilita.it

Umbria
www.umbriamobilita.it/servizio-di-trasporto-pubblico-locale

Lazio
www.cotralspa.it

Rieti area
www.asmrieti.it

### Train
Tren Italia (national train system)
www.trenitalia.com

## APPENDIX B – USEFUL CONTACTS

TFT (Upper Arno Valley system)
www.trasportoferroviariotoscano.it

**Pilgrim credential**
Ordering Via di Francesco *credenziale*:
piccolaccoglienzagubbio@gmail.com
www.piccolaccoglienzagubbio.it/contatti.html

**Italian language resources**
Italian grammar and vocabulary
https://onlineitalianclub.com

**Websites for other major St Francis pilgrim routes**
Cammino di Assisi
www.camminodiassisi.it/EN (English)

Di Qui Passò San Francesco
www.diquipassofrancesco.it/En (English)

Via di Francesco
www.viadifrancesco.it (Italian)

St Francis Sacred Valley (Rieti area)
www.camminodifrancesco.it (Italian and English)

Franciscan Trail (Diocese of Gubbio)
www.ilsentierodifrancesco.it (Italian)

**Emergency telephone numbers**
Remember always to use the Italian country code (39) if you are calling from a non-Italian number.

12 – Telephone directory assistance

112 – One-call emergency service phone line

113 – Direct line to local police

115 – Fire department

116 – Italian Automobile Club roadside assistance

117 – Finance police (if you've been cheated)

118 – Medical emergencies (ambulance)

1515 – Forest Fire Service

# APPENDIX C
## Language tips

English is commonly spoken in the tourist cities of Italy, but the opposite is true in rural areas. Here are some pronunciation tips and sample phrases that might help for those times when sign language won't do.

### Italian pronunciation guide

Unlike English, Italian pronunciation is very regular. If you follow these rules you'll be able to pronounce most all words.

| Letter | Sound | Example |
|---|---|---|
| Vowels | | |
| a | Like 'a' in 'father' | *mamma* |
| e | Like 'a' in 'say' | *sera* |
| i | Like 'e' in 'meet' | *amico* |
| o | Like 'o' in 'post' | *sole* |
| u | Like 'oo' in 'food' | *uno* |
| Single consonants | | |
| c | c – before an 'i' or 'e' always sounds like 'ch' in 'church' | *ciao* |
| c | c – unless before 'i' or 'e' like 'k' | *casa* |
| g | g – before 'i' or 'e' like 'g' in 'general' | *giorno* |
| g | g – always like 'g' in 'goal' unless before 'i' or 'e' | *gusto* |
| h | h – always silent | *hotel* |
| r | r – rolled like 'r' in Spanish | *Roma* |
| z | z – like 'ts' in 'cats' | *grazie* |
| Combined consonants | | |
| ch | like 'k' | *anche* |
| gh | like 'g' in 'goal' | *spaghetti* |
| gli | like 'lli' in 'million' | *figlio* |
| gn | like 'nyuh' in 'canyon' | *gnocchi* |
| sc | before 'i' or 'e' like 'sh' in 'shut' | *pesce* |
| sc | like 'sk' in 'skip' unless before 'i' or 'e' | *scala* |

Emphasis in Italian generally goes on the syllable between a double consonant, for example *gatto* (GAH-toe 'cat'), *dubbio* (DOOB-ee-o 'doubt'), *freddo* (FRAY-doe 'cold').

## Appendix C – Language tips

**Here are some basic useful phrases:**

| | |
|---|---|
| *Good morning (or good day)* | Buongiorno |
| *Thank you* | Grazie |
| *Thank you very much* | Grazie tante |
| *You're welcome* | Prego |
| *Please* | Per favore |
| *Yes* | Sì |
| *No* | No |
| *Excuse me* | Mi scusi |
| *I'm sorry* | Mi dispiace |
| *I don't understand* | Non capisco |
| *I don't speak Italian* | Non parlo italiano |
| *I don't speak Italian very well* | Non parlo molto bene italiano |
| *Do you speak English?* | Parla inglese? |
| *Speak slowly, please* | Parli piano, per favore |
| *Repeat, please* | Ripeta, per favore |
| *What's your name?* | Come si chiama? |
| *My name is…* | Il mil nome é… |
| *How are you?* | Come va? |
| *Where is the subway?* | Dov'è la metropolitana? |
| *Is the tip included?* | Il servizio è incluso? |
| *How much does that cost? (sg/pl)* | Quanto costa/costano? |
| *Do you have Wi-Fi?* | Avete Wi-Fi? (pronounced as in English) |
| *What is the password?* | Qual é la chiave? |
| *Can you help me?* | Mi può aiutare? |
| *Where is the bathroom?* | Dov'è la toilette? |
| *I would like to make a reservation* | Vorrei fare una prenotazione |
| *…for tonight* | …per stasera |
| *…for tomorrow night* | …per domani sera |
| *…for a single room* | …per una camera singola |
| *…for a double room* | …per una camera doppia |
| *…with a double bed* | …con un letto matrimoniale |
| *May I have a pilgrim stamp?* | Posso avere un timbro pellegrino? |
| *Is there a laundromat nearby?* | C'é una lavanderia nelle vicinanze? |
| *Do you have a laundry service?* | Avete un servizio di lavanderia? |
| *Is breakfast included?* | La colazione é inclusa? |

## THE WAY OF ST FRANCIS — VIA DI FRANCESCO

| | |
|---|---|
| *What time does the restaurant open?* | A che ora il ristorante aperto? |
| *What is the local specialty?* | Qual é la specialitá locale? |
| *May I have the check?* | Potrei avere il conto? |
| *I would like…* | Vorrei… |
| *Good evening* | Buonasera |
| *Good night* | Buonanotte |

*The narrow, medieval streets of Gubbio have helped earned it the distinction as one of the most beautiful towns in Italy (Stage 12)*

# APPENDIX D
*Index of St Francis stories*

| | |
|---|---|
| Stage 1 | Basilica Santa Croce; The early years of Francis |
| Stage 2 | Francis and nature ('Canticle of the Sun,' Part 1) |
| Stage 3 | Francis and the leper |
| Stage 4 | Francis hears 'Rebuild my church' |
| Stage 5 | Francis receives the stigmata at La Verna |
| Stage 6 | Francis and the dove seller |
| Stage 7 | A test of obedience |
| Stage 8 | The bandits of Montecasale |
| Stage 9 | Francis renounces his earthly possessions |
| Stage 10 | Francis experiences failure |
| Stage 11 | St Francis and Lady Poverty |
| Stage 12 | Francis and the wolf of Gubbio |
| Stage 13 | Francis retreats to Gubbio |
| Stage 14 | Francis learns a lesson in humility |
| Stage 15 | The death of Francis ('Canticle of the Sun,' Part 2) |
| Stage 16 | Francis preaches to the birds |
| Stage 17 | Francis sells his father's cloth |
| Stage 18 | A letter by Francis |
| Stage 19 | The flaming chariot |
| Stage 20 | Francis at Lago Piediluco |
| Stage 21 | The Beech Tree of St Francis; Revelation at Poggio Bustone |
| Stage 22 | The miracle of the wine; Francis at the Holy Valley of Rieti |
| Stage 23 | Francis and the Sultan |
| Stage 24 | Francis and Clare |
| Stage 25 | Young Francis and the beggars |
| Stage 26 | The canonization of Francis |
| Stage 27 | Francis is called to Rome |

# APPENDIX E
## *Further reading*

### Biography

Francis of Assisi and Clare of Assisi, *Francis and Clare: The Complete Works* (trans. Regis Armstrong, OFM CAP, and Ignatius Brady, OFM), Paulist Press, 1982. A compendium of all writings of these two beloved children of Assisi.

Saint Bonaventure, *The Life of St Francis of Assisi* (TAN Edition), St Benedict Press, 2010. Authoritative in the early days.

Thomas of Celano, *The First Life of St Francis*, Society for Promoting Christian Knowledge, 2000. The most influential of the historical biographies.

GK Chesterton, *St Francis of Assisi*, Hodder and Stoughton, 1923. A brief and inspirational biography.

Father Omer Englebert, *St Francis of Assisi: A Biography*, Franciscan Herald Press, 1965. The most comprehensive, authoritative, and readable of the hundreds of biographies.

Adrian House, *Francis of Assisi: A Revolutionary Life*, Hidden Spring, 2001. Modern and fact-filled, but quite readable. A little skeptical, but also reverent.

Paschal Robinson, *The Writings of St Francis of Assisi*, Dolphin Press, 1905. An adaptation of Robinson's translation of the Spoleto letter of St Francis is included in the text.

E Gurney Salter, *The Legend of Saint Francis by the Three Companions*, Forgotten Books, 2012. Attributed to Brothers Leo, Rufino, and Angelo as the first biography of Francis, written by witnesses to his life.

Augustine Thompson, *Francis of Assisi: A New Biography*, Cornell University Press, 2012. Well documented, thorough, and accessible.

*The Little Flowers of Saint Francis* (trans. Thomas Okey), Dover, 2003. A classic collection of St Francis' sayings and legends, gathered by his followers.

### Fiction

Nikos Kazantzakis, *Saint Francis* (trans. PA Bien), Loyola Classics, 2005. As only Kazantzakis could, this fictionalized biography describes the inner turmoil of the holy man.

Joan Mueller, *Francis, the Saint of Assisi: A Novel*, New City Press, 2010. A novelized biography by a professor of theology and Christian spirituality.

### Modern spiritual lessons

Richard Rohr, OFM, *Eager to Love: The Alternative Way of Francis of Assisi*, Franciscan Media, 2014. This prominent and beloved author and Franciscan priest proposes a Franciscan model for a new mysticism.

Jon M. Sweeney, *The St Francis Prayer Book: A Guide to Deepen Your Spiritual Life*, Paraclete Press, 2004. A basic introduction to Franciscan spirituality.

## Other guidebooks

Franciscan Pilgrimage Programs, *Pilgrim's Companion to Franciscan Places*, Editrice Minerva Assisi, 2002.

Linda Bird Francke, *On the Road with Francis of Assisi: A Timeless Journey Through Umbria and Tuscany, and Beyond*, Random House, 2005. Reflections on St Francis' life and journeys.

Frank J Korn, *A Catholic's Guide to Rome: Discovering the Soul of the Eternal City*, Paulist Press, 2000. An extremely helpful guide to the historic sites of Christian Rome.

Roch Niemier, OFM, *In the Footsteps of Francis and Clare*, St Anthony Messenger Press, 1999. A devotional guide to sites around Assisi, including stories of Francis and Clare.

Angela Maria Seracchioli, *On the Road with Saint Francis*, Terre di Mezzo Editore, 2013. A guide to Franciscan sites with rich details from the life of St Francis by a pilgrim pioneer. Details the Di Qui Passò itinerary from La Verna to Poggio Bustone.

Lucinda Vardey, *Traveling with the Saints in Italy: Contemporary Pilgrimages on Ancient Paths*, Castle Quay Books, 2005. Organized by region, this comprehensive guide details the biography, beliefs, and pilgrim sites pertaining to Italy's most notable saints.

## Travelogues

Russ Eanes, *Pilgrim Paths to Assisi: 300 Miles on the Way of St Francis*, The Walker Press, 2023.

## Films and videos

*Brother Sun, Sister Moon*, dir. Franco Zeffirelli, Paramount, 1972.

*The Sultan and the Saint*, dir. Alex Kronemer, 2016 (www.sultanandthesaintfilm.com).

# NOTES

# NOTES

## DOWNLOAD THE ROUTES IN GPX FORMAT

All the routes in this guide are available for download from:

**www.cicerone.co.uk/1167/GPX**

as standard format GPX files. You should be able to load them into most online GPX systems and mobile devices, whether GPS or smartphone. You may need to convert the file into your preferred format using a conversion programme such as gpsvisualizer.com or one of the many other such websites and programmes.

When you follow this link, you will be asked for your email address and where you purchased the guidebook, and have the option to subscribe to the Cicerone e-newsletter.

www.cicerone.co.uk

# LISTING OF CICERONE GUIDES

## BRITISH ISLES CHALLENGES, COLLECTIONS AND ACTIVITIES

Great Walks on the England Coast Path
Map and Compass
The Big Rounds
The Book of the Bivvy
The Book of the Bothy
The Mountains of England and Wales:
 Vol 1 Wales
 Vol 2 England
The National Trails
Walking the End to End Trail

## SHORT WALKS SERIES

Short Walks Hadrian's Wall
Short Walks Lake District — Keswick, Borrowdale and Buttermere
Short Walks Lake District — Windermere Ambleside and Grasmere
Short Walks Lake District — Coniston and Langdale
Short Walks in Arnside and Silverdale
Short Walks in Nidderdale
Short Walks in Northumberland: Wooler, Rothbury, Alnwick and the coast
Short Walks on the Malvern Hills
Short Walks in Cornwall: Falmouth and the Lizard
Short Walks in Cornwall: Land's End and Penzance
Short Walks in the South Downs: Brighton, Eastbourne and Arundel
Short Walks in the Surrey Hills
Short Walks on Dartmoor — South: Ivybridge and Princetown
Short Walks on Exmoor
Short Walks Winchester
Short Walks in Pembrokeshire: Tenby and the south
Short Walks in Dumfries and Galloway
Short Walks on the Isle of Mull
Short Walks on the Orkney Islands
Short Walks on the Shetland Islands

## SCOTLAND

Ben Nevis and Glen Coe
Cycling in the Hebrides
Cycling the North Coast 500
Great Mountain Days in Scotland
Mountain Biking in Southern and Central Scotland
Mountain Biking in West and North West Scotland
Not the West Highland Way
Scotland
Scotland's Best Small Mountains
Scotland's Mountain Ridges
Scottish Wild Country Backpacking
Skye's Cuillin Ridge Traverse
The Borders Abbeys Way
The Great Glen Way
The Great Glen Way Map Booklet
The Hebridean Way
The Hebrides
The Isle of Mull
The Isle of Skye
The Skye Trail
The Southern Upland Way
The West Highland Way
Walking Ben Lawers, Rannoch and Atholl
Walking in the Cairngorms
Walking in the Pentland Hills
Walking in the Scottish Borders
Walking in the Southern Uplands
Walking in Torridon, Fisherfield, Fannichs and An Teallach
Walking Loch Lomond and the Trossachs
Walking on Arran
Walking on Harris and Lewis
Walking on Jura, Islay and Colonsay
Walking on Rum and the Small Isles
Walking on the Orkney and Shetland Isles
Walking on Uist and Barra
Walking the Cape Wrath Trail
Walking the Corbetts Vol 1 South of the Great Glen
Walking the Corbetts Vol 2 North of the Great Glen
Walking the Fife Pilgrim Way
Walking the Galloway Hills
Walking the John o' Groats Trail
Walking the Munros
 Vol 1 — Southern, Central and Western Highlands
 Vol 2 — Northern Highlands and the Cairngorms
Walking the West Highland Way
West Highland Way Map Booklet
Winter Climbs in the Cairngorms
Winter Climbs: Ben Nevis and Glen Coe

## NORTHERN ENGLAND ROUTES

Cycling the Reivers Route
Cycling the Way of the Roses
Hadrian's Cycleway
Hadrian's Wall Path
Hadrian's Wall Path Map Booklet
The Coast to Coast Cycle Route
The Coast to Coast Map Booklet
The Coast to Coast Walk
The Pennine Way
Pennine Way Map Booklet
Walking the Dales Way
The Dales Way Map Booklet

## LAKE DISTRICT

Bikepacking in the Lake District
Cycling in the Lake District
Great Mountain Days in the Lake District
Joss Naylor's Lakes, Meres and Waters of the Lake District
Lake District Winter Climbs
Lake District: High Level and Fell Walks
Lake District: Low Level and Lake Walks
Mountain Biking in the Lake District
Outdoor Adventures with Children — Lake District
Scrambles in the Lake District —
 North
 South
Trail and Fell Running in the Lake District
Walking The Cumbria Way
Walking the Lake District Fells —
 Borrowdale
 Buttermere
 Coniston
 Keswick
 Langdale
 Mardale and the Far East
 Patterdale
 Wasdale
Walking the Tour of the Lake District

## NORTH-WEST ENGLAND AND THE ISLE OF MAN

Cycling the Pennine Bridleway
Isle of Man Coastal Path
The Lancashire Cycleway
The Lune Valley and Howgills
Walking in Cumbria's Eden Valley
Walking in Lancashire
Walking in the Forest of Bowland and Pendle
Walking on the Isle of Man
Walking on the West Pennine Moors
Walking the Ribble Way
Walks in Silverdale and Arnside

## NORTH-EAST ENGLAND, YORKSHIRE DALES AND PENNINES

Cycling in the Yorkshire Dales
Great Mountain Days in the Pennines
Mountain Biking in the Yorkshire Dales
The Cleveland Way and the Yorkshire Wolds Way
The Cleveland Way Map Booklet
The North York Moors
Trail and Fell Running in the Yorkshire Dales
Walking in County Durham

Walking in Northumberland
Walking in the North Pennines
Walking in the Yorkshire Dales:
   North and East
   South and West
Walking St Cuthbert's Way
Walking St Oswald's Way and
   Northumberland Coast Path

## DERBYSHIRE, PEAK DISTRICT AND MIDLANDS

Cycling in the Peak District
Dark Peak Walks
Scrambles in the Dark Peak
Walking in Derbyshire
Walking in the Peak District —
   White Peak East
   White Peak West

## WALES AND WELSH BORDERS

Cycle Touring in Wales
Cycling Lon Las Cymru
Great Mountain Days in Snowdonia
Hillwalking in Shropshire
Mountain Walking in Snowdonia
Offa's Dyke Path
Offa's Dyke Map Booklet
The Pembrokeshire Coast Path
Pembrokeshire Coast Path Map Booklet
Scrambles in Snowdonia
Snowdonia: 30 Low-level and Easy
   Walks — North, South
The Cambrian Way
The Snowdonia Way
The Wye Valley Walk
Walking Glyndwr's Way
Walking in Carmarthenshire
Walking in Pembrokeshire
Walking in the Brecon Beacons
Walking in the Wye Valley
Walking on Gower
Walking the Severn Way
Walking the Shropshire Way
Walking the Wales Coast Path

## SOUTHERN ENGLAND

20 Classic Sportive Rides in South
   East England
20 Classic Sportive Rides in South
   West England
Cycling in the Cotswolds
Mountain Biking on the North Downs
Mountain Biking on the South Downs
The North Downs Way
North Downs Way Map Booklet
Walking the South West Coast Path
South West Coast Path Map Booklet
   — Vol 1: Minehead to St Ives
   — Vol 2: St Ives to Plymouth
   — Vol 3: Plymouth to Poole
Suffolk Coast and Heath Walks
The Cotswold Way
The Cotswold Way Map Booklet
The Kennet and Avon Canal
The Lea Valley Walk

The Peddars Way and Norfolk
   Coast Path
The Pilgrims' Way
The Ridgeway National Trail
The Ridgeway Map Booklet
The South Downs Way
The South Downs Way Map Booklet
The Thames Path
The Thames Path Map Booklet
The Two Moors Way
Two Moors Way Map Booklet
Walking Hampshire's Test Way
Walking in Cornwall
Walking in Essex
Walking in Kent
Walking in London
Walking in Norfolk
Walking in the Chilterns
Walking in the Cotswolds
Walking in the Isles of Scilly
Walking in the New Forest
Walking in the North Wessex Downs
Walking on Dartmoor
Walking on Guernsey
Walking on Jersey
Walking on the Isle of Wight
Walking the Dartmoor Way
Walking the Jurassic Coast
Walking the Sarsen Way
Walks in the South Downs National
   Park
Cycling Land's End to John o' Groats

## ALPS CROSS-BORDER ROUTES

100 Hut Walks in the Alps
Alpine Ski Mountaineering Vol 1 —
   Western Alps
The Karnischer Hohenweg
The Tour of the Bernina
Trekking the Tour du Mont Blanc
Tour du Mont Blanc Map Booklet
Trail Running — Chamonix and the
   Mont Blanc region
Trekking Chamonix to Zermatt
Trekking in the Alps
Trekking in the Silvretta and Ratikon
   Alps
Trekking Munich to Venice
Walking in the Alps

## FRANCE, BELGIUM, AND LUXEMBOURG

Camino de Santiago — Via Podiensis
Chamonix Mountain Adventures
Cycling London to Paris
Cycling the Canal de la Garonne
Cycling the Canal du Midi
Mont Blanc Walks
Mountain Adventures in the
   Maurienne
Short Treks on Corsica
The Grand Traverse of the Massif
   Central
The Moselle Cycle Route
Trekking in the Vanoise
Trekking the Cathar Way

Trekking the GR10
Trekking the GR20 Corsica
Trekking the Robert Louis Stevenson
   Trail
The GR5 Trail
The GR5 Trail —
   Vosges and Jura
   Benelux and Lorraine
Via Ferratas of the French Alps
Walking in Provence — East
Walking in Provence — West
Walking in the Auvergne
Walking in the Briançonnais
Walking in the Dordogne
Walking in the Haute Savoie: North
Walking in the Haute Savoie: South
Walking on Corsica
Walking the Brittany Coast Path
Walking in the Ardennes

## PYRENEES AND FRANCE/SPAIN CROSS-BORDER ROUTES

Shorter Treks in the Pyrenees
The Pyrenean Haute Route
The Pyrenees
Trekking the Cami dels Bons Homes
Trekking the GR11 Trail
Walks and Climbs in the Pyrenees

## SPAIN AND PORTUGAL

Camino de Santiago: Camino Frances
Costa Blanca Mountain Adventures
Cycling the Camino de Santiago
Mountain Walking in Mallorca
Mountain Walking in Southern
   Catalunya
Spain's Sendero Historico: The GR1
The Andalucian Coast to Coast Walk
The Camino del Norte and Camino
   Primitivo
The Camino Ingles and Ruta do Mar
The Mountains Around Nerja
The Mountains of Ronda and
   Grazalema
The Sierras of Extremadura
Trekking in Mallorca
Trekking in the Canary Islands
Trekking the GR7 in Andalucia
Walking and Trekking in the Sierra
   Nevada
Walking in Andalucia
Walking in Catalunya —
   Barcelona
   Girona Pyrenees
Walking in the Picos de Europa
Walking La Via de la Plata and
   Camino Sanabres
Walking on Gran Canaria
Walking on La Gomera and El Hierro
Walking on La Palma
Walking on Lanzarote and
   Fuerteventura
Walking on Tenerife
Walking on the Costa Blanca
Walking the Camino dos Faros
Portugal's Rota Vicentina

The Camino Portugues
Walking in Portugal
Walking in the Algarve
Walking on Madeira
Walking on the Azores

## SWITZERLAND
Switzerland's Jura Crest Trail
The Swiss Alps
Tour of the Jungfrau Region
Trekking the Swiss Via Alpina
Walking in Arolla and Zinal
Walking in the Bernese Oberland — Jungfrau region
Walking in the Engadine — Switzerland
Walking in the Valais
Walking in Ticino
Walking in Zermatt and Saas-Fee

## GERMANY
Hiking and Cycling in the Black Forest
The Danube Cycleway Vol 1
The Rhine Cycle Route
The Westweg
Walking in the Bavarian Alps

## POLAND, SLOVAKIA, ROMANIA, HUNGARY AND BULGARIA
The Danube Cycleway Vol 2
The High Tatras
The Mountains of Romania

## SCANDINAVIA, ICELAND AND GREENLAND
Hiking in Norway — North
Hiking in Norway — South
Trekking the Kungsleden
Trekking in Greenland — The Arctic Circle Trail
Walking and Trekking in Iceland

## SLOVENIA, CROATIA, SERBIA, MONTENEGRO AND ALBANIA
Hiking Slovenia's Juliana Trail
Mountain Biking in Slovenia
The Islands of Croatia
The Julian Alps of Slovenia
The Mountains of Montenegro
The Peaks of the Balkans Trail
The Slovene Mountain Trail
Walking in Slovenia: The Karavanke
Walks and Treks in Croatia

## ITALY
Alta Via 1 — Trekking in the Dolomites
Alta Via 2 — Trekking in the Dolomites
Day Walks in the Dolomites
Italy's Grande Traversata delle Alpi
Italy's Sibillini National Park
Ski Touring and Snowshoeing in the Dolomites
The Way of St Francis
Trekking Gran Paradiso: Alta Via 2
Trekking in the Apennines
Trekking the Giants' Trail: Alta Via 1 through the Italian Pennine Alps
Via Ferratas of the Italian Dolomites: Vol 1
Vol 2
Walking in Abruzzo
Walking in Italy's Cinque Terre
Walking in Italy's Stelvio National Park
Walking in Sicily
Walking in the Aosta Valley
Walking in the Dolomites
Walking in Tuscany
Walking in Umbria
Walking Lake Como and Maggiore
Walking Lake Garda and Iseo
Walking on the Amalfi Coast
Walking the Via Francigena Pilgrim Route — Part 2
Walking the Via Francigena Pilgrim Route — Part 3
Walks and Treks in the Maritime Alps

## IRELAND
The Wild Atlantic Way and Western Ireland
Walking the Kerry Way
Walking the Wicklow Way

## EUROPEAN CYCLING
Cycling the Route des Grandes Alpes
Cycling the Ruta Via de la Plata
The Elbe Cycle Route
The River Loire Cycle Route
The River Rhone Cycle Route

## INTERNATIONAL CHALLENGES, COLLECTIONS AND ACTIVITIES
Europe's High Points
Walking the Via Francigena Pilgrim Route — Part 1

## AUSTRIA
Innsbruck Mountain Adventures
Trekking Austria's Adlerweg
Trekking in Austria's Hohe Tauern
Trekking in Austria's Stubai Alps
Trekking in Austria's Zillertal Alps
Walking in Austria
Walking in the Salzkammergut: the Austrian Lake District

## MEDITERRANEAN
The High Mountains of Crete
Trekking in Greece
Walking and Trekking in Zagori
Walking and Trekking on Corfu
Walking on the Greek Islands — the Cyclades
Walking in Cyprus
Walking in Malta

## HIMALAYA
8000 metres
Everest: A Trekker's Guide
Trekking in the Karakoram

## NORTH AMERICA
Hiking and Cycling the California Missions Trail
The John Muir Trail
The Pacific Crest Trail

## SOUTH AMERICA
Aconcagua and the Southern Andes
Hiking and Biking Peru's Inca Trails
Trekking in Torres del Paine

## AFRICA
Kilimanjaro
Walking in the Drakensberg
Walks and Scrambles in the Moroccan Anti-Atlas

## NEW ZEALAND AND AUSTRALIA
Hiking the Overland Track

## CHINA, JAPAN, AND ASIA
Annapurna
Hiking and Trekking in the Japan Alps and Mount Fuji
Hiking in Hong Kong
Japan's Kumano Kodo Pilgrimage
Japan's Kumano Kodo Pilgrimage
Trekking in Bhutan
Trekking in Ladakh
Trekking in Tajikistan
Trekking in the Himalaya

## TECHNIQUES
Fastpacking
The Mountain Hut Book

## MINI GUIDES
Alpine Flowers
Navigation
Pocket First Aid and Wilderness Medicine

## MOUNTAIN LITERATURE
A Walk in the Clouds
Abode of the Gods
Fifty Years of Adventure
The Pennine Way — the Path, the People, the Journey
Unjustifiable Risk?

For full information on all our guides, books and eBooks, visit our website:
**www.cicerone.co.uk**

# CICERONE

Trust Cicerone to guide your next adventure, wherever it may be around the world…

Discover guides for hiking, mountain walking, backpacking, trekking, trail running, cycling and mountain biking, ski touring, climbing and scrambling in Britain, Europe and worldwide.

Connect with Cicerone online and find inspiration.

- buy books and ebooks
- articles, advice and trip reports
- GPX files and updates
- regular newsletter

cicerone.co.uk